# IN PRAISE OF TOMATOES

# IN PRAISE OF TOMATOES

## A YEAR IN THE LIFE OF A HOME TOMATO GROWER

### STEVEN SHEPHERD

HarperCollins*Publishers*

IN PRAISE OF TOMATOES. Copyright © 1996 by Steven L. Shepherd. Illustrations copyright © 1996 by Suzanne Dixon Mallory. All rights reserved. Printed in the United States of America. No part of this book may be used or reproduced in any manner whatsoever without written permission except in the case of brief quotations embodied in critical articles and reviews. For information address HarperCollins Publishers, Inc., 10 East 53rd Street, New York, NY 10022.

HarperCollins books may be purchased for educational, business, or sales promotional use. For information please write: Special Markets Department, Harper-Collins Publishers, Inc., 10 East 53rd Street, New York, NY 10022.

FIRST EDITION

Designed by Laura Lindgren

Illustrations by Suzanne Dixon Mallory

Library of Congress Cataloging-in-Publication Data

Shepherd, Steven L.
        In praise of tomatoes: a year in the life of a home tomato grower / by
    Steven Shepherd. — 1st ed.
        p. cm.
        ISBN 0-06-017484-6
        1. Tomatoes—California—San Diego—Anecdotes. 2. Vegetable gar-
    dening—California—San Diego—Anecdotes. 3. Shepherd, Steven L. I. Title.
    SB349. S48  1996
    635'.642—dc20                                                        96-11755

96 97 98 99 00 ❖/RRD 10 9 8 7 6 5 4 3 2 1

*To Susan and Gabe,*
*who put the joy in my tomato growing*

❖ ❖ ❖

Shall we not find fascination
in the earth's daily doings?

—Stephen Jay Gould

# ODE TO TOMATOES

The street
filled with tomatoes,
midday,
summer,
light is
halved
like
a
tomato,
its juice
runs
through the streets.
In December,
unabated,
the tomato
invades
the kitchen,
it enters at lunchtime,
takes
its ease
on countertops,
among glasses,
butter dishes,
blue saltcellars.
It sheds
its own light,
benign majesty.
Unfortunately, we must
murder it:
the knife
sinks

into living flesh,
red
viscera,
a cool
sun,
profound,
inexhaustible,
populates the salads
of Chile,
happily, it is wed
to the clear onion,
and to celebrate the union
we
pour
oil,
essential
child of the olive,
onto its halved hemispheres,
pepper
adds
its fragrance,
salt, its magnetism;
it is the wedding
of the day,
parsley
hoists
its flag,
potatoes
bubble vigorously,
the aroma
of the roast

knocks
at the door,
it's time!
come on!
and, on
the table, at the midpoint
of summer,
the tomato,
star of earth,
recurrent
and fertile
star,
displays

its convolutions,
its canals,
its remarkable amplitude
and abundance,
no pit,
no husk,
no leaves or thorns,
the tomato offers
its gift
of fiery color
and cool completeness.

—Pablo Neruda

# CONTENTS

# BEGINNINGS

I T BEGINS THIS YEAR even before the calendar turns, as I sit at my kitchen table in late December studying a seed catalog. This particular catalog, from Tomato Growers Supply Company, features more than two hundred varieties of tomato, and I want them all. How could it be otherwise, their names are so seductive? Champion and First Lady, Costoluto Genovese and Wanda's Potato-Top. The Boy family—Toy, Big, Better, Wonder, and Ultra. Names that beg questions—Porter's Pride and Arkansas Traveler. (Who was Porter and of what was he proud? Who was the Arkansan, and where was he traveling?) Names that bear homage to love— Marion and Dona. Names that speak of ethnic and regional loyalties—Super Sioux, Dutchman, Plainsman, and Creole. And the beefsteaks, colossi whose names bear witness to the observation by Garrison Keillor that gardening is a competitive sport: Bragger, Whopper, Dinner Plate, Abraham Lincoln (could there be a more majestic name for a tomato?), and, my favorite, Mortgage Lifter. Tomatoes, tomatoes, tomatoes. I am made drunk by tomatoes.

Still, reason must prevail. Our space is limited, and I can't grow them all. Moreover, I have a problem: Because we have little space, I have grown tomatoes in the same place for as long as we have lived in this home—more than six years now. This is not a good practice, and last year it began to catch up with me. Probably, it was before that. My first few years the crops were spectacular, a joy to tend and to reap. I had big fruits and plenty of them, so many that I gave lots away—everyone who visited left with tomatoes—and I made things like ketchup (which didn't help, because instead of having lots of tomatoes I simply had lots of ketchup). But the last few years the yields have been less bountiful, the fruits smaller and fewer, my joy struggling with anxiety.

Last summer was particularly disappointing. The tomatoes were few and far between and the plants sickly, with no vigor. I consulted by phone with my father, a plant pathologist, and he suggested that I might have nematodes—microscopic worms that live in the roots and create strings of knotty swellings. The definitive diagnosis is to pull up the plant to look for these swellings, but at first I was hesitant to do this, since it's hard on the plant. Soon afterwards, though, *Sunset* came out with an article entitled "When Plants Die Mysteriously . . . Suspect Nematodes." My plants weren't dead yet, but the sick specimen in the illustration looked strikingly similar to those in my yard: stunted in stature and with yellowed, wilting leaves. It was by then mid-August and the plants had pretty much stopped producing, so I yanked one up and sure enough, its roots were strewn with nodules and swellings. I had nematodes.

The remedy is twofold, the first step being to fumigate the soil. In the interest of political correctness, I did inquire at the nursery about possible nontoxic solutions to the problem. They told me I might try seeding the soil with beneficial nematodes; these were meant to displace the harmful nematodes, and it might work, they said, but could take years. Because a central part of my approach is to do whatever works, and because I was made to understand that these years I was waiting would be without tomatoes, I considered the second option I was given, which was to buy a bottle of Vapam. Vapam was recommended by most sources I consulted (my father included), but apparently it had some nasty qualities because the chemical was being taken off the market and what was then for sale was all that would ever be available. So I bought it.

Home, I spaded the soil, mixed the Vapam with water, and saturated the infected soil of my tomato patch. I then covered the area with black plastic, sealing in the fumes and killing everything in it—plant and animal alike. The soil would be sterilized and next year I could again plant tomatoes.

I left the plastic in place for two weeks, but there was a hole in my attack about which I could do nothing. We have no backyard and my tomato patch consists of a long rectangular planter box in my front yard. It is in the only spot I have with good sunlight and is bounded by my driveway, the sidewalk, and a similar plot that belongs to my neighbor. When first we bought our house, my and my neighbor's two parcels were undifferentiated swaths of grass separating our driveways. After we had lived in our house a few months and I had thought about things, I decided this was the only place I could grow tomatoes, and so I took out the grass. I was pleased when, several months later, my neighbor took out *his* grass and put in tomatoes, followed later by fava beans, lettuce, eggplants, and a miscellany of other vegetables.

A few years later we restuccoed our house, and shortly thereafter my neighbor restuccoed his—using the same contractor and the same color. Obviously he and I shared some interests, and in the years since we have traded fruits and vegetables. He has an apricot tree and a tangerine, and he has often brought us bowls of fresh fruit. In the first year we grew tomatoes my crop far exceeded his and I kept him supplied. Talking, however, has been more difficult. My neighbor is seventy-nine years old. He was born—he has told me this repeatedly—in Milwaukee. Albert's family, though, was Italian and by the time he was six his father had earned enough money to return to Italy and buy some land. Whatever English Albert may have learned he apparently forgot, and when, after the Second World War, he and his brother returned to the United States he didn't take up the language again. Albert and I have spent an excruciating half hour confirming that, yes, the Atlanta Braves were playing in the World Series, and our conversations now are pretty much limited to hand signals and exuberant exclamations of "Bella!" whenever the weather is nice. I have never conversed with his wife.

Albert's brother lives across the street from us. Vito's English is better than Albert's, and he and I have been able to talk—in a limited fashion. Vito worked in the construction trades, where he specialized in terrazzo. The walkway leading to his doorstep is terrazzo, as is his front porch, which is pink with a large green star and the word *Welcome* emblazoned across it. I have never been inside Vito's house, but I imagine there is terrazzo inside as well. This is because of the large quantity of terrazzo in *our* house. Our house was once owned by Vito's boss, also Italian, and we have terrazzo on our front porch, in our kitchen, and in our garage. (Because the shop they worked in sold marble as well as terrazzo, our house also has marble windowsills, a marble fireplace, and marble *subflooring*—an extravagance I have never quite understood.) Terrazzo is the hardest building material known to man and a glass or dinner plate dropped on it will miraculously powderize. It is also the coldest, and our kitchen floor is therefore high on my wife's list of things she would like someday to replace. Nonetheless, I have many a time borrowed tools from Vito and in return I have given him tomatoes, both plants and fruit. Every morning he drives away for coffee (neither his nor Albert's wife drives) and before he goes he always hails me.

Next to Vito lives a woman who is 104 years old. I have seen this lady only once in the seven years we have lived here. This occurred one night when her housekeeper knocked frantically on our door and said the woman could not get from her chair to her bed and that she, the housekeeper, had recently injured her back and could not help her. Could I? I went over and got her into bed and the thing I remember most is that she was heavier than I would have expected. Frail she was not, but I guess it pays to be sturdy if you are going to live 104 years. Aside from her age, this woman is most well known in our neighborhood for having earned a master's degree while in her seventies and for having lived continuously in her house since she purchased it new in 1922—for two thousand dollars. The latter generates much envy, because prices have risen considerably in the interim.

Next to the 104-year-old are John and Rose, my favorite neighbors. John and Rose, unlike Albert, were born in Italy, in Mazara del Vallo, Sicily. There they were also betrothed, but their engagement was interrupted for five years when Rose's father was able to bring his family to the United States. Here Rose became a citizen, and as soon as she could, she returned to Italy and married John so that he too could become an American and join her.

John and Rose speak good English, but even so there are many things about them I do not fully understand, rich and wonderful things borne of different upbringings. Their front door, for instance, is rarely used. Friends and family, of which there is a constant stream, all enter through a side door. With the exception of strangers, whom I can now identify by the lost expressions they acquire when wandering bewildered on John and Rose's front steps, use of the front door is apparently reserved for formal occasions. Formal entrants through the front, intimates through the side. It is, perhaps, a permutation of the distinction drawn in the Romance languages between the formal and informal forms of you: *tú* and *usted* in Spanish, *tu* and *Lei* in Italian.

The first few years we lived across from John and Rose, Rose wore nothing but black. It took me some time to realize this—that she only wore black. They had had three sons and before we moved to the neighborhood one had died of leukemia while still a teenager. From then on Rose had worn black, for she was in mourning. That it took me so long to realize this was because I had never lived among people whose clothing conveyed such meaning, and I had never known someone who had entered a formal state of mourning. Slowly, though, I began to understand, and when, two years ago, I spotted Rose in a blue dress I did realize that I was witnessing a significant event; later, when I asked John about it, his primary expression was of great relief.

I do know the name of John and Rose's hometown because for many years they ran a nearby deli and pizza shop named Mazara's. They have since sold the shop, but Rose retains the cooking skills she practiced there. One day every summer John drives to a local produce vendor and returns with dozens of lugs of tomatoes, which he stacks on a dolly and trucks inside his house.

Rose cooks these into sauce, which they freeze and use year-round. Once, before I'd seen this, I took John a bag of fresh tomatoes. He seemed appreciative, but a little bemused, and a few hours later we were called to our front door by a knock. There stood John and Rose, he holding a large platter with swirls of pasta covered by tomato sauce made from our tomatoes, and she a basket of fresh-baked sesame-seed rolls. They were reticent about coming in, so we stood on our doorstep and chatted about tomatoes. After a time I went to our kitchen to retrieve a particularly large and handsome Supersteak. That particular tomato remains to this day my magnum opus, bigger than a softball and without a blemish. I was quite proud of it. I had meant only to show them this wonder of nature, to let them too bask in its glory, but overwhelmed and a little embarrassed by the richness with which my earlier gift-giving had been rewarded, I suddenly thrust the monster into John's hands and bade him take it. I was a little shocked at myself for doing this, but later as we sat before Rose's meal my qualms began to dissipate. (But not to disappear. In my mind's eye that tomato, the one that got away, has never stopped growing and is now as big as a basketball.) Rose's sauce was exquisite. It consisted, I believe, of little more than tomato and basil, lightly cooked and with a purity of flavor I'd never have thought possible. I have since tried to duplicate that sauce and have come a long way from my throw-in-everything-and-cook-it-all-day beginnings, but Rose's sauce is not to be equaled.

Tomatoes, then, have helped me know my neighbors.

But neighbors, specifically Albert, are also responsible for the problem before me. My Vapam treatment has probably rid the soil in my tomato patch of nematodes. But it could have had no effect on the soil in Albert's patch, which is no doubt equally infested and from which his nematodes will have free access to my tomatoes. This means I must employ as well the second strategy suggested to me by the nurserymen and others, and choose only varieties that are resistant to nematodes.

The disease-causing agents to which tomato breeders have managed to endow their plants with resistance are denoted in catalogs with letter codes; $V$ for verticillium wilt, $F$ for fusarium wilt, and so on. These can be listed in combination, and to obtain nematode resistance I must choose only from varieties whose names include coding combinations that contain N.

This N means that a gene named Mi has been bred into the tomato plant. The Mi gene, which gets its name from the M. incognita nematode, causes the tomato root cell upon which a nematode is feeding to self-destruct, releasing in the process a toxic burst that kills the nematode. This gene originally came from a wild tomato, and it represents a good example of the value of preserving a plant's genetic diversity and of protecting its wild and rare varieties from extinction. It was first successfully incorporated into a commercial tomato variety, the Hawaiian Anahu, in 1958, after nearly thirty years of work by breeders.

Because I would like my "main" tomato to have large quantities of good-sized fruit and to bear for an extended period, the first choice I make is the Champion VFNT Hybrid. Champion is an indeterminate: it will continue to grow and set fruit until the vine dies. This is in contrast to determinate varieties, which harbor the sp—or self-pruning—gene, and whose fruit tends to ripen all at once and whose vine size is limited. The sp gene causes flower clusters to form at the tips of the stems (thereby halting growth), and is the result of a spontaneous mutation that took place in Florida in 1914—one of over twelve hundred natural mutations known to have occurred this century. This same mutation may well have appeared before, but it was then that an observant physician noticed a singularly bushy specimen among the plants in his tomato patch and saved its seeds. Those seeds are now a part of the lineage of the vast majority of the tomato plants grown each year. But successful though it has been, the self-pruning gene still in my opinion has great untapped potential, for it could be put to welcome good use in suburban lawn grass, bougainvillea, and adolescent boys.

Continuing my selections, I choose for sheer size a packet of Burpee's Supersteak VFN Hybrid, described by Tomato Growers as "the modern version of the old-fashioned beefsteak." Elsewhere I have found it described as having "huge fruit with wonderful flavor and texture. If you grow Supersteak you will never again grow the old-fashioned beefsteak varieties." But I of course am not tempted to do this; I want merely to reproduce the Adonis I gave to John.

For variety, I pick Lemon Boy (a yellow member of the Boy family), Heartland, and California Sun (living in San Diego, how can I resist such a name? It sounds as if developed by the Beach Boys). All are VFN hybrids. The latter two are described as dwarf indeterminates; this sounds to me incongruous, but they're said to do well in containers, and there I'll try them, containers being one way to circumvent my lack of space. I've no experience with any of these.

Every tomato garden must have at least one cherry. Cherries are the most flavorful of tomatoes and one of the best parts of summer is walking by the tomato patch while on some unrelated chore, grabbing a handful of warm fruit, and popping them in your mouth in quick succession, the new entrants rolling and slipping in the juices of the old. In years past, I have planted the Sweet 100. They produce huge quantities, having been bred to form clusters that are the height of geometric economy, with long central stems off which radiate branching pairs of fruit-bearing stemlets. But Sweet 100, like most cherries, is not resistant to nematodes. As such, I select the Sweet Chelsea VFNT Hybrid. Again, I've not tried this variety before, but it is said to have "jumbo-sized cherry tomatoes with extra sweet taste" and resistance to ten diseases. How can I go wrong?

Finally, and mostly out of curiosity, I choose several varieties said to do well in baskets. These include Pixie, Basket King, and Floragold Basket—a yellow-cherried dwarf determinate that must be tiny indeed, for I can supposedly put three in a single twelve-inch pot.

My choices represent a mixture of the standard and the experimental—of promise and experience. Hopefully some will be winners—enough to make up for those that aren't. Hopefully I'll have licked the nematode problem, and hopefully things will turn out. But how could they not? For no matter what happens, I'll be growing tomatoes.

I also order a bottle of Tomato Bloom Spray. This is a plant hormone that is supposed to increase yields by reducing the propensity of tomato blossoms to fall off the vine. Whether it actually works I do not know. Mostly I buy it out of impulse and because it is consistent with my urge to coax every possibility from my little plot. It speaks, perhaps, to an interventionist bent towards gardening. Or to a wish to let no potential go untapped.

In addition to these selections I make for myself, I purchase a gift for a friend. Each year Tomato Growers offers a sampler collection of heirloom varieties. Heirlooms, also called open-pollinated or old-fashioned tomatoes, are what tomatoes used to be before the introduction of modern hybrids. They tend to lack disease resistance but can reliably reproduce themselves from generation to generation. In contrast, hybrids are the result of manual pollination between diverse parental lines. The purpose of hybridization is to emphasize combinations of traits not otherwise easily obtainable—like multiple disease resistance and large, noncracking fruit—and to benefit from the phenomenon known as hybrid vigor. The downside is that, like mules—the big, strong hybrid of a donkey and a horse—hybrids can't reproduce. Or rather, they can't reproduce themselves. Instead, the seeds of a hybrid will lead to a disparate crop of plants with an unpredictable mixture of traits more closely resembling those of their grandparents—the hybrid's parents.

Nonetheless, heirlooms offer colorful history and extraordinary variety. These are the tomatoes with the wonderful names, the ones grown in a single family for ten generations, the ones with ribs and ruffles and bulges and streaks of rainbowed colors, and among many tomatophiles they have acquired a pronounced romantic cachet. My friend, for instance, bemoans the flavor of today's hybrids and recalls the fruit of her youth as superior. I do not argue with her; to me, the difference between homegrown and store-bought is so large that other possible differences are hardly worth quibbling about. Instead, I buy for her the heirloom sampler, which contains seeds for Mortgage Lifter, Brandywine, Watermelon Beefsteak, Pineapple, and Cherokee Purple—said to be a dusky rose and purplish fruit first cultivated in Tennessee by the Cherokee. I expect my gift will result in the return to me of at least a few fruit during the season, and that way she and I can discover together how well these heirlooms live up to reputation and memory.

As I finish compiling my order, my mother walks through the kitchen and asks what I am doing. She and my sister are spending the holidays and have been with us for the past week. They live together, my mother and my sister, in my mother's condominium near Berkeley, in the San Francisco Bay Area. My mother has filled virtually in all three dimensions the entire volume of this condominium with furniture and bric-a-brac, much of it retained from the days of my childhood and her marriage to my father, and where she does not have things she has plants. She is forever snipping off stems and branches of plants, wrapping them in wet paper towels, and taking them home to start as cuttings in pots. Such plants fill her house and her back patio as well—the only outdoor space she has. And so it does not surprise me that as I retire for the evening I leave her poring over the catalog, and in the morning I find a list of seeds she wants to buy.

Most of her selections are varieties that I too have chosen, and we will divide and share them when the seeds arrive. But some are unique, and she wants also to order a few peppers, which have made their way into the catalog by virtue of their botanic.kinship with tomatoes. I fill in the order form, write the check ($32.25), and deposit the envelope in the mail.

Between us, and counting the heirlooms, we have ordered fifteen packets of seeds. This is somewhat embarrassing. Tomato Growers promises about thirty seeds per packet, which means we have just obtained the potential to produce some five hundred plants and many tons of tomatoes. On the other hand, they won't all grow; redundancy is part of the key to success and it is for this reason that a single tomato plant can produce as many as twenty-five thousand seeds. Besides, it's Christmas.

Three weeks later my order arrives. From the packets we are sharing, I pour half the seeds into hand-labeled paper envelopes; I then reseal the originals and mail these and her other selections to my mother. The heirlooms I set aside to give to our friend when next I see her. Beyond this, there is not much to do. It is January and too early for planting.

This same day I also receive the new Park Seed Company catalog. Park, of course, is a large and well-established company and they offer seeds for a wide range of flower and vegetables, all shown in glossy color photographs. I flip through the catalog, perusing the cannas, the corn, and the lilies. But it is to the tomatoes I am headed. This year Park is promoting a new beefsteak-sized hybrid called the OG 50 Whopper. The name is meant both to inspire awe and to honor the fiftieth anniversary of *Organic Gardening* magazine, and they have devoted several large and enticing photographs to this tomato. But the object of my interest is smaller.

The Sweet Million FNTL Hybrid is a cherry tomato available only from Park and about which I have read a great deal. It is billed as a successor to the Sweet 100 and by all accounts is a tremendous improvement. Unlike the Sweet 100, it is resistant to nematodes. Its fruit are supposed to be sweeter than sweet and not to crack. And the plants are said to be prolific beyond description.

For its reputed many good qualities, I want this tomato. But mostly I want it for its name. Such promise! I have grown and liked the 100, and if the Million is as much better as its name implies, it will be a ten-thousandfold improvement. (For this same reason, I look forward to the next generation in the line. If it represents an equal magnitude improvement, it will be called the Sweet Ten Billion, or, more neatly, the Sweet $10^{10}$.)

Rationally, I don't need the Sweet Million. With the Sweet Chelsea seeds just arrived I'll have cherries aplenty. But I'd prefer the Million. Momentarily I waver. I could start both and identify the best performer before deciding which to transplant. But do I really need more tomato seeds?

To help sway me, Park is offering a free "Tomato Culture Sheet" with every order. I have on a shelf a folder with newspaper and magazine clippings saved over the years, and an excellent and now falling apart manual by Walter Doty and A. Cort Sinnes from Ortho Books, all telling me how to grow tomatoes. This is more information than I'll ever need; John, Albert, and Vito all grow tomatoes without recourse to any printed reference. But I am always seeking additions to my collection, and accordingly, I sweep restraint aside and send in the $2.80 for seeds, postage, and handling. Millions I will have.

## FEBRUARY 20

I plant my seeds today. Roughly, they should take a week to germinate and another eight or nine before they are ready to transplant. I have in the past experimented with setting out nursery-bought transplants as early as late February or mid-March. But these attempts to speed up the clock have been less than successful, and whether I've put them in the ground in late winter or mid-spring, I have generally always begun to harvest fruit around the first week of July. This year, therefore, I have decided not to try and push things, but rather to aim for a transplant date of late April.

This means I should plant sometime over the next few weeks. Ideally, I'd prefer to wait a bit, but in this matter I am not a free agent. In three days I will be leaving on a nine-day trip for work, and I would like to start the seeds before I leave rather than after I return. The days before my departure will be harried, so today, a Sunday, is beginning to appear the best of a quickly shrinking set of choices. In truth, I have even less leeway than this, for if today is the day, I must be finished by 11 A.M. This is because we are having brunch with my wife's family, and the remainder of our day is in one way or another obligated.

The beginning of a job under the pressure to complete it as rapidly and efficiently as possible—the shoehorning of an activity into the briefest snippet of time—is the surest way I know to rob a task of its intrinsic pleasures and to convert it to something odious or to another form of workaday drudge. Washing dishes. Shopping. Clearing a desk or the garage. All can be relaxing and satisfying when done at a leisurely pace. When, that is, done without having to be hurried so that another chore can then be hurriedly started and hurriedly finished. But in the main, it has been many years since I have had the luxury of lingering at the grocery store or of washing dishes absentmindedly.

And so I will plant the tomatoes without wasted motion, my satisfaction consisting only of knowing that there will be opportunities later to enjoy what I have done. My planting flat is a rectangular, black plastic tray with egg-carton-like cells, ten wide by six deep. In addition, I have three disposable plastic six-packs saved from the purchase of last year's impatiens. These I set on the floor of our patio and fill with sterile seed starting mix. I have two four-quart bags of mix ($2.49 apiece) and I open them over the trays and spread their contents with the palms of my hands, the soil light, clean, and moist. There is a difference, my father used to tell me, between soil and dirt, and part of that difference I know now is that soil can feel clean but dirt cannot. When I have leveled the surface, I sprinkle it lightly with water and tamp the trays until the soil in each cell has dropped just below the rim.

In the matter of labels I have generally used whatever is at hand, resorting one year to cannibalizing the trimmed ends of the foil packets in which my seeds came, cutting them into joined strips like matchbooks: one strip for the Celebrities, two for the Champions, and so on. This year I have set aside a plastic milk jug, and I now take the jug into the kitchen and cut the flat panels from its sides with a knife. These I cut into strips, and these I then take back to the patio, along with an indelible marker.

I begin with the California Suns, opening their paper envelope and emptying the seeds into the palm of my hand. They are almost weightless, like flecks of parchment, and it seems as though they would float away were I merely to look at them too hard. Instead of looking, however, I pick up a few between thumb and forefinger—my fingers thick and clumsy in the manipulation of their lightness—and begin to sprinkle them into the cells of the planter tray's first row. I drop two, three, sometimes four or five into each cell, and when I reach the end of the row I take up a strip of milk carton, write "California Sun" on it, and insert it into the last cell in the row.

I repeat this process for each row in the flat and for each packet of seeds. When I have finished, I sow the plastic six-packs. These I will give away. I have no particular recipients in mind, and plan them as gifts primarily because I have soil, seeds, and containers to spare, and because I have faith they will be wanted. Nonetheless, I feel a certain responsibility towards their eventual owners, and for this reason I plant in the six-packs combinations that are self-complementing (reds and yellows, bigs and smalls) or somehow unique. In one I plant only cherries.

When the seeds are spread and the labels in place, I sprinkle a few handfuls of soil lightly over the seeds, raising the soil in each cell flush with the rim. With a half-pint watering can, I drizzle the trays with water and set them in the sun for the great unfolding to begin. Then I clean up, first the patio, then myself. The whole has taken less than an hour.

On our way to brunch I instruct my son, within my wife's hearing, to set the seed trays outside in the sun during the day while I am gone and to bring them in the garage at night. And keep them watered.

I repeat this message several times before I leave on my trip. And then I write it down.

## DAVIS

I grew up in a town surrounded by tomatoes. Davis, California, lies fifteen miles west of Sacramento and the Sacramento River, which gave the city its name and drains the great Sacramento valley, bringing water from as far north as Mount Shasta, two hundred miles distant and visible from Davis on a clear, clear day. From the foothills of Mount Shasta to Davis, and for another three hundred miles to the south, the valley is flat. Absolutely flat. And hot. Hot so that heat waves shimmer up from the ground in summer.

These are the things tomatoes like—heat, space, and water—and a great industry has arisen here around the farming and processing of tomatoes. Each year, the average American eats eighty-five pounds of tomatoes, fifteen in the form of fresh, recognizable tomatoes and the remainder in soup, juice, ketchup, and the like. This amounts to twelve million tons of tomatoes per annum, which are grown on 750 square miles of land. Of all the tomatoes grown in the United States, 85 percent are grown in California, and of these, a fifth are grown in Yolo County, of which Davis is a part. Each year, over one hundred square miles of Yolo County are planted in tomatoes—equal in their entirety to four times the area of Manhattan.

When I was a child, the fields across from our house were planted with tomatoes and variously with corn, sorghum, and alfalfa. One year there were sheep. The frontiers of these fields have receded as the town has grown, from the nine thousand who lived there in 1960, when I and my family arrived, to its current fifty thousand. But always the town has remained surrounded, and from all directions the roads lead in through fields of tomatoes miles on edge.

The people of my hometown have not accepted their encirclement without resistance. Next to the railroad tracks and not far from where I played Little League baseball is a large Hunt's tomato cannery, flanked now by dozens of huge steel storage tanks. The cannery is the town's sole industrial facility and in the summer, when the tomatoes are harvested and the plant never closes, plumes of steam rise from its stacks and its lights illumine the night. It is then that the cannery is the destination of an unending stream of trucks from the fields. Each pulls two flatbed trailers and lashed to each trailer is a fiberglass bin; tomatoes are piled high in each bin and as the trucks wend their way towards the cannery tomatoes roll off and accumulate on and by the sides of the roads. This is how it comes to be that during the harvest the roads to Davis are paved with tomatoes.

After I graduated from high school and during my first few years of college I worked for a small construction company owned by a friend's father. We were engaged in converting farmland to housing, and the first tract I worked on was directly across from the Hunt's cannery. Here, in August and September, the air was redolent with the sweet, cloying smell of tomatoes being cooked by the ton into sauce, paste, and ketchup.

But despite the millions of tomatoes that have been crushed, skinned, and stewed at the cannery, it is not here that the people of Davis have had their greatest effect on the tomato. Rather, it is across town that their efforts to transform the tomato were first plied in earnest. It was here, at the campus of the University of

California, that the notorious "square" tomato was developed. This was a project undertaken to complement the school's earlier work on the mechanical tomato harvester. The harvesters lessened the growers' need for migrant workers—the dark-skinned *braceros* who were housed in camps, hauled in buses, and spent untold hours bent in the sun—and they thereby helped change the social stew. The harvesters, huge contraptions ungainly as peddlers' wagons, have insatiable appetites for tomatoes and engulf whole plants at a time in multiple rows; on a quiet summer's night, they can be heard in fleets in the distance, squealing, squeaking, clanking, and grinding as they chew their way through the fields. My sister, on nights long ago, worked on the harvesters, standing for hours at a stretch on narrow gangways next to a rushing river of tomatoes, sorting the green from the red, the bad from the good.

Still today the university tends the tomato. On its faculty are chemists and biochemists, botanists, engineers, and breeders; physiologists, virologists, and pomologists—dozens of -ologists and nonologists with whose children I went to school and whose life's work is the tomato. Doyen of them all is Charles Rick, who spent half a century studying and collecting tomatoes in all their variety and who still, well into retirement, oversees the Tomato Genetics Resource Center, which makes available to researchers and breeders around the world seeds with thousands of variations of the tomato's one thousand genes.

There is, though, one gene Rick cannot provide. That gene was made, patented, and is now owned by a small biotechnology firm located equidistant from the university and the cannery. Calgene, Inc., was started in 1980 by a group of researchers and investors, and it is here that the people of Davis have mounted their most audacious effort yet to bend the tomato to their will.

The gene Calgene made is the antisense polygalacturonase gene, also called the Flavr Savr. The Flavr Savr is in some ways an attempt to undo much of the university's work; it is meant to redeem the fresh, grocery-store tomato, which distributors are now able to supply year-round and undamaged to produce sections throughout the country, but without color, taste, or texture, or any resemblance whatsoever to the fruit I grow in my yard. The Flavr Savr gene addresses this problem by slowing the rate at which a tomato softens as it ripens. By delaying softening, Calgene can grow and sell tomatoes that have been allowed to ripen on the vine and don't need to be picked green and gassed to ensure they survive their trip to market.

At least that's the plan.

For nearly a decade, Calgene has been working to obtain regulatory approval to sell its tomato. The company probably now has on its staff as many lawyers as scientists. People have been mixing plant genes for thousands of years (it's what happens when a breeder makes a hybrid), and random new genes create themselves daily. But the Flavr Savr, if approved, will be the first food in the grocery store with a gene designed and built by humans.

If it is successful, there will be many to follow. Waiting for Calgene to pave the regulatory way are companies with genes that will make snap peas sweeter, vegetable oils less saturated, and beans—perhaps—less gassy. And these are only the most plebeian of the possibilities. My father, who studies the use of viruses as a means for introducing genes into plants, speaks of the day when insulin is harvested from corn, and on the radio I have heard of potatoes that produce plastic rather than starch.

Naturally, not everyone is thrilled at the prospect of plastic potatoes or vegetables that make their own antifreeze. Concerns have been raised about superplants that could escape farmers' fields and take over the roadsides; about pesticide-equipped plants that have the eventual effect of producing pesticide-resistant bugs (as our doctors have produced antibiotic-resistant bacteria); about modified foods with unexpected nutritional compositions; and about the corporate ownership of DNA. But mostly the concerns are philosophical and tinged with a primal queasiness: we're at the core of life, goes the argument, and shouldn't be mucking around.

Because it is first, and because it will set a precedent, Calgene's tomato is at the focal point of this debate. Boycotts have been planned and suits have been threatened. And the government has tread cautiously. For the Department of Agriculture, Calgene has conducted field trials, demonstrating that its tomato won't take over the universe. For the Food and Drug Administration, it has shown that the Flavr Savr is "substantially equivalent" to a regular tomato, and it has won the right to sell genetically engineered produce without having to label it as such. Genes, said the FDA, won't be considered food additives.

This decision was considered a major victory until Dan Quayle got involved. Quayle trumpeted the policy as an example of the unshackling of American industry from excessive regulation, but in the process he made it sound as if the safety concerns were mere nuisance details that could be disposed of by governmental fiat. That Calgene didn't need to prove its tomato safe could have been construed as an indication that it *wasn't,* and to ward off this possibility the company turned around and asked the FDA to treat the gene as an additive so the tomato *could* be labeled and said explicitly to be safe. This has caused added delay, and at the outset of this eighth year of the company's regulatory odyssey the FDA has yet to rule and the fate of the Flavr Savr remains in limbo. Whether it will ever reach market—whether it will be a tomato that spearheads the new millennium—is unknown.

And so, tomatoes have changed the people of Davis, and the people of Davis have changed the tomato. And now, many years later, I am finding that from this town I have been sent into the world with tomatoes in my heart and tomatoes in my blood.

# MARCH

## MARCH 5

THE PLANTS SPROUT at different rates. The first came up while I was still away—away in Virginia Beach, where it rained heavily and then, on the day I left, snowed. While I was gone my wife kept me informed of the tomatoes' progress, sending a fax telling me there were as yet no sprouts but that come July we'd be "up to our necks in tomato-hood!" She told me too that a friend of ours had been laid off. The woman's husband also lost his job recently—both had worked among the disappearing remains of San Diego's aerospace industry—and the times ahead will be difficult for them and their two children. They are, however, resourceful, and will manage. Moreover, they are Republicans, and they can take comfort in the lessening government role in their professions and in the workings of the unfettered marketplace.

My son also sent his greetings, telling me he, his mother, and his aunt had been watching the winter Olympics and that Kerrigan "got the silver!" Adorning the missive was an image of a saxophone—an instrument my son plays. It made me miss them terribly, as I waited out the wet days in a run-down hotel in a boarded-up town in the off-season and watched the Atlantic, an unfamiliar ocean with a greenish gray, milky cast.

The first of the sprouts came up the first of March. These were Chelseas and Pixies, and of these there are now three to five plants per cell in the seed tray. They are an inch tall on average, with slender stems, and on some the two embryonic leaves, the cotyledons, are pinned at their tips by the still-clinging seed coat—their thin blades opening out to the world and then bowing back to meet at the seed coat. In their form these remind me of the Buddha, arms overhead, elbows out and palms together, hands pointed skyward.

Next quickest are the Supersteaks, Champions, Basket Kings, and Heartlands; each has three to four half-inch sprouts per cell. Slowest are the Lemon Boys, California Suns, and Sweet Millions—of which I now have eight.

When evening comes, and after they have spent a full day in the sun of our patio, I bring the plants indoors for warmth and safekeeping.

## MARCH 6

Overnight, more Lemon Boys and California Suns. Also another Million. I love counting the Millions and noting their new appearances, for as I do—one million, two million, three million, four—I feel enriched. It is a cheap way to grow wealthy.

If you watched closely enough, if you had the patience and the time, I imagine you could see the seeds break the surface. A small bit of white stem emerging first, followed soon after by the seed-coated head. At this stage, curved neck protruding and head all but buried, I am reminded of flamingos, with long looping necks, and heads tucked under wings, hiding from the world.

The notion of hiding flamingos (absurd, really, in their pinkness) brings to mind a form of hide-and-seek my son and I still play. The conceit of the game is that if you can't see them, they can't see you. In the mornings the two of us "hide" from my wife as we hear her approach, leaping into bed, pulling the covers over our heads, and announcing as we do, "Hide!" Covered, we wait expectantly for her to find us, two enormous lumps in the bed, hidden from view—after all, we can't see her, how could she see us? As she comes nearer, circling the bed and wondering aloud where we could possibly be, the tension grows (Will she pounce?) until finally, unable to bear it any longer, we throw back the covers, revealed, and she reacts in shock: "*There* you are!"

What most reminds me of the flamingos, and the nascent tomatoes, is how the game has evolved. Now, my son and I can "hide" simply by lowering our heads and covering our eyes. We can do this even while standing in the middle of the kitchen floor; hiding for all the world to see.

Heavy rains and lightning storms are predicted for today, and with them comes a conundrum. After setting the seedlings outside in the patio in the morning, I begin to fret at the first sprinkling. Should I put them back? This would seem prudent, but doing so will deprive them of the day's sunlight and the opportunity for growth.

As a compromise, I put the plants on the front porch. Here, they'll be sheltered from the rain but can take advantage of what little light there is. My worries are eased by this decision, but I suspect my father would tell me my conniving is pointless. Plants have light thresholds below which they will not begin to photo-synthesize, will not build sugars, will not grow. And on this dark and clouded day, where I put my tomatoes is probably irrelevant.

### MARCH 7

More Millions. More rain. Same quandary. My porch certainly provided protection from the rain, but overnight a new concern has come to mind. Our front porch is less than ten feet from the sidewalk, and it has occurred to me that while I am away at work my trays of tomatoes could easily walk off with some malevolent passerby. How likely this is I do not know. Probably the chance is remote (it being possible that I have inflated somewhat the value of my young crop and the temptation it poses). But rather than run the risk, I decide today to put the tomatoes inside the patio, positioned against a wall and protected from the rain by the over-hang roof.

This proves less than satisfactory, for I find at the end of the day that the seedlings have been slightly battered by the rain and are all leaning slightly to one side. Fortunately, they will recover.

## MARCH 8

In the plot where I will eventually plant my tomatoes the rain reveals myriad flecks of white strewn across the soil. They are bits of eggshells, remnants of a diagnosis and experiment made on a previous crop. The ends of my tomatoes had been turning black and mushy, and I made the diagnosis—blossom-end rot—with the aid of my Ortho book, which also said the cause was erratic watering or a lack of calcium in the soil. Of the two, the calcium deficiency was the more palatable, because the alternative suggested a deficiency on my part and not on the earth's. The recommended remedy was to dig crushed limestone into the soil, but about this time I read elsewhere that eggshells could also be used as a source of calcium. This seemed the more wholesome approach, and I decided to address the problem with eggshells.

For more than a year I collected eggshells. I kept them in a one-quart plastic yogurt container that lived on top our refrigerator. When I had shells to add, I'd pop the lid—the smell was spectacular—throw on the new additions, and crush them down as I replaced the cover. The whole operation took only a second or two. When the container would accept no more, I would take it to my tomato plot, dump the contents on the ground, and turn them into the soil.

I plowed in dozens of dozens, but the next season I again had blossom-end rot. The problem, I suspect, was that the calcium in the shells is virtually insoluble in water and will take decades, if not centuries, to become available to the plants. My father suggested this might be the case, but even after I asked him about it, I kept up with the therapy a while longer. I figured it couldn't hurt, and might help some. But mostly I was hoping for magic.

## MARCH 9

Our annual neighborhood homeowners' association meeting is tonight. My neighborhood consists of thirteen small and puzzle-shaped blocks just east of Balboa Park, San Diego's main municipal park and home to the well-known zoo. In 1911, when the neighborhood's streets were graded, the work was done with teams of mules. To distinguish the tract, the developer incorporated a rose-colored tint into the sidewalks, and with that simple step he gave our neighborhood an identity that still endures. Our sidewalks give us definition and cohesion. They tell us where the neighborhood begins and where it ends; who's in and who's out. I can tell my son he may ride his bicycle within the neighborhood, and he knows he can ride as far as there are pink sidewalks and no further. And once a year it is our sidewalks that lead us to gather in the home of a neighbor and behave as a body politic.

There are this evening about fifty of us, along with our city councilwoman, who has come as a guest. Some years ago the street lights in San Diego were changed from white to yellow so as to minimize the effect of the city's nighttime glow on astronomers using the great 200-inch telescope at the Mount Palomar Observatory, fifty miles from downtown. Ever since, there has been a clamor to change the lights back, and the issue has been a subject of constant debate—the "yellows" proclaiming the need to make sacrifices for science, the "whites" saying the yellow light is dingy and oppressive.

Tonight two of my neighbors take up the issue, hoping to influence the councilwoman, and the exchange is on the verge of becoming heated when she steps in and urges restraint—"before you start lobbing tomatoes at each other." This is tomatoes as ammunition, tomatoes as metaphor, and on hearing her, my thoughts drift.

Tomatoes have long been a presence in art and literature. Tomatoes were the substance of the soup in Warhol's can, and Neruda praised them in verse. Tennessee Williams wrote of tomatoes (and of love and wartime remembrances) in *The Mattress by the Tomato Patch*, and Fannie Flagg used them to bind together generations, a town, and two remarkable women in *Fried Green Tomatoes at the Whistle Stop Cafe*.

On September 18, 1851, tomatoes helped make journalistic history when they were covered on the first page of the first issue of the *New York Times*, the prose quaintly stodgy even then:

LONG ISLAND—VEGETABLES The State of Long Island is some on tomatoes. We were shown the other day, a tomato raised by Mr. Frederick Rowland of Hempstead, one of those vegetables which measured 22½ inches around it and weighed 2 pounds 3½ ounces. Who can beat it?

Tomatoes have appeared frequently in movies. Brando's Don Corleone died in his tomato patch. And they were the stars in *Attack of the Killer Tomatoes*, the worst movie ever made, and doubly notorious for having been filmed in San Diego.

Nor have tomatoes been neglected in song. In 1983, "Homegrown Tomatoes" earned Guy Clark a spot on the country charts. And in 1937, as part of the score for *Shall We Dance?* George and Ira Gershwin gave the world "Let's Call the Whole Thing Off":

> *You like po-ta-to and I like po-tah-to,*
> *You like to-ma-to and I like to-mah-to,*
> *Po-ta-to, po-tah-to,*
> *To-ma-to, to-mah-to!*
> *Let's call the whole thing off!*

And I wonder, Could Dan Quayle have spelled tomato?

## MARCH 11

My wife and I go to the post office today to submit passport applications. A sales counter has been set up in the lobby to sell special-issue stamps, books, and other philatelic paraphernalia, and on our way out I wander by, looking for hummingbird stamps.

I had never seen a hummingbird until I moved to San Diego. My wife, before she was my wife and while we were still courting, had a feeder outside her apartment, and I became enthralled with the speed and maneuverability of these little creatures. Aerial acrobatics is a phrase used often in books on hummingbirds, and they perform these seemingly without end; it's their life's work. In the desert in early spring the hummingbirds (Costas, with jewel-bright purple gorgets) will sit squeaking and chirping on the topmost branches of the palos verdes, their branches green and swollen from the winter rains. Suddenly, one will shoot skyward. At the top of its climb it will dive straight down with a shrill whistling that rises in pitch as the bird falls; the whistling stops as the bird pulls abruptly out of its dive and begins a new ascent, its course an elongated figure eight in the sky. It's a flight of courtship, and after several loops the bird will resume its post on the same branch on the same tree.

I can only presume these displays produce results, for once when hiking with my son in the desert I came across a hummingbird nest, no longer in use. Made of grass, tufts of fuzz and feathers and the tiniest of twigs, its hollowed inside no bigger than a walnut shell, I freed it from its perch and carried it cupped in my hand back to our car. Today it sits in a display box on our mantel.

After my wife and I were married, we rented an upper-floor apartment with a large picture window by the kitchen table. We fastened a hummingbird feeder to the window with suction cups and watched during our meals as the birds came within inches of our faces and drank from the feeder. Endless battles raged as one bird laid claim to the feeder and, having fed, took watch in an overhead branch. At another's approach, the current owner would swoop violently down on the intruder, chattering angrily with gorget flared and claws outstretched; a flurry of barrel rolls and high-speed flybys would ensue and off they'd go, the intruder fleeing, the owner pursuing. Ownership reestablished, the victor would return for a sip and then to his post—the whole cycle to be repeated within minutes. Occasionally we'd visit the hummingbird enclosure at the zoo, where we'd see the same behaviors save with more brightly colored "exotics" from South America and more truncated flight patterns.

Several years ago the post office issued a set of stamps featuring different hummingbirds. In my office at home I have on the wall a pair of posters showing hummingbirds and their favorite flowers, and I think every now and then of mounting and hanging the hummingbird stamps as well. But I am not sure I have the whole set, and this is why I stop at the post-office stand.

As I approach, the clerk is involved in an even-paced routine of withdrawing items from the display counter for inquiring customers, making sales, and engaging in pleasant banter. When it is my turn, I ask about the stamps. He says five had been issued—I have the full set—and then the clerk tells me he is fascinated by hummingbirds.

He lives in a small town in the mountains on the edge of the desert. For three months, he tells me, he'd had a hummingbird with colors unlike any he'd seen before: a ruby-throat, but with an all-dark body, almost black. Momentarily I am confused. Did he have this bird caged? Did he keep it inside? No, he says, it was wild, but had been coming to his feeder, and he had been watching it.

Relieved, I tell him the bird could not be a ruby-throat because ruby-throats are found only east of the Mississippi. His bird sounds more like a Costa, or perhaps a rufous. But gracefully he ignores my attempt to play expert, and he asks instead whether I and my wife have ever been to the hummingbird enclosure at the zoo. He could spend hours in there, he says, watching the birds. Yes, we say, we have been there, and we too have spent hours watching.

And there it was: the recognition, rich, humbling, and electric—as always—that someone I had not been prepared to see, someone I'd have thought I had little in common with, shared with me a deep interest. In something ordinary, and without seeking it, we had found a connection.

I have had similar encounters regarding tomatoes.

## MARCH 13

Our home is about five miles from San Diego Bay and ten miles from the ocean. According to the *Sunset New Western Garden Book*, I live in climate zone 23—"one of the most favored gardening climates in North America." Most of the time, says *Sunset*, this zone "is under the influence of the Pacific Ocean; only 15 percent of the time is the determining influence from the interior. A notorious portion of this 15 percent is on those days when hot and extremely drying Santa Ana winds blow down from the hills and canyons from the mountains and deserts."

Today is such a day. It starts calm and still, like yesterday, but as the morning progresses, the wind picks up and the temperatures rise. Papers in my office curl, and the skin of my hands begins to feel dry and dusty as the wind sucks the moisture out of all things, living and nonliving alike. By noon the temperature on the floor of my patio (where the tomato seedlings sit) is one hundred and twenty degrees.

Santa Anas are Southern California's counterpart to the siroccos that blow off the Sahara and onto Italy and southern Europe. John has told me that the last time he and Rose visited their relatives in Sicily in summer there was a sirocco. It was, he said, so hot that they spent the nights alternating between roaming the balcony, seeking fresh air, and lying directly on the tile floors. Afterwards, they vowed never to return in summer.

I have read that in traditional cultures, it is acknowledged that tempers will be short and arguments quick to become violent during a sirocco. A measure of lenience, therefore, is shown in the punishment of crimes committed during the winds. Perhaps our judges, too, should adopt such forbearance, for we can be equally incitable. "When the Santa Anas blow," wrote Raymond Chandler, "meek housewives finger their carving knives and eye the backs of their husbands' necks."

But the Santa Anas have their beauty. When first they begin, and if you are far from the inland passes where the air is forced through from the deserts, the air takes on a stillness and clarity that can be startling. There is a visual compression of distances, such that the Coronado Islands, twelve miles offshore and in Mexican waters, appear but a short swim away, and the mountains to the east lie like a backdrop behind the buildings of downtown. Colors, too, are affected. The ocean takes on the deepest of cobalt blues, and the palms and the grass of the golf course in Balboa Park acquire a brilliant emerald green; at sunset the reds and oranges have their turn, as the horizon appears almost in flame, until extinguished by the cool dark of night.

Later, as the Santa Ana progresses, the air will begin to foul, filling with dust, haze, and a yellow-brown smog that floats low and dirty over the ocean and sends creeping fingers into the canyons. This is when the Santa Anas become oppressive.

The worst Santa Ana I have ever experienced was five and a half years ago during Labor Day. The winds that day were exceptionally fierce, with temperatures in the shade well over a hundred, and a half dozen fires broke out around the city. Smoke darkened the sky, as if dusk had come at noon, and at the Naval Training Center, barracked recruits detected a funny smell in the air and were overcome with shortness of breath, wheezing, and weakness; several fainted, some were given CPR, and the county medical emergency plan was activated for the first time ever. Thirty-two hospitals were put on alert, scores of ambulances were called, and four hundred recruits were evacuated for treatment and observation. Later, it was concluded that the recruits, under the influence of the strange environmental conditions, had succumbed to an episode of mass psychogenic illness.

Also known as mass hysteria, mass psychogenic illness has a history traceable to the Middle Ages. The dancing manias of France and Italy were early examples. A mania would begin when someone ran to the town square writhing and twisting and claiming to have been bitten by a tarantula. Others would join in—one sixteenth-century French outbreak involved hundreds of dancers—and the frenzy would continue nonstop for days until the dancers fell from exhaustion. The only known cure was music, for which the tarantella was written. Today, outbreaks are not uncommon in offices, factories, or schools—any place conducive to the quick transmission of anxieties and vague discomforts. Indeed, the episode at the Training Center was notable not so much for its occurrence, but for the fact that it struck a population of would-be warriors rather than a class of impressionable grade-school girls. But such is the power of a Santa Ana.

I developed a fuller appreciation for the harshness of that Labor Day past when I and my family returned home from an outing to find a small lime tree I had planted in a container in our patio in a state of catastrophic wilt and minutes from death. I hosed it off immediately and drenched the surrounding soil, but the tree's survival was in doubt for weeks afterwards. For years its trunk bore noticeable scars from the heat, but eventually the tree recovered, and today it is a handsome specimen with deep green leaves and fruit that is exquisite when squeezed into a glass of iced, bubbling mineral water.

The lime tree taught me the value of watering during a Santa Ana, and I do so today with the tomato seedlings. This done, they are happy to be left in the heat and the sun, greedily soaking up what my father calls thermal units.

The tallest of the seedlings are now about one and three-quarter inches high. The Sweet Millions are the shortest and but a quarter of an inch. All the plants have tender purplish red stalks sheathed in almost-invisible tiny white hairs, and on many this same burgundy coloring extends to the underside of their two leaves. Several days ago I stopped bringing the trays indoors at night, and because all the seeds that are going to sprout have now done so, I take inventory. This is what I have:

### Sprouted Seedlings: March 13

| | Count | |
|---|---|---|
| VARIETY | MAIN FLAT | GIFT PACKS |
| California Sun | 14 | 12 |
| Lemon Boy | 9 | 3 |
| Champion | 21 | 0 |
| Chelsea | 23 | 14 |
| Supersteak | 9 | 2 |
| Floragold | 15 | 5 |
| Pixie | 25 | 9 |
| Basket King | 13 | 2 |
| Heartland | 24 | 7 |
| Sweet Million | 16 | 9 |
| TOTAL | 169 | 63 |

When I have finished, I retreat inside. For I too am soaking up thermal units, but less happily than the tomatoes.

## MARCH 14

The Santa Ana continues. Yesterday the official high temperature was the highest recorded for that day in forty-seven years. Today, following its predictable pattern, the air has turned an awful yellowish brown.

At midday I water the tomatoes. The surface of the soil in their trays has dried completely and not to water would be fatal. Also, I rotate the trays. The seedlings have all bent to one side as they track the sun across the sky, and I turn them to "correct" their leanings. Most likely they would eventually straighten themselves, but the impulse continually to correct things—or as my wife would say, to control them—is one of my most dominant traits.

Shortly after this my son serenades the seedlings. This is not his intention, but that is nonetheless what happens. Ten years old and playing the saxophone for seven months now (ever since the day he came home from school and told us he had signed up for band and needed a saxophone—"tomorrow"), he steps out to the patio to play, I suppose for the sun and the warmth. He has worked out the notes to a few bars from two songs—"Can't Help Falling in Love," recorded by Elvis Presley and known best in our house through a reverent version sung on the radio one Sunday afternoon by Garrison Keillor, and the spiritual "Swing Low Sweet Chariot"—and he alternates between the two, playing each two or three times before switching to the other. As he plays, he occasionally pulls the instrument from his mouth and sings a few words or a verse or, if he hits a string of notes that pleases him particularly, he repeats it, varying the repetitions and dawdling a bit, stretching the notes and following them up and down the scale, wherever they take him.

As he plays, I am struck simultaneously with the realization of why making music is called "playing," and with a memory of him eating cookies when he was a toddler. He would take ten minutes or more to eat a single cookie, taking small bites and chewing them thoroughly, savoring each mouthful in utter serenity. This was not deliberate or an affectation, it was simply that for him, then, the happiness evoked by eating a cookie was complete.

When he finishes, he packs up the instrument and comments that with a little improvement perhaps he could play for money in the park. This is a reference to a boy we heard playing the sax one afternoon in Balboa Park some months ago. He had a collection of jazzy riffs he played proficiently and with enthusiasm; his father had obtained an entertainer's license for him, and over the course of the afternoon the boy had managed to fill his case with a considerable quantity of coins and bills donated by passersby as impressed with his verve as with his virtuosity.

"Yes," I tell my son, "you could play in the park. It just takes practice."

I myself am musically unskilled and illiterate, and I want desperately for him to learn to play. I chauffeur him to lessons and try at every turn to encourage him, but I must also fight constantly against my urge to goad and to nag. The session he has just finished, although wonderful, lasts just fifteen minutes. I would like him to play longer, but I refrain from saying anything more. For him to succeed, I must let him bend and follow the sun as he will, for I can't turn him as I turn the tomatoes.

## MARCH 15

Regional tomato conceits abound. This morning my wife tells me of a recent conversation with a colleague on the East Coast. She had mentioned that we had tomatoes growing, and he was immediately interested. He could remember, as a child in New Jersey, stopping with his family to buy fresh tomatoes from farmers at roadside stands. They would be wearing bib overalls, and on these they would polish a tomato before consuming it in great watery bites, juice running down their chins. Ah, he had said, no doubt our tomatoes would be good. But we would never know the joy of a Jersey tomato.

Perhaps not. But I have known many other people who were just as passionate about the tomatoes of their youths. No matter when or where they grew up, all have insisted that the tomatoes they once knew were the best there ever were. Better than any from anywhere else, and better than any grown today.

I am sure these were good tomatoes—all of them. But I am sure, too, that these are idealized memories of tomatoes much improved through constant favorable comparison with the cardboard spheres in the supermarkets and as a function of our tendency to believe that few things in life are as good as they used to be. I, for one, remember one summer when I was in high school and my family went away for an extended vacation, leaving me in charge of the harvest from our large garden. I pumped gas that summer (my first full-time job) and every evening when I came home from work I would gather up sweet corn, peaches, and tomatoes; occasionally, a watermelon. Of these, along with a fried hamburger patty, I would make dinner, eating as much as I could hold. At the time I'd not yet had sex (that was still years away), but it would have been impossible then to convince me that anything could have been more sensuously satisfying than those meals.

At 12:15 P.M. the Santa Ana begins to break. A foghorn sounds in the bay. Wisps of fog blow in from the ocean, gray and laden with moisture. And a cool front passes through my office.

The first time I witnessed the dissolution of a Santa Ana was a fall afternoon years ago when I was a student at the University of California, San Diego. The UCSD library is a truly breathtaking structure, one of the few in San Diego for which I go out of my way while on outings with out-of-town visitors, driving up through the eucalyptus groves that hide it from view, until, suddenly, there it is—and my guests gaze in awe, while I am treated to the sight of their dazzled and appreciative expressions.

Completed in 1974, the library's form is that of a gemstone on a raised setting. The first and second floors are out of sight below ground, while the third consists only of stairs and elevators in a concrete peduncle. Atop this stand sits the fourth floor, square but for notched corners. The fifth is similarly shaped but larger, so that its edges extend beyond those of the floor below, and the sixth is larger still. The seventh and eighth floors reverse the plan and are each progressively smaller. The skin of the building is reflective plate glass, and when standing inside these windows on the sixth, outermost floor, the effect is of being suspended in space, for there is nothing in front, above, or below you.

It was from there that I watched the retreat of that long-ago Santa Ana. Taking a break from my studies I stood at the window, mesmerized as always by the view, bleached white after days of heat, dryness, and smog. As I watched, a fogbank appeared through the trees, coming in from the ocean. It pushed silently towards the library, its face a gossamer mist, and then it passed all around me, an evanescent plane. And when it was past, I was enveloped in coolness and moisture and quiet, and the Santa Ana was gone.

Late in the day I go for a walk. In yards everywhere I notice California poppies—our state flower—in bloom. They are a magnificent plant, with deep, velvety orange petals and masses of lacy silvery gray leaves that look like carrot tops.

Poppies are wildflowers, and this time of year they can be seen in abundance along roadsides and in great swaths across hillsides throughout the state. But the flowers I see are not wild. No doubt they were planted from packaged seeds purchased mail order or from nurseries, and the thought of this suggests to me that somewhere there are breeders hard at work developing "Super" and "Improved" varieties. It suggests the poppy is being domesticated.

This is a path the tomato started down centuries ago and on which it continues today. The wild, unadulterated tomato came from a thin strip of land along the western slopes of the Peruvian and Ecuadorian Andes. According to Charles Rick, who served as the source for a brief history in my Ortho book and who has himself written hundreds of articles on the tomato, these ancestral tomatoes were vigorous plants with small red fruit. They can still be found today growing like weeds in their native homeland, unchanged but for the acquisition of a modern scientific name— *Lycopersicon esculentum* variety *cerasiforme*.

The tomato seems not to have been domesticated while in South America. But somehow the plant wound up in southern Mexico, and there, under the care of the Maya and other Mesoamerican peoples, the tomato was tamed. By the time Cortés arrived, these early growers—by selecting and growing those plants they liked, and by preserving and perpetuating the occasional favorable mutation—not only had increased the fruit size to the proportions of today but had also enhanced its diversity, such that tomatoes could then be had in yellow and with bulging, pepperlike lobes. We know this because the earliest European references to the tomato are of large, yellow fruit.

The Aztecs called the fruit *xitomatl* and the Spanish called it *tomate*. But once in Europe, the tomato took on a profusion of names. The Italians, who showed an early fondness for the fruit, called the tomato variously *mala peruviana* ("Peruvian apple"), *pomo d'oro* ("golden apple"—which survives today as *pomodoro*), *pomo dei mori* ("Moors' apple," suggesting the fruit reached Italy via Morocco), and, in Latin, *poma amoris* ("apple of love"). The French, less profligate in their naming, called it *pomme d'amour*. The English, too, called them *love apples* for a time—the recurrent mixing of "love" and "apple" in the names being due to the propensity of sixteenth-century botanists to refer to any unfamiliar fruit as an apple and to the belief by some that the tomato had aphrodisiac qualities.

The plant is known to have been cultivated in the American colonies by 1710, and by the end of the eighteenth century, Thomas Jefferson wrote that he had seen tomatoes in Virginia gardens. (They had also gained by then the name by which we now know them, *tomato* having arrived by way of Jamaican slaves.) Jefferson was an active promoter of the tomato and its improvement, and is known to have sent or received seeds from France, Spain, and Mexico. He and other early tomatophiles were sufficiently successful that by 1839 enthusiastic recommendations for the pickling, stewing, and daily use of tomatoes were appearing in popular farmers' magazines.

## DAILY USE OF THE TOMATO

Cut up with salt, vinegar and pepper (as you do cucumbers) and eat away as fast as you can.

*The Genesee Farmer and Gardener's Journal* (September 21, 1839)

In 1870 the first commercially developed tomato variety was introduced. The Paragon was bred in Reynoldsburg, Ohio, by Alexander Livingston, who labored twenty years to rid his product of the bumps, ruffles, and ridges introduced by the Maya. Compounded in the twentieth century by the advent of hybridization techniques, the success of the Paragon (which can still be had today) set off a riot of breeding and varietal development that shows no signs of slowing. Every year new tomatoes are introduced, and by one estimate there are now as many as 16,000 distinct varieties.

Whether the story of the poppy will prove so rich only time will tell.

## MARCH 16

I am cast this afternoon without warning upon the Information Superhighway. It happens when I visit a friend in her office and find her at a computer terminal, a caught-in-the-act look on her face. During lunch, she tells me, she has been logging onto the Internet, exploring user newsgroups. It's fascinating, she says. Almost addictive. Would I like to see?

Newsgroups are groups of people who use the Internet to spread and retrieve information from among others with shared interests. To show me the breadth of topics addressed, she begins to scroll through listings of different groups and their interests. There are thousands. There are scientific and academic groups for every conceivable discipline, groups for animal lovers, groups for sports fans, groups for fans of every movie, musical, and TV entertainer that ever was, and groups—lots of groups—for people with different sexual interests.

As the screens scroll by, I become a little panicky. All of this has been going on without me. Moreover, I realize immediately that I am behind and will never catch up. It is as though I have been put in the movie *Koyaanisqatsi* and sent on a high-speed tour of the Library of Congress, the sole point being to impress me with how much I don't know and never will.

Seeking the solace of the familiar, I ask if there is a group for gardeners. Silly question. My friend finds a group called *rec. gardens*;

some sixteen thousand messages have been posted since the group was founded, and more than three thousand are still available for scrutiny. Each message has the Internet address of its sender, a posting date, and an *RE:* notation telling what the message is about. We begin to read.

A first-time homebuyer wants to know what kind of lawn mower to get, and in response, Vince says that when he first bought his home he "went out and got the biggest and baddest mower there was. But now, every time I mow I have to schlep out that mower and pray the engine starts. When this mower craps out, I'm going to get the $89 electric model at Home Depot." Vince has a canned signature line noting that the "Opinions expressed may not be correct but at least they're mine," and below that he has appended a quote:

> *"There is no satisfactory substitute for excellence."*
> —DR. ARNOLD O. BECKMAN

Someone else is seeking information on the effect of moonlight on plant growth. And Gary is "confused." He is planting Silver Queen sweet corn, a hybrid, and he has received conflicting information about whether he can save some of his crop for use as seed. He asks for clarification, and the response he receives strikes me as a model of clarity and crispness:

> Hybrids will not come true from seed. The varieties you describe are $F_1$ hybrids. The seeds from them would be $F_2$ hybrids, and 50 percent of them would be the same as the parent. The other 50 percent would revert to one of the inbred parents of the hybrid, which are usually VERY inferior to the hybrid. $F_3$ and higher generations get much more complicated. Cross-pollination from other varieties complicates this picture further.

Of tomatoes, there is plenty. There are requests for growing tips, requests for recommendations on the best varieties for drying (Principe Borghese, says one respondent), and questions on techniques for frying (no replies). And we stumble upon a debate-in-progress about tomatoes in China.

The instigator has been seeking information about the use of tomatoes in Sinic cuisine. Why, he asks, haven't tomatoes been incorporated into Chinese cooking? Theories are proffered ("perhaps it has to do with the New World origins of the tomato and the traditional nature of Chinese food"), and one respondent, citing the example of beef tomato, notes that tomatoes do appear in Chinese dishes made in Hawaii. But the most thunderous response comes from someone who says the premise of the question is wrong: Tomatoes *are* used in China, he says. In fact, China harvests about four million tons a year.

This brings a sharp retort from the original inquisitor. Four million tons, he says, is about eight pounds per person, enough, perhaps, to satisfy the country's need for ketchup. And to support his original contention, he closes with this:

To get an idea of how familiar tomatoes are in China, consider the Chinese names for tomato:
    1. fānqí—strange/foreign eggplant
    2. xīhóngshì—western red persimmon

He convinces me (after all, *I've* never seen a tomato in a Chinese meal), but at this point I am no longer able to judge. I turn away and stagger from my friend's office, reeling from information overload.

## MARCH 18

Today I notice the seedlings' first true leaves. They have appeared in ones and twos out the tops of the plants, and unlike their embryonic predecessors, these are covered with tomato hairs. Tiny though they are, the new leaves also hint at the shape they will take when fully grown.

This is, I suppose, a transition, like a child's first steps (the baby thereby becoming a toddler). And I wonder, are they no longer seedlings?

## MARCH 19

The nights have been warm since the Santa Ana, and we have begun to open the windows again as we sleep. We are for this reason perhaps more sensitive than usual to noises outside. And so it was that my wife and I were especially attentive last night when we began to hear rustling noises as we were falling asleep. At first I thought it was my neighbor to the rear of us out for his evening constitutional with his dog, Dan, a frail and ancient Airedale. The rustling persisted, however, and just as I was trying to decide how long I should let my reticence against snooping get the better of me before I did the reasonable thing and got up to see what was going on, I realized the sound was rain. It fell slowly at first, but quickly the drops became fat and the sound an unremitting staccato. And as it did, I sat up in bed—my tomatoes were being pelted.

I ran to the patio in my underwear, rain falling about me. I put the tomatoes in the garage, locked up, and returned to bed, rescue complete.

The rain continued throughout the night and has fallen most of the day. In San Diego, where the average annual rainfall is less than ten inches, rain is almost always welcome, and many times during the day I step out to the porch to watch and listen and to feel the cool moisture of the air.

## MARCH 20

Spring arrives today at 12:48 P.M. Pacific Standard Time. The sunrise is due east, and the sunset will be due west. Night and day will be of equal length, hence the term *equinox*.

I would not know these things were it not for books, radio, and the newspaper. I suppose there was a time when people knew them intuitively, when the information was in their bones. But today we've largely forgotten because the knowing is less critical. Still, the information is there, and when rediscovered it strikes a chord.

In celebration I survey my estate. It doesn't take long: we have less than five hundred square feet of lawn surrounded by a few beds of flowers and shrubs, a small fern garden, and, for shade, a cluster of drought-tolerant melaleuca trees from Australia. In one of the flower beds we have a dwarf Navel orange, bedecked at the moment in white blossoms (beloved by bumblebees). The pink powder puff is living up to its name. The California lilac is in bloom. (This time of year in the hills outside San Diego you can buy bunches of wild lilacs from trucks pulled to the side of the road—their back ends filled with fragrant masses of fresh-cut white and purple flowers.) And we have irises. The Japanese iris have blooms. The buds of the Douglas iris are swelling. And the Dutch iris are just beginning to show blue; in a few days they'll have flowers—my and my wife's favorite. I am satisfied.

On my tour I also spot a nutsedge, and afterwards I head to my garage for the herbicide—Roundup. One of the first Internet messages I read was from someone whose plaintive request was for help in getting rid of nutsedge. He had a new garden, and it was "doing OK except for the invasion of the nasty weed, nutsedge." What could he do?

I first learned about nutsedge when we landscaped our yard five years ago. We had hired a contractor to do the work and a landscape architect to draw the plans, and at first it all looked wonderful: new grass, new bushes, new trees. Everything neat and tidy and ready to grow into our own botanical wonderland. But within a few weeks a profusion of grasslike weeds began to appear in the planting beds. Soon the same weed was coming up through the lawn, its presence in the grass betrayed by its rapid rate of growth and lighter shade of green.

Dismayed, I called the contractor, who took some samples and had them identified by a nursery. Nutsedge, they said, probably purple. To find out more I checked out a copy of a nicely titled book called *The World's Worst Weeds*, by LeRoy Holm. The first chapter was devoted to purple nutsedge, and the first sentence got right to the point: "*Cyperus rotundus*," it said, "is the world's worst weed." Elsewhere it said that large tracts of the world's agricultural land had been abandoned because of invasion by nutsedge and that the weed was "generally held to be well nigh indestructible."

Over the next few months I found out why. The top of the plant has long grassy leaves, and from this surface structure a thin rootlike rhizome extends eight to twelve inches down into the soil to a tuber about the size and shape of a peanut. Lateral rhizomes spread out from this tuber to form new tubers, which in turn send out new rhizomes which form new tubers. It's a fiendishly effective arrangement. The whole mass grows at an exponential rate, and seemingly everything that might be done to curb it serves only to make it grow faster. The tops, for instance, can be easily pulled, but doing so simply stimulates the tubers to send out more rhizomes. Likewise, digging up the tubers breaks the interconnecting lattice of rhizomes and causes the tubers that remain (you can never get them all) to send out more rhizomes at a faster rate. All of this Holm's book told me, but I had to learn for myself.

After we had identified the menace, the contractor began sending out crews to weed. I supplemented the effort with my own labor and by hiring neighborhood kids looking for work. The latter I gave up on when I began finding plants we had just paid to put in—ferns, lilacs, and clumps of Mondo grass—squashed, trampled, and uprooted; anything in the ground, it seems, was fair game. Hoping to obtain more discriminating help, I hired the teenage son of a friend. But this was equally ineffectual, for he spent the bulk of his time talking with his girlfriend, whom he had induced me also to hire; moreover, he had the unappetizing habit of drinking from the kitchen faucet by suckling the end of the tap. (My God, I had thought, he's untamed.)

But despite the assault, the weeds only grew faster. Often a new crop would await me in the morning in the very spot we'd cleared the night before. In desperation I called an expert at the University of Georgia, who said the only sure remedy was to excavate the top two feet of soil. Because of this method's likely detrimental effect on our new landscaping I chose instead to go with chemicals. Early in the affair I had tried Roundup, but in the frenzy of new sproutings it had seemed to have little effect. Now, though, I resolved to intensify my efforts.

Roundup is one of the most remarkable herbicides ever developed. My father, who speaks of it fondly, calls it a "wonderful chemical." It will kill anything green, is considered harmless to animals, and becomes inactive on contact with soil. The label also says it is effective against nutsedge, and I figured I only needed to up the dosage.

I planned war, and as a first step I had the contractor remove the new lawn, leaving bare dirt in its stead. Then I began to spray. Every day I sprayed. I sprayed and I sprayed. My theory was twofold: I wanted the tops to absorb enough chemical to transmit an effective dose to the tubers, and I wanted no tops to live long enough to produce food for the tubers. Over the next four and a half years I went through two sprayers, two gallons of the most concentrated Roundup available (enough, said my father, to kill a forest), and a period of intense guilt when I stepped inadvertently on my neighbor's lawn after having doused my shoe with spray and then watching as a footprint of dead grass developed within a few days.

Eventually the rate of new sproutings slowed, and I tapered my sprayings to once a week. In time the sproutings were few enough that I could identify the appearance of new individuals— and spray them immediately. And after many false determinations, I came finally to believe that the area where my lawn belonged was weed-free. Isolated appearances continued in other parts of the yard (hence my need to spray today), but two months ago I called the contractor and had our lawn reinstalled.

Roundup has made a fortune for its developer, Monsanto. Farmers use it in great quantities, and they would like to use even more. But it must be applied with precision lest it kill everything in the area, friend and foe alike. (Early in the battle, when the nutsedge was thick, my wife and I would work in tandem, she gathering up and pulling out of the way the plants we wanted to preserve, sometimes shielding them with cardboard, and I applying the nozzle of my sprayer point-blank to the leaves of the nutsedge.) To surmount this obstacle, scientists at Monsanto are, in a curious twist, working feverishly to find a gene that will protect plants from its effects.

The incorporation into desirable plants of a gene for Roundup resistance would make it possible to weed fields whole-sale. Tomatoes are a prime focus of this effort, and the day will come when the farmers around Davis plant their fields with Roundup-resistant tomatoes and do their weeding with Roundup-dispensing airplanes, leaving in their wake fields that are free of green save for the rows of bushy plants with the red fruits headed for the cannery.

## MARCH 22

My neighbors behind me (owners of Dan the Dog and a now gloriously flowering avocado tree) set out their tomatoes today: four transplants, four to five inches tall and a bit ragged from handling. Each is perched on a mounded hill and dwarfed by a wire cage towering expectantly overhead. I know this because my neighbors have put their tomatoes where they always do: in a square patch of ground in the middle of their front lawn. It's the place where a coral tree once flourished until, tired of its incessant need for pruning, they pruned it all the way to the ground and dug out its roots. The spot lay fallow until they finally decided to put it to good use and planted it with tomatoes.

Growing food in the front yard is not unusual in my neighborhood, where space is precious. On the short walk to the bus stop to pick up my son from school, I pass lemon, orange, and tangerine trees, figs, loquats, bananas, grapes, and patches of fava beans (enormous fat things with pods over a foot long; a great favorite among my Italian neighbors); mixed in among the flower beds I see also lettuce, beets, broccoli, onions, peppers, parsley, cilantro, fennel, and basil.

Among all this bounty, the most unusual crop I know of was tended by John a few years ago. I first became aware of it one night when I saw John in his front yard with a coffee can into which he was tossing things that landed with a plunk. Wandering over, I discovered the plunking objects were snails; he was collecting them for transfer to a holding pen formed by a ring of coarse rock on the ground. No doubt escape was easy for the more athletic of the mollusks, but enough apparently stayed captive to provide John and Rose with an occasional meal. How she cooked them I do not know, for I never got the recipe.

## MARCH 23

Our "last winter storm" is predicted for tomorrow and the temperature has turned chilly. This of course is relative. According to the newspaper, this has been the "one winter in ten" when all five of the Great Lakes freeze over, and even now the ice is as thick as forty inches. But in anticipation of a cold night I bring in the tomatoes nonetheless.

My son helps me with this task, and as he does so he asks what I would do if the tomatoes died. He is referring to the risk posed by the cold, but his question makes me a little worried, for it seems perhaps the seedlings are a bit yellow. This observation leads me in turn to think about "medical student's disease"—an affliction affecting many doctors early in their training and whose symptoms are those of whatever disease they are currently studying. It speaks to the ability of suggestion to influence our perceptions, whether it be of pain or the color yellow.

But I keep these thoughts to myself, and in answer to his question I tell him, "I don't know. Probably buy more."

Momentarily I am stricken with guilt at the thought I might so casually replace with stand-ins from a nursery these plants I have raised from seed. But it is, after all, only tomatoes I am after, not transcendence, and my commitment to them can only reasonably go so far.

## MARCH 24

On my way to the bus stop today I pass the owner of Dan the Dog, and I ask him about his new plants. He is a large man, reminiscent of Burl Ives in appearance; his youth was spent in the Long Beach naval shipyard, and he lives now on a monthly government check sent in trade for a case of asbestosis.

He tells me the transplants came from one of our Italian neighbors, a man who worked as a private cement contractor and acquired his own disability via a ruptured disk in his back. As treatment he had an operation, and for months afterwards he labored at recovery, hobbling repeatedly around our block, hands clenched tightly to the grips of his walker, face in a grimace, stopping every few yards to rest and catch his breath, his pace slower than that of the two-year-old granddaughter who accompanied him. This year the contractor had sown seeds from tomatoes he had grown the year before; he had done so by scattering a handful amongst the flowers in his backyard, and of the many that had sprouted, he had offered the owner of Dan the Dog to help himself. As to their variety, Dan's owner says simply they are "big ones."

This is a utilitarian view of tomato growing: you grow what's available, eat what results, and it will be good because it will be fresh and you grew it. There's not a lot of fussing to it. It's a view I envy but have not been able to emulate. On the contrary, I have more than once plucked out a volunteer because I didn't know its ancestry; even if I had, I still wouldn't have wanted it because it would have been the unpredictable child of a hybrid.

Instead, the course I follow fits somewhere between two different continua, one emphasizing output, the other process. The first might best be characterized as the relentless pursuit of technical optimization: the use of precise schedules for watering and fertilizing, of meticulous soil preparation, and the selection of varieties matched exactly to current needs and circumstances. The other recognizes in any activity the potential for self-realization in the pursuit of mastery, be it hitting a baseball, maintaining a motorcycle, or growing tomatoes. I am too much a dilettante and have too many competing demands to be close to either of these endpoints, but they are the directions towards which my proclivities lie.

## MARCH 27

The clouds today are high, white cotton balls floating in from the Pacific, the sky beyond a deep blue. Sunlight glints off windows and water.

It was on a day like today that I came to San Diego. My grandparents were leaving on a six-month cruise—the last they ever took—and needed a housesitter. For the first week I was here a breeze blew in from the ocean, carrying with it just a hint of moisture. The wind's coolness, the sun's warmth, the light sparkling off buildings and water, and the feeling of being alone and on my own for the first time was an exhilarating combination.

I stayed the six months, then moved to a small studio and stayed to finish college. It was during that time that I met my wife, and when I got my degree, she and I went away together so she could complete another year of school. We came back after that year, ostensibly so I could begin yet another round of school (school then held the key to dreams), but primarily because I had fallen in love with San Diego. On our return we rented an apartment in which we stayed for seven years. All this was before I ever knew I would grow tomatoes.

I planted my first tomato on a day that was also such as this. How could it have been otherwise? It was the same time of year, and—meteorologically—no other kind of day is so full of promise and inspiration. In the center of our apartment complex was a barren concrete patio and one day I got it into my head that I could grow tomatoes there in containers. I had three five-gallon paint buckets, and after I drilled holes for drainage in the bottom of each I set off for the nearest nursery.

I wasn't so finicky then about varieties, for the simple reason that I didn't know enough to be otherwise. I relied on the advice of the nurserywoman, and she sold me potting soil, stakes, fertilizer, and the requisite three plants. The spot I was forced to use received too little light, and I don't recall that my yields were overwhelming. But the plants did become a conversational centerpiece of the apartments, and I repeated the process during each of the remaining years we lived there.

## MARCH 28

I telephone my mother today, and she gives me an enthusiastic accounting of her tomatoes. Her plants are now "about three inches tall and with leaves a couple of inches long." This news makes me envious, for my plants are no more than an inch and a half on average. Moreover, I'm still concerned about their yellow tinge—tomato grower's disease it wasn't. The plants seem not to be thriving, and I suspect they are not getting enough light. Of all the things a plant needs, sunlight would seem the easiest to provide; however, our patio is bounded on all sides by a six-foot fence and overshadowed by a large and sprawling ficus. Started from a sapling by a previous owner, the tree is overgrown and should be removed, but taking it out now would require significant effort, and so I let it remain. Similarly, I have toyed briefly with the idea of putting the tomato seedlings on the roof, but this seems a bit eccentric and so I let them too remain.

Though different than mine, my mother has had her own pleasures and travails. She too planted her seeds in a tray with multiple rows, and those in one row did not survive. Half her seeds she gave to a couple with whom she square dances, and she is now treated to regular news of their progress. I have observed that the passing on of tomatoes, be they fruit, plant, or seed, is one of the great joys in their growing. The urge to give them to friends, neighbors, passersby, and complete strangers is virtually irresistible and may well be inborn. It is, I suppose, a form of the passing on of life's sustenance, bounty, and promise, all at one time.

She was growing peas as well, but these were eaten by snails, and as a preventative she has now sprinkled snail powder around the bottoms of her tomato pots. She is, though, using the powder sparingly. This frugality is prompted by a concern that she may soon lose her job. The company for which she works is moving its offices to Georgia. Briefly, she too considered relocating. But then she wound up bedridden with the flu, and the time in bed, relying on friends and my sister to run errands, shop, and generally keep her going, led her to rethink the value of the roots she has established since she and my father divorced—and of the difficulty of doing so again.

She has decided to remain and to hope the company might find her a place in a small contingent that will stay behind. But I am astounded that she ever considered going. She is sixty years old, and I can only imagine that starting alone and anew at that age would have none of the luster it had for me when I left Davis and came to San Diego.

## MARCH 29

The thing that consumes a person can be anything, of course. In the paper this morning there is a story about a Los Angeles physician who was shot in his driveway as he was returning home from delivering a baby. The man had a wife, two young children—and a passion for bonsai. A photograph shows him and his daughter in his backyard amid a dozen miniature trees.

Fortunately, he recovered. And so it was with relief and some embarrassment that he was able to ponder his words, potentially his last, as he was taken away in the ambulance. These were a request to his wife to water his bonsai. "I wish," he said later, "it had been something more meaningful. Like 'Take care of my children,' or 'I'll see you in the next life.'"

No doubt he'll be forgiven this, but I have been moved by his experience to promise my wife that should I face similar circumstances I will not speak of tomatoes.

## MARCH 30

In the mail today I receive a new seed catalog. It's an engaging publication, and though I have no more need for its wares, I can't resist a look.

Several pages are devoted to tomatoes, including a sidebar on growing tips, and in them I learn that I can have "larger, earlier, and better-flavored fruit" if I remove two-thirds of the flowers from heavily-bearing plants. Seeds, I learn, are viable for three years. And I discover a host of new and wonderful names: Stupice, Saucy, Sweetie, Aunt Molly's, and a beefsteak named Large. Large is as simple as a name can be, but the deft one-upsmanship of the true tomato cognoscenti is revealed in the fruit's description. "Compared to other bragging size tomatoes," says the catalog, "these are the most handsome."

Many of the offerings are designer varieties with origins from around the world (Stupice is from Czechoslovakia—when there was a Czechoslovakia), and in many cases the name of the breeder is provided. This is a level of tomatodom I have not previously encountered, and so it is perhaps not surprising that I begin to grow demoralized as I read. I come across technical terms I can't pronounce and can't find in the dictionary. And when they recommend the Dutch Monix for making sauce, but add that "the serious sauce maker should conduct his or her own variety trials," I quietly close the pages. This is a catalog, it says on the cover, for the "master gardener," and clearly I (with my pale and yellow seedlings) am but a dabbler.

I do have friends and neighbors who consider me an "expert" on tomatoes. But this only demonstrates the adage that an expert is someone who knows more about a subject than you do. I have cystic fibrosis, and like everyone who has CF, I was born with the disease and have lived with it my whole life. I have also written about it, and as a result I have had people call me an expert on this as well. Compared to someone who can't pronounce the name, yes, I know a great deal. But compared to my doctor, who has treated hundreds of patients and seen many die, or to a scientist who studies the disease's molecular foundations, I know next to nothing. And knowing a little of the magnitude of what they know and I don't, I have found these misapplications of the word "expert" painfully embarrassing, like the apprentice mistaken for a master, an artisan for an artist—or a home tomato grower for a Charles Rick.

## MARCH 31

The man whose house fronts my son's bus stop has a beautiful yard. A large and willowy Chinese elm provides shade. From river rock he has built a birdbath into which a trickle of water flows. And his lawn is immaculate, with ever fine, delicate blades of grass. Prior to the nutsedge debacle, I once stopped and asked what kind of grass he had in his lawn, thinking I could plant the same and thereby reproduce his results. It was, he said, ryegrass— which he re-seeded every spring. This explained the texture of his lawn and at the same time convinced me that such a lawn was going to take more work than I could conceivably give, and that I would have to settle for the coarser stuff.

Every year this gentleman plants tomatoes. He too is short on space, and he plants them in his front yard in three fifteen-gallon containers that never move and over which he has built a trellis. I have never inspected the affair too closely—it is some distance removed from the street—but he appears to get good yields of sizable fruit.

As we walk past the house today I notice that the containers are newly occupied. Indeed, the owner is standing on his front porch with leftover transplants in his hands as we approach. I ask what variety he has planted and note as I do that I've always thought he had nice crops. They are, he says, Better Boys. "I've always had good luck with them." And then, acknowledging my compliment, he adds that to eat them all, he'll "need help in the summer."

For a man with three plants, it's a fine boast.

# A P R I L

FOR TWO WEEKS now it has been spring. Even before it became so there were days of glory—days, as Paul Simon says, of miracle and wonder. But now the signs are more tangible, more personal. In our yard the Dutch iris are blooming. My wife has begun to wear shorts. The drone of lawnmowers is omnipresent. And in the stores there are flats of cheap, fresh strawberries—big gorgeous red things, and sweet, from San Diego's own North County.

Further signaling spring's arrival, my son today plants impatiens. My wife has purchased a half dozen six-packs of cream-, salmon-, and rose-colored hybrids and they are to go amongst the ferns at the north end of the house, a spot where they will receive as much shade as possible (their likes being opposite those of tomatoes). My son has done this before, and as a consequence the job is now his—as are the resulting flowers.

In preparation, he gathers his tools—hand trowel, gloves, and a two-gallon watering can into which I mix liquid root stimulator. These and the flowers themselves he transports to the planting site via skateboard. Outbound he kneels, his weight over the rear wheels, hands grasping each side of the board's front end, cargo positioned beneath him; the loading takes place in the patio and once everything is arranged he vrooms down the driveway and makes a great swooping curve onto the sidewalk. A few pushes with his foot and he arrives at his destination, where he offloads and begins his return journey. The return trip he makes prone—face forward, legs trailing, and arms swept back against his side. There is a great deal of to and fro, but eventually he gets to the planting. This he does leisurely, digging and shaping each hole individually, first with the trowel and then with his fingers, settling the plant in position and snugging it up by gently patting the surrounding loosened soil. Each new occupant in our yard is christened with a sprinkling of the hormone-laced water, and as he works, his hands and knees—pretty much all of him—become suitably dirty.

Meanwhile, I thin the seedlings. I have long been avoiding this task, for it involves removing much of what I have been endeavoring to produce. But it can no longer be postponed, and hoping to reduce the legginess of my crop, I now select for preservation in each of the planting tray's cells the seedling with the largest ratio of leaf length to stem, discounting in this calculation the long-bladed cotyledons. Those seedlings not selected I snip away with a pair of sharp scissors, and when finished I am left with a handful of almost weightless, trash-bound clippings. In addition, I have on my hands the unique acrid smell of tomato foliage and the following counts of survivors:

THINNED SEEDLINGS: APRIL 3

| | Count | |
| VARIETY | MAIN FLAT | GIFT PACKS |
| --- | --- | --- |
| California Sun | 6 | 4 |
| Lemon Boy | 6 | 2 |
| Champion | 6 | 0 |
| Chelsea | 6 | 2 |
| Supersteak | 6 | 1 |

| VARIETY | *Count* | |
| --- | --- | --- |
| | MAIN FLAT | GIFT PACKS |
| Floragold | 6 | 2 |
| Pixie | 6 | 3 |
| Basket King | 6 | 1 |
| Heartland | 6 | 2 |
| Sweet Million | 6 | 1 |
| TOTAL | 60 | 18 |

I have reduced by two-thirds the number of plants to which my sowing gave rise. Of those that remain the tallest is about two inches and the shortest about one. This means there has been no appreciable height increase in the last three weeks, and the slowness of the plants' growth, their legginess, and the yellowness of their leaves all cause me concern.

This concern is heightened by the comparisons invited with six new nursery-grown plants added inadvertently to my collection last night. I obtained these newcomers while touring a friend's garden. On the ground lay the still half-full six-packs in which his newly planted tomatoes had been purchased, and impulsively he offered them to me. I knew as he did so that I would not use them—the identifying markers had become separated and there was no telling which plants were which. But what could I say? One doesn't decline an offer of free tomatoes.

These new plants are all about four inches tall and have branching stems with multiple leaves. The leaves are a deep green and the plants are sturdy. The contrast with my seedlings is striking, and reinforces the impression that mine are floundering. Tomato seedlings, my Ortho book tells me, like twelve or more hours a day of direct sunlight; other sources say six will do, but the more the better. In my patio, safe from theft but too well shaded, my plants are probably getting three or four hours at most.

Be that as it may, I resolve to give my seedlings three weeks to shape up. April 24 will mark nine weeks since I planted them and if by then they are not ready to transplant, I will look for replacements. I feel better having made this decision; hopefully I will now feel less antsy as I spy almost daily new and brawny-looking tomato plants in nooks and crannies throughout the neighborhood.

## APRIL 5

On the Internet today I tap into a discussion about leggy tomato plants. Jeffrey writes that he started his seedlings three to four weeks ago, and "they are growing very fast. Too fast, they are getting very leggy." He has them in a furnace room, where the temperature is seventy-two, and he has close-hanging fluorescent lights that are on fourteen hours a day. He fertilizes lightly, has thinned, and is careful in their watering. "But still they stretch."

His problem is far from my own—my seedlings certainly aren't growing too fast. But a response he gets gives me pause. Jeffrey's troubles, says Lena, are caused by too much nitrogen and not enough light.

> Early in the year window light is not sufficient; more true the more north. Standard fluorescents are a suitable supplement; set them 2 to 3 inches above the foliage (no more) and leave them on 16 to 24 hours per day (no less).

Apparently, Jeffrey's fourteen hours are not enough. I have already realized my plants aren't getting enough light. But what impresses me about this interchange is the amount of effort Jeffrey has expended to still provide inadequately for his plants' needs. Never have I thought about hanging artificial lights for my seedlings. Never have I thought of putting them in a furnace room or a greenhouse (of which I have neither). Never have I seen a coldframe. And the process of "hardening" (acclimatizing seedlings to the outdoors) seems an unnecessary nuisance.

Perhaps I am just lazy. Or perhaps my view of gardening is closer to that of my utilitarian neighbor's than I had suspected. But there may be another explanation, and this I glean from a second Internet posting. It seems that a well-known electronic gardener is planning on moving, and she is being wooed by people around the country. She has been invited to Northern California. But "Naw," says a rival, move to Alberta, where I can look out my window and see some of the same snow that fell in November. Gardening here takes artistry and finesse. In California it's like shooting trout in a rain barrel.

Being provided for can rob people of their initiative. And so it is, I suppose, even with tomato growing. It has simply been the case that for me, here (where the gardening is probably the easiest in all of California), complacency has always sufficed: the tomatoes I have planted have always grown, without resort to manipulation.

Clearly, though, this approach is not now working. If the seeds I have planted are to produce tomatoes, I must do something different, and today—as I show my son's baby-sitter the seedlings and he confirms that, yes, they do seem a little pale and, yes, the purple coloring on the stems and underleaves is a little dramatic—I decide to put the plants on the roof. Eccentric or not, they need the light.

Still, propriety remains a concern, and I wait until the baby-sitter (a college student who drives a four-wheel-drive pickup, plays drums in a band, and impresses my son to no end) leaves before making the move. When he has gone, I dig out my ladder, prop it against the house, and begin hoisting the flats on top of the roof. Most of our roof is pitched, but over our kitchen we have a level section and this is where I make the seedlings' new home.

At dinner I tell my wife and son of the relocation. The tomatoes, I inform them, are now but a few feet overhead. This in turn prompts a prolonged and repeated duet of harmonized verses from Gerry Goffin and Carole King's "Up on the Roof," made popular in the 1960s by The Drifters.

Apparently this is to be our anthem for the weeks ahead.

### APRIL 6

Surely the tomatoes must now be happy. They spent the whole day in full sun.

## APRIL 8

On the radio today it is announced that Calgene's Flavr Savr has passed another hurdle. A scientific advisory group has reviewed the evidence and found the tomato "as safe as any other." However, it is still by no means certain that the Food and Drug Administration will accept the scientists' findings and approve the Flavr Savr for marketing. That decision is expected within ninety days, after which, if favorable, it will be another month before the tomato itself appears in stores. This of course will be an event of far greater substance than the pen-and-paper rite of regulatory passage, and I await with curiosity and anticipation the fruit's arrival in the produce section and then in my salad.

Late in the afternoon I spy John in his front yard. Venturing over, I ask if he would like some tomato plants, and when he says yes (what else could he say?), I retrieve the plants given to me earlier in the week and hand them over, confident their wanderings have come to an end.

For a while we talk about the tomatoes, but eventually John asks if I would like to see the work he has just finished on his house. Indeed I would. In the seven years we have lived across from John and Rose, I have been inside their home only once, and that for but a brief time. Things forbidden have of course an exaggerated appeal, but even from the outside John and Rose's home invites attention. In our neighborhood the houses are primarily Craftsman bungalows or tile-roofed Spanish Revival fortresses. But John's house renounces these architectural themes and evokes instead the Mediterranean. No doubt it, too, was once a cottage, but over time it has acquired stucco, stonework, columns, arches, and ornamental plaster medallions. The latter John makes from molds he has brought from Italy, and from similar molds he has cast the decorative concrete fencing that surrounds his front yard. This fencing resembles a lattice of wooden boughs, and copies of it and the medallions are in such demand within the local Italian community that John has created for himself a part-time business devoted to their production.

Before we begin, I return home to summon my wife and son, who would never forgive me were I not to inform them of such an opportunity. With John in the lead, we enter through the front door—the only time I ever have done so. Inside we are greeted by Rose and the rich, warm smell of baking in progress. The front door opens directly onto the living room, and it is here that John has been working the last month. It is a room unlike any I have ever seen, and immediately my wife and I are entranced.

The carpeting is new and salmon colored. Through it a tile pathway curves from the door to the quarters beyond, and to one side of the path the floor has been raised by half a step. The freshly painted walls are a light gray, save where they meet the ceiling and where John has inserted an ornamented plaster cove molding, painted white. The ceiling itself is a shade darker than the walls, and from its center hangs a chandelier. A white medallion encircles the base of the chandelier, and smaller matching medallions have been placed in counterpoint elsewhere on the ceiling. On the wall is a portrait of the son John and Rose lost to cancer.

The room is neat and proud, precisely conceived and executed, and we are effusive in its praise. Emboldened, John and Rose invite us to view their bedroom, where John also has done some recent work. Here the motif is satin and gold. The bed—neatly made, as ours never is—is covered with blue satin, and loops of gold braid adorn the matching curtains. Here, too, John has made plaster coving for the ceilings and walls; the coving has a raised relief of looping braid that John has painted gold to complement the curtains. A wedding picture of John and Rose in Sicily, young and radiant, hangs on the wall, and again my wife and I are profuse in our compliments. But here we do not stay, for this is too private a place to linger.

As we leave, Rose presses into our hands a plate of Italian cookies. These are the source of the aroma we first smelled upon our arrival, and the cookies she gives us are as warm as her smile. There are fingers and twists, some covered with sesame seeds and some with colored sprinkles of sugar. There are scallops filled with apricot jam, scallops filled with figs, and there are wondrous marzipan swirls topped with fruit. We offer her thanks upon thanks, both for the tour and for the pastries, and we begin to lighten the plate's load even as we cross the street. They are, as I would have expected, sublime—and an admirable trade for six tomatoes in need of a home.

## APRIL 9

The seedlings' increased exposure to sunlight is having its desired effect. The plants' foliage is darker and more healthy looking than a week ago. But there are drawbacks to rooftop gardening and today they become apparent.

As continued protection against chill, I have been bringing the tomatoes down from the roof and inside the garage most nights. This morning soon after waking I restore them to their spot on the rooftop. But a few hours later it begins to drizzle, and as it does I become afflicted by a paroxysm of indecision. The rain at first is soft—more a mist, really, soundless and peaceful. In this form it poses no threat, but should its intensity increase I would have to pull the trays back down for shelter. Of course, this might not happen and I might get away with leaving them as they are; if the rain gets heavier, I can bring them down later. But this last thought prompts a harsh internal lecture on the foolishness of even considering climbing a wet, precariously placed ladder onto a slippery roof in a driving rain to "save" a bunch of tomatoes.

It would be tough to explain if I fell and broke my neck during such an escapade. Remembering the bonsai doctor, I wonder what I would say if it were tomatoes and not a gunman that brought me down. So prudence prevails and I haul the tomatoes back down while the mist is still light. Later, the wisdom of this decision is borne out when it rains heavily for several hours. Up or down, the tomatoes weren't going to get much sunlight anyway.

## APRIL 14

The tomato discourse on the Internet has been slow the last few days. Instead, hot topics have included "sex and plants" (a clever

RE: line intended to encourage comment about plant gender and its possible bearing on a nonflowering amaryllis), tips on the best flowers to attract hummingbirds, and the proper use of soaker hoses. But today a tomato question is posed that generates considerable interest. From the Medical College of Virginia someone asks, "What is your favorite sweet slicing tomato? If you could choose a tomato to just pick up and eat like an apple, which one would it be?"

Rich, in New Jersey, replies emphatically that the tomato of choice is the "Rutgers. . . . Perfect hand size, great taste, the classic Jersey tomato." From British Columbia, the Stokes Ultra Boy—"a large beefsteak with lots of flesh and a very good producer"—gets a vote. And Patty, in Chicago, writes that at an heirloom crop festival two years ago

> I really liked both an Ecuadorian and a Peruvian type of tomato someone was growing. Due to our horrible cold, rainy spring, and my lack of space for starting seeds, I just threw some seeds in my vegetable plot. They took off eventually, growing all over the place. They put out clusters of fruit ranging in size from smaller than cherry to smaller than Early Girl, but were delicious and more productive than our standard varieties.

I doubt these South American varieties were true slicing tomatoes. Ultra Boy's endorsement sounds like it came from a catalog. And though I myself am not prone to regional tomato biases, I would hate to leave the "classic Jersey tomato" winner by default. But I expect there is more yet to be heard on this subject.

### APRIL 15

Late this afternoon I am called to the front door by a neighbor asking if he can look at my tomatoes. I am on the verge of telling him, "Yes, but they're on the roof," when he tells me that he actually wants to look not at my plants but rather at my planter box. This request is an unnecessary courtesy given that the box is right next to the sidewalk and available for all to see.

But given that he has asked, I assent and together we go to inspect the box.

In truth, it is nothing special. It was built by the landscape contractor who put in my lawn and didn't take out my nutsedge. It consists of redwood two-by-twelves set on edge, with four-by-four posts in the corners, and a two-by-six lip around the top; very simple. In addition to the eggshells, I've filled it over the years with a variety of commercial soil amenders and one season I threw in several bags of sewage sludge composted by earthworms. This product is a favorite among San Diego gardeners, but its availability is in constant jeopardy: the sanitation department that makes it is under continual pressure from nearby homeowners to cease its production. The smell, I gather, is a bit much.

My neighbor tells me he is interested in the box's design because he is building his own planter in his backyard. He asks if I will be putting in tomatoes this year and I reply that, yes, I will, but I am waiting for my seedlings to become big enough to plant. He is impressed by this—that I am growing tomatoes from seed—and in this conversation (since I don't allude to their desperate location, their woes of yellow, or my resolution to replace them soon if need be) I get to play the master gardener that some catalog writers would know I am not. As to his own plans, my neighbor tells me he is going to grow three Better Boys. They are, he says, all he has room for, and were given to him by his next-door neighbors—remnants of a six-pack they had purchased for themselves.

Like a vegetable chain letter, this passing on of tomatoes helps knit the neighborhood together. Certainly we need this. A walking route I sometimes take through surrounding neighborhoods leads me along Twenty-eighth Street, near the golf course. There is a house on this street with an enormous and stately sago palm in its front yard. The plant is probably eight feet tall, which makes it a veritable giant for this slow-growing but successful species. (Sagos have been around for some two hundred million years—since before dinosaurs and before insects—and they form large forests in Papua, New Guinea, where they are harvested for their edible pith.) The plant's slow growth and exotic nature make it a valuable commodity in nurseries and among landscape architects, and five-foot crated sagos can have price tags of well over a thousand dollars. The specimen on Twenty-eighth had caught my attention after my father came for a visit several years ago and spent much of his time collecting seeds from sagos around town—including sagos at the zoo and sagos at local nurseries. (Like my mother, my father is an inveterate plant collector. Our back fence is covered with a variegated ivy started from a cutting taken from a plant at my father's house, which he in turn started from a cutting he made from a plant growing on Winston Churchill's grave; it's known in our family as the Churchill ivy.) Beyond its size, the Twenty-eighth Street sago was noteworthy for having fresh seed, and when one day I noticed this I stopped at the house, introduced myself, and asked if I might collect some seed. The owner of the house, a middle-aged and congenial woman, said yes and she went on to tell me that this sago had been planted by her father in the early days of World War II. He had purchased it from a Japanese—whether a U. S. citizen or not she did not say—who was being forced to a "relocation camp" and was given but days to sell all that he owned. Her father had paid ten or fifteen dollars for it; she couldn't remember exactly how much. Under the circumstances, of course, it was strictly a buyer's market and the woman's father had probably done the man a favor by paying him anything at all, but even then it was only a trifling amount.

The neighbor who came to look at my planter box is of Japanese descent. He has a wife and two young children. He teaches elementary school and spends many a weekend hour listening to Dodger games and weeding nutsedge from his lawn and flower beds (he, being a gentle man, is unwilling to resort to chemicals and outright warfare). He is quiet, friendly, and an important part of the neighborhood. At times I think of him and I think that were it fifty years ago, it would be he who was forced from his home, he who was forced to give away or to sell for a pittance his treasured belongings. And at such times I feel a mixture of shame, incredulity, and doubt. How could that have happened? And were it to happen again, what would I do?

## APRIL 16

My son has fallen under the influence of Pablo Neruda—he could do worse—and has announced his intention to write his own book of odes. He is going to be busy, however, for he has also just started a mystery novel in collaboration with my wife. Called *Downshift,* it is about a mother-and-son investigative team—based on whom, I can't imagine. The duo has been called upon to unravel a suspicious accident involving the prototype of a Detroit truck manufacturer's new sixteen-wheeler; evidence has been found implicating a competitor, and further developments are pending.

Often I get annoyed at my son's lack of interest in his schoolwork and the cursory manner in which he performs many assignments; rarely does he apply to this work his full range of abilities. Yet I must admit that little of what he is asked to do is inspiring, and as I listen to him hatch his ideas or watch him write his stories and poems, tinker for hours on the computer, and fall asleep at night while reading a book, leaving a light on, I can't help but think that he is allocating his time, energies, and enthusiasms appropriately. So far he has written an ode to cats and an ode to rain, and this morning he adds an ode to tomatoes.

## ODE TO TOMATOES

Dark ground,
pulls me,
envelops me,
our rapture,
caused by life,
of a seed.
I must sacrifice the soil,
offer it,
give it,
to the seed.

The seed lands,
the ground,
in awe,
praises,
the majesty,
demands from me,
I give.
It receives
my gift,
to please me,
and
itself,
it grows.
Love
surrounds it,
nourishes,
it is bribed
to
come out
and see
the world.
Naive sprout,
lost,
in the
darkness,

the
vastness,
the
strangeness,
of
the ground.
Blinded,
it
pops out,
shock,
around it,
the
lettuce cheers,
the
carrots rejoice,
the
world sings
Lord King,
the tomato,
makes
itself
known.
Hallelujah!

—Gabriel Shepherd

He decorates the page with a pair of large, red oblate fruit—beefsteaks perhaps, green-stemmed and splitting open at the top. They would make wonderful sandwiches. The poem itself is in places ponderous and I think heavy on the commas, but it has some imaginative twists and turns and bears re-reading; it is a fine first draft. Coaxing my son to revise and edit, however, poses for me the same hazards as urging him to play his saxophone: How to stimulate without nagging? How to prompt reconsideration without criticizing? How to nourish this "naive sprout"? And all while remembering that he is but ten years old.

## APRIL 18

More Internet votes have come in for "the tomato to pick up and eat like an apple." Dona and Carmello both get a nod, as does Brandywine. And Heather from Santa Cruz, California, endorses Lorissa:

> My ultimate favorite tomato. They're dense, about the size of a tennis ball and are both sweet and tangy. Unfortunately, the grower has stopped propagating the seeds. I do have three seed packets in my freezer and six young seedlings waiting to go into the ground. A very good tomato to eat fresh, sliced with a touch of basil and black pepper. They also freeze well for winter soups.

I have never heard of Lorissa, but there is no doubting Heather's devotion.

Curiously, many respondents have felt compelled to offer two votes, one for the requested large slicing variety and another for their favorite cherry tomato. There are fans of Sweet 100s, Yellow Pears, Tigerettes ("a visual delight in the garden . . . the tomatoes start out yellow and when ripe are bright orange-red with stripes; to top it off they are wonderfully tasty and fleshy"), and Pink Capri. But voices for the Millions are quiet. I wonder, Should I worry?

In the physical world, the weather is sunny and warm (a high today of seventy-three degrees), and the seedlings seem happy. The tallest are about two and a half inches, and most are now a deep healthy green. The plants' stems have thickened, and all are less wispy-looking. Many have their first pair of true leaves and are beginning to form their second. So they're making progress. But when I look at the plants of my neighbors, many a foot high now, it is beginning to seem inevitable that soon I'll be making a trip to the nursery.

## APRIL 19

The Muse has possessed my son, and today he adds two new odes to his collection: "Ode to a Ship in a Bottle" (also a Neruda title) and "Ode to Birds Singing" (his own invention). In addition, he adds a stanza to his tomato ode; it's not as strong as the rest of the poem but does show a willingness to revise. Perhaps I should tell him of Donald Hall, whose unfinished poem "Another Elegy" has seen more than six hundred drafts. Or perhaps I shouldn't.

## APRIL 22

A natural experiment is under way in the neighborhood, the results of which bear directly on my seedlings. The owners of Dan the Dog put their tomato transplants, each four to five inches tall, in their front yard exactly a month ago. Not until March 31 did the gentleman at the end of the street plant his Better Boys in the fifteen-gallon black plastic containers. These also were four to five inches at the time.

The conditions experienced by these two groups of plants have differed in two main respects. One is their exposure to light: the afternoons of my next-door neighbors' plants are spent in the shade of our melaleucas, whereas the Better Boys have lived their lives in full sun. The other is their exposure to heat. The average high temperature the past month has been sixty-six degrees, but the Better Boys, in their sun-exposed energy-absorbing containers, have no doubt been warmer than the plants in my neighbors' front lawn.

The result of these differences has been dramatic. The Better Boys are now twelve to sixteen inches tall, with multiple stems and flowers. In contrast, my neighbors' plants are perhaps eight to ten inches, single-stemmed, slightly yellow, and have among them only one flower. So it is again confirmed: tomatoes like light and heat. By placing them on the roof, I have tried over the past two weeks to give my seedlings as much sun and warmth as possible. But their deprived infancies may have harmed them irreparably: the tallest is still less than three inches. And thus their judgment day fast approaches.

❧   ❧   ❧

I receive in the mail today yet another gardening catalog. It is, though, unlike any I have seen, and resembles most closely the *National Enquirer.* Every page is filled with gargantuan vegetables that look as if they were escapees from a 1950s radiation experiment. One picture shows a cabbage on the verge of devouring a small child, placed onboard to help illustrate the vegetable's enormity. "Challenge the record of a 123 lb. cabbage," says the caption. There are colossal peppers, humongous onions, gigantic ears of corn, and "Tomatoes as big as grapefruits—too big to fit on this page."

Purchasers of these alleged Goliaths are encouraged to "challenge the world record of a 6¼ pound tomato" and are promised submission forms for the *Guinness Book of World Records* with every order. But unchallenged winner of the ersatz prize is the tomato-potato plant. This plant (a double landmine for Dan Quayle) is the Swiss army knife of vegetables: a tomato vine grafted onto potato rootstock. An accompanying photograph shows the "astonishing" result: a bedraggled green top with red, green, and yellow fruit, and down below a cluster of red potatoes.

Tomatoes and potatoes are botanically related, both being members of the Nightshade family, Solanaceae, as are peppers, eggplant, tobacco, and petunias. But relatedness, as many a human family member will attest, is insufficient reason for excessive closeness. The doubtful quality of its produce aside, the tomato-potato is a grotesquery that violates every precept of good taste. It should be banished.

## APRIL 23

There are many tomato varieties whose fruit departs from the standard red globe, but which in their uniqueness lack the off-putting qualities of the tomato-potato (also called a potamato). Today, for instance, my wife returns from a shopping expedition with a basket of yellow plum tomatoes. This is a cherry-type fruit with yellow flesh and a shape like a rugby ball.

I have never seen this variety before, but they remind me of the yellow pear tomatoes we grew in our backyard when I was growing up. As with other cherries, their flavor is better than that of full-sized store-boughts, with a tang that pricks at the sides of my tongue. But still they lack the fullness, the richness, the explosiveness, of a vine-ripened tomato. They offer the enticement of a kiss, but without the follow-through.

Later in the day I talk on the phone with my sister. It is raining in Northern California, and as we talk she asks if I can hear it—the steady sound in the background of falling water.

My sister has her own way of saying things and I am reminded of this as she updates me on the tomatoes she and my mother are growing. "Our tomatoes," she says, "aren't growing as well as some other tomatoes are growing—they're just sort of staying in dwarf." And by way of comparison, she says the tomatoes of the square dance partner with whom my mother shared her seeds already have flowers and are three times the size of theirs.

Hesitantly, I ask my sister how big her and my mother's plants are—the ones a third the size of their friends'. A foot high, she says, with stems half an inch thick. And when she in turn asks how big mine are, and I tell her, she says, "Wow, they're really stuck in dwarf!"

Yes, I think, I know.

## APRIL 24

It has been three weeks since I resolved to replace the seedlings if they were not ready by today. During this time—most of it spent on the roof absorbing the maximum possible sunlight—they have darkened in color but grown no more than an inch. Perhaps through ineptitude—inadequate provision of light and nonexistent safeguards against cold—I have permanently stunted them. Perhaps, like the emperor, the would-be master grower has been found to have no clothes. Perhaps. But regardless of what has happened, or why, if I want fruit by summer, I must get some robust plants in the ground now.

Today, however, the storm that yesterday was drenching my sister has arrived here. Outdoors, it is cold, wet, and uninviting. Neither nurseries nor tomatoes beckon, and my family and I stay inside and make soup and bread.

In the evening we go to hear a neighbor sing in Mendelssohn's *Saint Paul Oratorio*. In the choir he stands absorbed and composed, and as I watch I find myself wishing, as I often do, that I could more readily achieve the freedom from self-consciousness that grants him this momentary state of grace. On the program the baritone has received top billing, but it is the soprano, a young woman named Sylvia Wen, who most impresses me. Her voice is confident and strong and complements wonderfully the enormous organ of the church in which the performance takes place. As she begins her recitativos, I am shot through with shivers of joy. Afterwards I overhear more knowledgeable audience members who say Ms. Wen performs regularly with the opera and has the potential for great things. I am no judge, but I hope mightily that she fulfills this promise.

The day, tomato failures notwithstanding, has had its pleasures.

## APRIL 25

It remains cold and dreary, but in three days I will again be leaving on business for a week, and I feel a sense of urgency. Accordingly, my son and I visit Anderson's Nursery. Founded in 1928 and now a San Diego institution, Anderson's prices are higher than competing chain mega-nurseries. But they have no incessant loudspeakers ("Roses, pick up on line one!"), no forklifts threatening the unwary, and they'll answer questions.

In short, it's closer to gardening than to hell.

We head to the tomatoes, and I begin to review the selection. Their choices are fairly typical: Ace, Pearson . . . Sweet 100, and a local variety called San Diego. Unexpectedly, they also have Lemon Boys. As with my selection of seeds, I am still constrained by the need to pick varieties resistant to nematodes. The Champions are a little overgrown, and the Lemon Boys are small, but I reselect them both for the same reasons I chose them initially. In addition, I choose two sturdy-looking Celebrities, and a six-pack of leggy Beefsteaks.

The latter present a conundrum. Beefsteak is one of the most beloved of tomatoes, having given its name to the whole familiar class of extra large, red slicing tomatoes. But it is an heirloom and not disease resistant, which is why hybrid versions such as Super-steak have been developed. Nevertheless, the tomatoes I now hold in my hand are described by their labels as Beefsteak VFN, indicating they have resistance to verticillium and fusarium wilts and to nematodes.

Perhaps the classic Beefsteak has been improved and is now disease resistant. Or perhaps there are now two varieties of Beef-steak, one resistant and one not. There could be varying degrees of what breeders are willing to call resistance. Or it could be that the tomatoes before me are indeed VFN resistant but are not Beefsteaks. But which of these explanations (if any) is correct I have no way of knowing.

For clarification I am directed to Anderson's "tomato man." He tells me that as far as he knows, and despite the label, Beef-steak is not disease resistant. But to find out, he will call the plants' grower. In the meantime, ever desirous of a chance to reproduce the lost giant I gave to John, I choose to believe in the veracity of the plants' labels and proceed with their purchase.

While I have been so occupied, my son has found for himself a six-pack of strawberries (where we will put them I do not know), along with two packets of tomato seeds "For next year" (How can I say no?), and seeds for catnip. Our cat is wildly susceptible to this stuff. Every year at Christmas he receives a catnip-filled mouse and, forgetting his age, spends his entire morning in midair batting at the intoxicating rodent until we are forced to rescue its remains. Some months ago my wife came home from a shopping trip with a small catnip plant, which she put in our front yard. Our cat's first reaction was to eat portions of the plant. He then went nose-to-leaf with it. And then, like a hen upon an egg, he sat on the surviving remnants for long periods of time, during which he seemed serenely happy.

The bill, which includes a box of Stern's Miracle-Gro for Tomatoes, is $17.71.

## APRIL 26

Not entirely happy with yesterday's selections, I stop by a second nursery and scan their offerings. In the way of varieties, they have nothing that was not available at Anderson's; but they do have some better-looking Beefsteaks (also labeled VFN) and I select a leafy, dark green specimen in a four-inch pot. I also pick up some cilantro and a six-pack of basil—two herbs indispensable for full tomato appreciation—and a bag of earthworm-composted sewage sludge, the opponents of this operation having so far failed in their efforts to bring the activity to a halt. The bill for these supplementary purchases comes to $10.98.

## APRIL 27

I am leaving tomorrow and must plant today. The rain of the past few days has made the soil moist and perfect for planting. But off and on throughout the day it threatens to rain again, which would make the ground soggy and planting a mess. Over the past few weeks as I have fretted about sunshine, high and low temperatures, and the pelting of rain, it has occurred to me that this is what life is like for farmers: unremitting worry over weather and its effect on crops. Except farmers can't remedy their misjudgments with a trip to the nursery.

According to my father—and I have no reason to believe otherwise (every weed and tree attests to its correctness)—plant roots are fully capable of spreading wherever they need to go and don't need the soil broken up prior to planting. But it does seem a necessary part of the ritual, and I begin my planting by turning the soil. The planter box into which I will place the tomatoes is three feet wide by thirteen feet long; I have room in it for seven plants. Because the box is elevated and because I have previously worked sand and various amenders into the soil, the drainage is excellent. For the same reason, the soil is easy to turn; it takes me less than half an hour with a spade to turn over the soil in the entire box. I work methodically, starting at one end and working in rows that are three shovels wide. Then I spread the compost and repeat my end-to-end spadework, folding in the rich, black mixture before finally leveling the surface with a rake.

In years past, my turning of the soil would have revealed any number of tightly curled, fat white grubs of unsavory appearance. These we would have tossed in the street for the birds, but today there are no grubs, no pillbugs, no creepy-crawlies of any sort. This is the legacy of the Vapam I applied last fall, and I hope it means as well that there are no nematodes.

With the soil ready, I retrieve from storage the wire cages I will put over the plants. There are an almost endless number of ways to support tomatoes, reflecting in their diversity the great and ever-present human interplay of ingenuity, necessity, and habit. John, Albert, Vito, and my other Italian neighbors favor single-staking with lengths of steel rebar or wooden broomsticks. Other schemes include trellises, lattices, twine, poles and wires, and unmitigated sprawl. The latter is generally frowned upon, for fruit left on the ground are prone to rot and the contact between leaves and ground provides a pathway for disease.

Partly the reason I use cages is that they're the easiest of support systems. The plant grows and you can pretty much ignore it except occasionally to push inside an errant branch. There's no pruning and no tying. The first year I grew tomatoes here in our house I bought commercial cages: flimsy wire cones whose welds broke when I pushed them in the ground. Nor were they big enough. No commercial cage I have ever seen has been big enough to accommodate a full-sized tomato plant, and so the second year I made my own.

The cages I made were like the ones we had when I was growing up. In truth, this is probably the main reason I use cages: it's what my father did. Like him, I made my cages out of concrete reinforcing wire, the openings in which are six inches square. Each cage is twenty inches in diameter. From each one I removed the bottom two hoops so the freed uprights serve as stakes when driven into the ground, and when so inserted they stand four feet high. They took me an afternoon to build—an afternoon with leather work gloves, long-handled wire cutters borrowed from Vito, and long stretches of spring-loaded steel mesh uncoiled in the street. Now they're covered with rust. But they still work and will serve me for years to come.

With the cages convened, I stop work to pick up my son from the school bus. This morning I promised him I would not put the plants in the ground without him, and as we walk home I tell him about my progress. Before we start we fortify ourselves with lemonade, and then we place the cages, I holding while he drives them in with a rubber mallet. We put the cages touching, which will put the plants twenty inches apart. Ideally they should be farther—two to three feet is recommended—but I gamble that I get more fruit by squeezing in an extra few plants than if I left out the extras and provided the remainders more optimal conditions.

Next, we dig by hand (the earth fine and moist in our hands) a narrow trench down the middle of the box, bisecting each of the cages. In this we lay a flexible soaker hose. I began using a soaker hose two or three years after I started growing tomatoes, as a lazy alternative to the watering of each plant individually. Books and magazines offer no end of advice on when, how much, and what devices should be used to water tomatoes. But in general the rule is to water regularly and deeply. For me, I've found that once the plants are established, a once-a-week use of the soaker hose turned on all day at the slowest possible trickle works well.

Soil, cages, and hose ready, we proceed to the tomatoes themselves. My son plants the two Celebrities and the Beefsteak, all sturdy plants from four-inch pots. From their six-packs, I plant three Champions and a single Lemon Boy. When we are finished, the plants stand five to six inches above ground. I douse them with a heavy watering of Miracle-Gro, and while I do so my son plants the basil and cilantro in whatever open spaces he can find around the yard. And then we are done. Tomorrow I can leave in peace.

As we clean up, my son asks if I am just going to let the other tomatoes—the seedlings—die. There is in his voice a note of disbelief, a touch of pleading, and seeking to reassure him, I say, "No, I'm not going to do that." I couldn't abandon them so easily, and hopefully I will still be able to put some—the cherries in particular—in containers. Others I'll give away if they begin to grow. To facilitate this, and because I don't want my son or wife suffering misadventure by climbing the ladder while I am gone, I remove the seedlings from the rooftop. They will spend the next week on the patio.

The last thing I do is distribute the unused plants. My son's baby-sitter stops by, and to him I give the remainders of the Champion and Lemon Boy six-packs. To Albert I give the six-pack of Beefsteaks. I do this in part because he especially likes the big ones. But I do so also for reasons less altruistic. Albert has no more room than I, and on occasion he has planted sunflowers in his small space. These of course dwarfed my tomatoes and left them in shadow for much of the day. My hope is that if Albert plants tomatoes he won't plant sunflowers. And so I go next door and present him with the six-pack.

Later, before retiring for the night, I go outside and take one last look at our handiwork. As I do, I see that Albert's new Beefsteaks are already in the ground. If I am lucky, there will be no sunflowers.

### APRIL 29

My travels put me in a rental car headed southeast from Washington, D. C., to Norfolk, Virginia, a part of the country through which I have never journeyed. It is late in the afternoon as I leave Washington, and for the first thirty miles the traffic is stop-and-go. The pace is interminable and reminds me of Los Angeles, which is not good. With the traveler's vulnerability to things different, I am greatly confused by the road signs. Every exit is quadruply labeled, with both compass directions and alphanumerics, and the freeway I am on seems randomly to change its name, this variably being the road to Norfolk, Newport News, Virginia Beach, and Portsmouth. Supposedly, these cities are all in a line at the end of the same road, but the changing signage leads me to wonder—my confusion heightened by the density of the traffic around me—if perhaps there are four parallel roads to these places and I am unwittingly hopping back and forth among them.

But what I am most struck by are the signs' historical resonances. A native Californian, my knowledge of much of our nation's past has been acquired secondhand through books and movies and lacks the intimacy of place. And so I am filled with awe as I pass turnoffs for Manassas (site of the First and Second Battles of Bull Run), Spotsylvania, Chancellorsville, Fredericksburg, and Richmond, capital of the Confederacy. So much history in so few miles.

At Fredericksburg I pull off the freeway and find my way to the battlefield site. It is late and a light rain is beginning to fall, but still I take the self-guided tour and walk down the Sunken Road, where Confederate forces crouched behind a four-foot stone wall in December 1862. Behind the road is a steep slope, at the top of which the Confederates placed their cannon. The position allowed the Rebel gunners to aim their shot directly over the heads of their own riflemen, and the combination of artillery and infantry gave them complete control of the open plain upon which the Union forces tried to advance.

It would be hard to imagine a better defensive position, and the Confederates repulsed seven Union charges. Fifteen thousand Union soldiers died here, and in the aftermath Robert E. Lee wrote, "It is well that war is so terrible; else we should grow too fond of it."

In the summer before the battle of Fredericksburg, Mrs. Robert E. Lee was captured by Union troops. As an indication, perhaps, of the civility that was then still possible in the midst of war, or perhaps as a matter of professional courtesy, General George McClellan kept his counterpart's wife no longer than necessary. Within a few days safe transit was arranged, and Mrs. Lee was allowed to return to Virginia.

In her carriage she carried with her two tomatoes, acquired in Washington and given by Mrs. Lee to the Confederate officer who escorted her home. Tomatoes were hard to come by in war ravaged Virginia, and Mrs. Lee knew they would be welcomed. Clearly they were, for the recipient of the tomatoes, Captain W. Roy Mason, saved the seeds. He planted these and shared them with others, and soon the Lee tomato spread throughout the state. Even today it can still be found—a reminder of the vast intercourse in small and common things that helped to bind us even in the midst of our greatest dispute.

# MAY

MAY 4

I**T'S GOOD TO BE MISSED.** My wife's employer held a conference while I was gone, and her attentions were not on the hearth. When I return, dishes are unwashed, the refrigerator is bare ("No milk!"), potted plants are dry, the living room smells of dead flowers, the lawn is unmowed, the car battery is dead, my son, having chosen the time of my absence for his only earache of the year, is on antibiotics—and the seedlings need them, having acquired tiny black spots on the leaves and green, aphid-looking things on a few stems.

Fortunately, all this is fixable. The dirty dishes yield to soapy water, and the dry plants to plain. The battery I jump. The seedlings I spray with insecticidal soap and malathion. This mixture is too harsh for some plants, and the tips of the Churchill ivy are burned by it. But it's what's in the sprayer, and the seedlings are becoming such a fiasco that I'm willing to risk it.

In contrast, the new nursery plants have done exceedingly well. Despite cool weather, they have gained leaf size, width across

74

the crown, and an average of two inches in height. As I am surveying them, Albert comes outside and joins me. Mysteriously, his plants have acquired a noticeable yellow tinge, and standing by our paired plots he points this out, making a sweeping, underhand motion from his plants to mine and saying, as he does so, "Green!" The word rolls heavily from his tongue. And then a miracle happens. He shakes his head and adds—and I understand—"I don't know. I use steer manure."

How I catch this I will never know. But clearly he had said that he used steer manure to fertilize his tomatoes.

This is tricky business. A university extension handout in my collection states that "If manure is used, it should be incorporated into the soil several weeks prior to planting, then irrigated thoroughly to allow time for decomposition to begin and to leech out harmful salts." And the tomato man at Anderson's had warned me against it just last week, saying manure would burn my new plants. (True to his word, the tomato man had also left me a message while I was gone: The Beefsteaks' grower had been as surprised as I to learn of the plants' "VFN" designation. The seedlings were ordinary Beefsteaks and *not* resistant to anything; it was the labels that were in error, these having been purchased from a commercial supplier and no one having bothered to check them.)

It would be impossible for me to explain to Albert the intricacies of steer manure. Even if I could, it would not undo the deed. So instead, I bring him into our garage, show him the box of Miracle-Gro, mix a two-gallon can, and give it to him so he can fertilize his plants. This makes him happy. But long-term, my guess is that the plants are going to have a rough time of it. And if they do, I suspect that in Albert's mind I will be partly to blame for having given him inferior plants.

### MAY 5

Today I stop by the friends to whom I gave the packet of heirloom seeds. In a whiskey barrel in their front yard I discover a flourishing tomato plant, with flowers and several sizable fruit, and I ask them eagerly if this is one of the heirlooms. "No," they tell me, none of those made it. This plant had "grown from compost."

Compost, I know from innumerable newspaper and magazine articles, requires layering, grinding, proportioning, cooking, turning, and meticulous effective incantation, and what my friends mean is that they had thrown some kitchen scraps out into the dirt in the barrel. Compost it probably isn't, but it has still proved fertile enough to have spontaneously generated this fine tomato plant. If the method were only reproducible (it being just as capable of having produced a squash or a pepper plant), I'd try it next year.

These same friends have just returned from a trip to Georgia, and they tell me they visited the town of Juliette. To get there, they had to "drive and drive and drive" on empty roads through unbroken pine forests. The town's great distance from anywhere was something of an economic hardship, and it had been "a month away from shutting down" when a film crew arrived to begin the making of *Fried Green Tomatoes*. Even the Whistle Stop Cafe had been closed and boarded up, but the film's success has apparently revived it. My friends had to take a ticket and wait for more than an hour before they could be seated to eat. Naturally, their meals included fried green tomatoes, and these could be ordered separately as well. Tomatoes, it seems, have saved the town—though Hollywood has helped, and the tomatoes themselves now come from Florida.

Declarations of tomato preferences have continued to accumulate on the Internet. Surprisingly, the trend of the first few days has held steady, with many varieties having supporters but few receiving more than one vote.

They're an eclectic group, these Interneters. There are boosters of the everyday (Better Boy, Big Boy, and Wonder Boy) and fans of the exotic ("My vote would be for the Russian Oxheart"). And there are those who take the pragmatic view ("The BEST tomato is the first one you pick after waiting for it to ripen since the last one last season. The tomato that reminds you why you do all of this!"). But still, a winner has emerged:

> My favorite is the Rutgers. A relatively old cultivar by today's standards (1928), it was perhaps the most popular

garden tomato in the U. S. for quite a few years. Open-pollinated, indeterminate, medium-sized fruits, good yield (sustained over a long harvesting time rather than maturing all at once), excellent flavor. Juicy but not watery, with a nice blend of tartness and sweetness. It has never disappointed me—it's the best salad tomato I know of.

Because this voter is from California and obviously less partisan than the New Jerseyite who tried earlier to steal the election, I am inclined to give increased weight to his opinion. Moreover, with the electorate so fractured, Rutgers has now amassed twice as many votes as its nearest rival. Rutgers wins the title of Internet Top Tomato.

But different forums produce different results. Not long ago *Sunset* asked its readers a similar question, and the variety most preferred was Early Girl, which "earned twenty-eight times more votes than most of the other varieties, and two and a half times the votes of its nearest rival, Sweet 100."

Early Girl's most prized trait was its early maturation. But the balance swings when the consideration is taste. Some years ago, *Los Angeles Times* garden writer Bill Sidnam reported on a taste test he had conducted among friends, chefs, and commercial growers. They used a twenty-five-point scale. And though they were outdoors in the full sun and open air (seed companies, says Sidnam, conduct their tests in darkened rooms under colored lights to prevent the confounding of appearance with taste), the group somehow managed to overcome this difficulty and to sample twenty-one different varieties. President, with a score of twenty-one, was judged the best.

Sidnam grew many of the tomatoes the group tasted, and naturally he has his own favorites. These include Supersteak, Lemon Boy, Better Boy, Brandywine, Early Girl, and Red Currant—"my youngest daughter's favorite." He has had ample opportunity to develop this list, for he grows some two dozen varieties each year and over the past forty years has grown over four hundred different kinds of tomato. This strikes me as an almost inconceivable luxury—having the time and the space to try and to grow so many tomatoes. And Sidnam would be the last to argue. "I really do," he says, "have fun."

## MAY 6

I am startled today to discover flower buds on several of the new tomatoes. Overnight, they have appeared in clusters at the plants' centers.

Literally, this is not true of course—the buds have been developing for some time. But such is the way we see plants grow. Seemingly they are static; they sit there and do nothing. Accordingly, our attentions wander, and when next we focus them, the plant in question has spurted up, sent out new leaves, popped into bloom, set fruit, or in any one of myriad other ways somehow changed. So the changes we notice are inevitably big, but I suppose it can be no other way.

Nor is this different from the way I see—or fail to see—my son grow.

## MAY 7

I am working in the front yard this afternoon when Albert approaches me with a great cluster of lemons from his tree. There are six in all, and he gives them to me—a reciprocal gift for the six Beefsteaks I gave to him and for my ministrations when they were ailing. Surprisingly, the plants have rebounded nicely and are now green and tall.

We don't need these lemons—we have our own tree and it has ample fruit. But still we will use them, and I am thankful for Albert's gift. Mostly, though, I am thankful for the absolution I have received of the guilt I might have borne for having given him suspect tomato plants.

## MAY 8

Today is Mother's Day, and as part of the celebration my son and I have planned a special breakfast for my wife. We will be having fresh-squeezed orange juice, a fresh fruit bowl (mangoes, strawberries, and kiwi), and coddled eggs topped with chives and tarragon from our yard. My son has also ordered orange brioches from a local pastry shop, and as he and I are climbing into the car to pick these up, he says, "Look, the tomato cages—they're gone."

And so they are. Looking puny and alone, the two tomatoes closest to the sidewalk, the Celebrities, have been stripped of their superstructures. This is a risk, I suppose, for anything I leave in the front yard, especially so near the sidewalk. But still I am furious. Who would steal some rusted wire cages? John, Albert, and Vito are all out tending their yards, and they commiserate with me. Kids, they surmise, are the culprits; they come through the neighborhood and tear things up, take things. This is true, and my neighbors routinely are the victims of teenagers who help themselves to their citrus trees. But my belief is that the cages have been taken by someone who wanted them for his own tomatoes. No doubt the thief had recognized my cages' superior design and construction, and decided to take mine rather than make his own.

As we restart our trip, my son, still too young—too innocent—to understand the finality of such an event, asks what I'm going to do to get the cages back. There is, of cours,e nothing I can do, and as I fume about it, I am reminded of a stream of related events.

The first tomato I grew in this house was stolen from me. I had been watching it grow riper by the day, my anticipation growing in proportion to the depth of its color, and finally one day I knew that on the morrow it would be ready—perfection would have been achieved. That next morning I eagerly went out to reap my reward for a crop well tended, and when I did so I found the precious fruit gone. My heart sank; not only had the tomato been taken but so had my trust in our new neighborhood. It was too much of a coincidence to believe that this one fruit, the only one ripe, had come to the attention of a random passerby; rather, it had undoubtedly been under observation by someone monitoring its development, much as I had been doing. A dozen suspects had leapt to mind (the guy who walked his dog early every morning; the guy who walked his two dogs late every evening; the newspaper man . . . ), and it so incensed me that I began to hatch irrational plans to catch or thwart the criminal. (I would sleep in the patio and spring out to confront him when next he struck. Or I'd post a phony *Poison!* sign announcing my recent use of some terrible toxic spray.) I harvested a great many tomatoes that year, and the cumulative weight of the many neighborhood courtesies and kindnesses extended us (that was the year John and Rose brought us the platter of pasta) so far exceeded the wound inflicted by that anonymous miscreant that my irritation at the incident eventually began to wane. Like retailers faced inescapably with "inventory shrinkage," I began to view such episodes as the unavoidable price of gardening next to the sidewalk.

But I have never accepted it as *right*. And so I was doubly annoyed when, several years later, I came home one evening to a report from my wife that she had driven up to find a *family*—on foot and clearly not from the neighborhood—leaving our premises with several bags of fresh-picked tomatoes. She had words with them, but to no avail. And we were left again with the feeling of rage and impotence that comes from being treated as suckers. (How could anyone be so foolish as to grow tomatoes in their front yard, there for all the world to take?)

Memories of the stories of others come tumbling as well. A tailor last week told me of a bucket of dirt taken from the side of her house. ("They'll steal *anything!*") The palm tree of a neighbor had been ripped from his front yard (an ugly gouge in the earth greeting my son and I the next day as we passed by on our way to the bus stop). And the tulips of my son's best friend's mother had been dug from her flower beds in broad daylight.

These memories mix themselves in a hot stew with my irritation at the theft of the cages, and so I am not surprised when I realize I've overshot the pastry shop by several blocks. I turn around, we buy the brioches, and return home. Here, we share the news with my wife (who shakes her head in wonder) and set the matter aside while we get on with preparing the breakfast.

Afterwards, I call *my* mother, who fills me in on events in her life. Her employer is proceeding with its relocation, and many people have already left. Her group will be among the last to leave, and she will have a job until the end of the year; however, she is beginning to read the want ads and to update her resume.

She tells me also of her tomatoes, which are "eighteen inches high and have flowers."

When we have finished talking, I return to the problem of the tomato cages. To replace them I will need a roll of concrete reinforcing wire, which means a trip to the mega-hardware store—"Homeowner's Hell," as Dave Barry calls it. To accommodate the roll of wire, I will have to take the backseat out of our station wagon. And I will need some heavy-duty wire cutters.

I begin the ordeal (this is not what I had planned for the day) by walking across the street and asking Vito if he still has the cutters I used when first I made my cages, and if so whether I might borrow them again. Yes, he says, I can use them anytime. That done, I proceed to dismantle the car.

Naturally the seat resists my efforts, but eventually I wrest it loose. As I am doing so, I am greeted by a local couple out for a Sunday stroll. We exchange greetings, and in the course of our conversation I mention the theft of my cages. They are sympathetic, and we repeat the same speculations I went through earlier with John, Albert, and Vito—vandals or renegade tomato grower?

The question would seem forever unknowable, but as they are leaving and round the corner, they call back to me with the answer. "Your tomato cages," they shout. "Here they are." And so they were, flung in some bushes across the street from Albert's house. The thieves had been mere curs with no care at all about the cages, their use, the quality of their construction, or much else about them except that they had been easy to yank up and toss about.

I am of course relieved by the cages' reappearance—I needn't spend the afternoon re-creating them. But having prepared the car physically and myself mentally to go to Mega-hardware, I decide to make the trip anyway to pick up some incidentals. This is a mistake. And hours later, after I have wandered the miles of aisles and evaded the dragster forklifts, as I stand with a pounding headache in the swarm before the cash register (which naturally goes "down" just as it is my turn to pay), I realize as I do every time I come here that I would be a happier person if I went always and only to our tiny, one-mile-away neighborhood hardware store and paid more money to choose from a smaller but still adequate stock of merchandise. Mega is not for the sane.

There is no joy in it, but deep in the store's bowels I do find something I've not found elsewhere: California Suns in four-inch pots. I buy two—stand-ins for the enfeebled seedlings—along with two bags of potting soil. The price, including soil, bailing wire, and a pair of leather gloves is $29.55—which seems a lot. Especially when you add in the pound of flesh.

After lunch and a short convalescence, I reinstall the two wandering cages and wire all seven together, thereby making their future removal an all-or-nothing affair. The potting soil I pour into fifteen-gallon black plastic buckets (hoping they'll do for me what they've done for the Better Boys down the street). I water the filled containers thoroughly. But the actual planting of the Suns I leave for a day less tiring.

### MAY 11

My plants' first flower has opened today, announcing itself ready for fertilization and the creation of fruit. Of course, like my first notice of the buds' appearance, this is but a contrived view of what in truth has been a seamless unfolding, ordained and begun from the first moment of the flower's formation, and indeed from the first moment the plant's seed was placed in soil, took on water, and began unfurling its genetic material.

Similarly, other events occur today which are but parts of their own unfolding but now intertwining stories. I plant the new California Suns. I fertilize. And another neighbor has planted his tomatoes.

Three houses to the east of us tomatoes have appeared in the yard of the contractor with the damaged back. His plants—kin to the big ones he gave the owner of Dan the Dog—occupy a raised, red-brick bed that borders the sidewalk. Unlike my patch, which harbors only tomatoes, this spot is home also to lettuce, peppers, basil, and grapes. A row of roses helps protect the tomatoes from the reach of casual passersby, but a pair of large, over-reaching olive trees also shields the plants from the sun. So the location is less than perfect. But even so, these thirteen plants, each tied neatly to a pastel-colored broomstick, and each grown from seed, represent one of the neighborhood's more prominent commitments to tomatoes.

## MAY 12

The common noun from which my name is derived is spelled *shepherd*, and in every phone book I have looked in the most common spelling of the name is the way that I spell it. *Shepherd* is, however, the *last* way strangers will attempt to spell my name, and invariably, when filling out a form or taking a message, they will offer up a litany of Shepard, Sheppard, Shepphard, Shepperd, Shephard, Shepeard, Shepheard, Sheperd, Sherperd, and Shapherd before I spell it for them—after which, more often than not, they will simply ignore what I've said and write it down the way they think I should spell it. Occasionally, my last name will be spelled right, but my first name will be spelled with a *ph*.

In the mail today I receive a new catalog. I try not to be swayed by its name, or by that of its publisher (Renee Shepherd), or the correct spelling of both, but in every respect *Shepherd's Garden Seeds* is an elegant work—a catalog that speaks of its makers' pride and pleasure in its undertaking.

The ink, paper, typography, and layout all invite readers to turn the pages and to look, and at every page, those who do so are rewarded. There are garden tips, original watercolor and pen-and-ink drawings, and fascinating recipes. The Cilantro Corn Pancakes sound particularly appetizing, and one recipe—Stir-Fry Cherry Tomatoes and Herbs—is clearly Sinic at least in inspiration.

All this is packaging, of course, but the catalog's promise is fulfilled in Shepherd's selection of seeds. They have ornamental popcorns, three dozen kinds of lettuce, mescluns, and salad greens, and two pages of edible flowers. And they have nineteen varieties of tomatoes, of which half are new to me, including Old Flame, Enchantment (bearer of crimson fruit likened by Shepherd to Fabergé eggs), and a Japanese variety called Pink Odoriko, said to have rose red fruits, heavy in the hand and "pretty as their name."

It is an exuberant, inclusive catalog. A catalog for master gardeners. For wanna-bes. And for everyone else.

# RENEE SHEPHERD'S RECIPE FOR STIR-FRY CHERRY TOMATOES AND HERBS

*Fast cooking perfectly marries the flavors of herbs and sweet/tart tomatoes.*

1 pint or about 3 dozen cherry tomatoes, stemmed, washed,
   patted dry
1 tablespoon butter
1 tablespoon olive oil
1 large clove garlic, minced
1 shallot, or two scallions, minced
1/3 cup chopped fresh basil
1 tablespoon chopped fresh oregano
Salt and freshly ground pepper

*In a large skillet, heat butter and oil. Add garlic and shallot (or scallions), and sauté for 2 or 3 minutes until fragrant. Add tomatoes and herbs, shaking pan continuously for 2 to 3 minutes, until heated through. Do not overcook. Season with salt and pepper to taste. Serve immediately.*
*Serves 4*

❧ ❧ ❧

Several weeks ago an Internet posting appeared that elicited two separate lines of response—one intended, the other not. An unknown Hoosier sent out the following:

Subject: Tall tomatoe (Indiana spelling)
  I have grown a Beefmaster tomatoe that was 11'5" from where the stem entered the ground to the tallest tip. It was one very long stake. Anyone out there with tall tomatoe stories?

Not surprisingly, the first group of responses concerns plant height. These include accounts of two-story tomato plants harvested from balconies, of plants coaxed through elm trees, and of cherries that climbed up *and then down* twelve-foot wire towers, the ring of truth provided by the correspondents' frequent lament that the plants' tallness seemed induced by a quest for light and was typically accompanied by poor or nonexistent fruit production.

But the second category of responses is less expected. It concerns spelling. Implicitly, the Hoosier has claimed that placement of an *e* on the end of *tomato* is acceptable in Indiana—exonerating by extension Dan Quayle of his famous gaffe. This claim has been challenged, and a debate has arisen on the subject of trailing *e*'s. Several respondents offer a general plea for the cessation of further "Quayle spellings." An Idahoan states "with all certainty that we spell *potato* without an *e*, although when we are talking about two potatoes the *e* is added." And from Colorado comes the observation, "I spell *tomato* WITHOUT the *e* as well as *potato* without the *e*. And you know what? I can't find *tomatoe* or *potatoe* in my *American Heritage Dictionary*." But this brings a rebuke from Jackie, who offers an all-encompassing explanation for the dictionary's omission and the idiosyncratic spelling habits of Indiana's favorite son:

> Thise ise because ite ise thee Americane Heritagee Dictionarye. Potatoe withe an 'e' ise the Englishe spellinge. Soe, it'se onlye incorrecte ife youe insiste one Americane spellinge.
>
> Whene Ie wase ae weee littlee girle mye teachere markede offe thirtye pointse frome ae majore teste becausee Ie usede Englishe spellinge one threee wordse. Ie saide, "Whye dide Ie gete ae 70e one mye historye exame, whene Ie knewe alle thee answerse?" Ande shee pointede oute thee "misspellede" wordse. "Ohe," Ie saide, "Ie usede thee Englishe spellinge." "Welle, we'ree note ine Englandee aree wee?" Ande Ie gote ae 70e, ore "C+e" ase mye Historye gradee fore thate terme. Grrrrrrrrre.

Sing with me now: "You spell potatoe and I spell potato, you spell tomatoe and I spell tomato. Potatoe! Potato! Tomatoe! Tomato! Let's call the whole thing off. . . ."

The V. P., it seems, was an Anglophile-e.

## MAY 15

At the grocery store today the talk is all of the weather. "It's depressing," says the checkout clerk. "It makes you just want to go home and hide."

"Yes, it does," says the man in front of me. "Yes, it does."

For the past three weeks the highs have been in the midsixties. It has been overcast constantly, and the drizzle has been frequent; today a heavy mist falls all morning. None of this is unusual. It results from what meteorologists call a heavy marine layer—a thin layer of ocean-born clouds that backs up against the mountains and blankets the Southern California coast—and it constitutes a seasonal weather pattern so predictable as to have been locally dubbed "June gloom." But its earlier-than-usual arrival and its unrelenting nature has had a cumulative and collective depressive effect, and we are all anxious for it to break.

For tomatoes, too, the weather has been less than ideal. The seedlings have been virtually dormant, but even so, those I intend to keep I must transplant today. Tomorrow I am leaving on business—back to Virginia for an encore of the talk I gave two weeks ago—and the day after I get back I depart with my family for ten days in Great Britain. For my son and me this will be a vacation; for my wife the trip will be a mixture of work and pleasure. A friend will house-sit while we are gone, and he will tend and water the tomatoes. But I don't feel that I can reasonably ask him to go up on the roof, and so I must now install them in their permanent homes without further ado.

Behind our house is a gravel-surfaced dog run patrolled on the far side of the fence by Dan the Dog and occupied on our side by a makeshift fort built by my son and his best friend. The site of battles, planning conferences, and engineering marvels, the fort is composed of loose boards, string, PVC pipes, various arma-

ments—a plastic crossbow among them—and whatever miscella-
neous building materials seem to have placed themselves at the
disposal of two boys, one ten and one eleven. Among the latter is
my supply of potting containers, which have been stacked to
make walls and columns, and to access this stockpile I must partially disassemble my son's fort. He is not around to consult with
me as I do this, but my conscience is assuaged by the knowledge
that he'll replace the pots by freely requisitioning from around the
house whatever else he needs.

From the fort I retrieve my two largest-available remaining
pots and eight one-gallon black plastic containers. These I fill with
the remainder of the potting soil from Mega-hardware. From the
roof I retrieve the seedlings for the last time. From my original
planting, I have now made several varieties redundant through
supplemental purchases. These I no longer consider candidates for
transplanting, and from the remaining varieties I weigh my
options.

The Sweet Millions are indeterminates, and if they ever take
off will become big, sprawling plants unsuited for container life.
Reluctantly, I conclude that this year I will have no Millions. The
Heartland is supposed to do well in containers, and so I pick the
heartiest of the seedlings and transplant it to the largest of my
waiting pots. For my next-largest pot I select the healthiest-
looking Chelsea; Chelseas are probably little better suited to containers than Sweet Millions, but without cherries there would be
no season, and so these I must have. Into three of the small pots I
put Pixies, and into another three I put Basket Kings. The last two
pots I fill with a pair each of Floragolds.

All the seedlings are still small—minute, really, in the case of
the one-inch-tall Floragolds—and they appear slightly ridiculous
in their new homes. But nonetheless I sprinkle them with Miracle-
Gro and arrange them neatly against the white stucco of our
house, hoping in this way to provide them a little added reflected
heat. Unfortunately, they will still be in the patio and their light
exposure will still be less than ideal; but I fear if I put them out
front they soon would take a sojourn like that of the cages. So
their home will be the patio. The decision embodies the tradeoff I

have made in most other realms of my life, a tradeoff I never like but seem always to make: security over the willingness to risk it all and try for the best.

So eighty-four days after I first filled my starting trays, my crop is in:

STARTING CROP: MAY 15

| VARIETY | COUNT | SOURCE | GROWTH HABIT | LOCATION |
|---|---|---|---|---|
| Celebrity | 2 | nursery | determinate | planter box (ground) |
| Beefsteak | 1 | " | indeterminate | " |
| Champion | 3 | " | indeterminate | " |
| Lemon Boy | 1 | " | indeterminate | " |
| California Sun | 2 | " | dwarf indeterminate | patio (pots) |
| Heartland | 1 | seed | dwarf indeterminate | " |
| Chelsea | 1 | " | indeterminate | " |
| Pixie | 3 | " | determinate | " |
| Basket King | 3 | " | determinate | " |
| Floragold | 4 | " | dwarf determinate | " |

I have 21 plants—9 from the nursery, 12 from seed. The latter are all I have used from the 500 or so seeds I purchased and from the 169 I sprouted. This is, perhaps, a profligate waste—all that DNA coaxed by water, light, and warmth to uncoil and begin the process of life, and so little to show for it. But this progression—500 to 169 to 12—is probably not much different than would have occurred in nature. Probably it is better. And indeed, the strategy that has brought me these 12 plants—success through reproductive excess—is the strategy of nature itself.

Moreover, the waste is not complete. The seedlings that are left over I will give away. For the gift packs, that was my intention. As with karma, some of these will come back to me—as lemons or cookies, or, as happens this afternoon, as odd and pleasing bits of information.

After the transplanting is finished, my son's baby-sitter, to whom I gave the leftover Champions and Lemon Boys, stops by for a visit. He is leaving for Spain in a few days and has come to say good-bye. We will miss him, for in the long string of baby-sitters we have hired, he has been among the best. He was fond of my son, and the two became companions, each gaining something from the other. Unfortunately, we learned again from him that our son's best sitters—the ones both stimulating and responsible—are also those most likely to be with us but a short time. It is they who are eager to get on with life and have the wherewithal to do so.

The tomato plants he got from us are "doing well," he says. He'll be leaving them in the care of his roommates. But the fate of one surprises me. Being an experimentalist and in college (and twenty years old and with a silver bead recently affixed to the side of his nose), he severed one plant from its roots. The top he placed in water with nutrients and a material he calls "rock wool," so that it might grow hydroponically. This one too is "doing well," having sprouted new roots which are spreading quickly through their liquid home. Why it was necessary to cut off the old roots I do not know—shaking off the dirt and rinsing them would seem to have sufficed. But I do know that for each of us, the way we grow tomatoes is as different as the way we lead our lives.

## MAY 16

Before I depart this morning, I flag down a neighborhood couple out for an early walk, he a newspaper reporter, she a lawyer, their infant son pushed along in a three-wheeled exer-stroller. Would they like some tomato plants?

They tell me they have never grown tomatoes ("It's not the sort of thing we've done before") but have no objection to trying. I bring them into the patio and give them two of the six-packs, one with California Suns, a Lemon Boy, and a Heartland, and the other one filled with determinate and miniature cherries. Because they are novices, I skip the details about names and growth habits and tell them simply that the seedlings in one of the six-packs will do well in containers—since they, like me, are short of space.

Perhaps I have done them a disfavor. They may become addicts, for they pursue their interests seriously. They have bicycled across Europe. They run marathons. And they play rollerblade hockey. But they themselves note that if they harvest only three fruits it will be three more than they would have had otherwise. And if they do acquire a passion for the culture of tomatoes, will harm have been done?

## MAY 19

Tomatoes today are front-page news. The *New York Times, Wall Street Journal, Los Angeles Times,* and *San Diego Union* all carry the news that the Food and Drug Administration has approved Calgene's Flavr Savr for sale. There are bold headlines, photographs, and explanatory graphics with twisting ladders of DNA and petri dishes filled with little colored squares and triangles.

The first sales are expected in ten days; the first stores to carry the Flavr Savrs will be in the Midwest and Northern California. This means I and my fellow San Diegans will have to be patient. But it means also there are fields of Flavr Savrs under cultivation right now—fields with reddening fruit that, says one article, will "give birth to a new era." I only wish I could see them.

In preparation for our trip to England tomorrow, I ask this morning a fellow parent at my son's bus stop if she would like some tomato plants. The answer is yes, and after she walks home with me, I give her the final gift pack, along with a half dozen selections from the main flat. Later, in one grand stroke, I offer the whole of the remains in the flat to Vito. There are nearly three dozen seedlings left, but he, like his brother, is interested primarily in the big ones, and so I mark for him with toothpicks the Supersteaks and Champions. The diaspora is now complete.

Also in preparation for our trip I water all of our plants and leave instructions as to their care for our friend who will be house-sitting. Most of the yard is on automatic sprinklers and should require little effort. However, the potted plants will need to be hand-watered, and in particular, the tomatoes in the containers will need water whenever the soil's surface dries out, perhaps as often as every day. The tomatoes in the ground can be watered with the soaker hose. In addition, we leave instructions concerning the mail, the cat, the garbage, the newspapers, the car alarm, the phone machine, and the refrigerator ("Eat everything in it"). My wife writes out a neat, detailed list and an itinerary and phone numbers where we can be reached.

Our friend is a combat veteran and college educated; we have known him for nearly twenty years. But still I am apprehensive. No matter his competence or intentions, he'll not do things as I would. He will maintain our home, but not nurture it. And unavoidably my thoughts are on the time years ago when we came back from a trip and there had been a Santa Ana, and our potted plants, tomatoes included, were wilted and near death.

### MAY 20 AND 21

At 8 A.M. we leave our house for the airport, from whence we will fly to Dallas, and then to London. It will be my third time this week in the Dallas/Fort Worth airport. A cab arrives at our house to pick us up, and as we load our suitcases, John, Albert, and Vito form an impromptu gathering on the sidewalk in front of our tomatoes to wish us farewell. For the first time in a long while the skies are clear and the sun adds to the warmth of the good-byes we receive—all accompanied by liberal assurances that our home will be looked after. Our friend the house-sitter is there as well, and they all wave as we drive away; we laugh as we go, and as we do I am aware that in this send-off is all that I have come to love about our neighborhood. My wife feels it too, and to her it brings tears.

The flight is long. Longer by twice than any I've ever made. As it proceeds we do all that one can do on an airplane—eat, read and fidget; retrieve and stow, stow and retrieve our luggage; bicker, eat, look out the window; listen to music, talk to the stewardesses, eat, watch the movie, and try to sleep. But the hours pass interminably, and our efforts to sleep are largely in vain.

One diversion is the reading of British newspapers, provided courtesy of the airline. I receive an *International Herald Tribune,* and in it I discover that interest in Calgene's Flavr Savr is not limited to the U.S. It fails to make the front page, having to compete with news of human-rights violations and with the death of

Jackie Onassis, but the story does appear on page three. The article is drawn from the same reports I read yesterday and adds nothing to what I've already learned. But I do note that *tomato* has been spelled without the trailing *e*.

We pass nearly over Greenland as we make our way east, and only then do I begin to understand just how far north the United Kingdom is—farther north than anyplace in the continental United States. Only then do I begin to understand the recent news reports for London of daily low temperatures in the forties. And only then, despite our recent cool and wet weather, do I begin to understand that London is not going to be like San Diego. "Toto," I think, "we're not in California anymore."

Eventually we begin our descent. It is, says the pilot, eleven degrees centigrade at Gatwick Airport; the obvious clouds and drizzle are apparently not worth mentioning. The day's first wave of international flights are all arriving at the same time (9 A.M. local time, 1 A.M. San Diego time—seventeen hours since we left home), and we must wait nearly an hour to have our passports checked. This done, my wife goes to find a luggage carrier, and my son and I approach a ticket counter to buy tickets for the train downtown. I request three tickets—two adult and one child—and the agent responds with a comment that seems to have something to do with my mother. Or his. I can't tell which.

"I'm sorry," I say, "could you repeat that?" He does, but again he asks about my mother, and again I ask him to repeat himself. We do it a third time, and this time my son translates: "He said, 'You don't have two adults, do you?'"

"Yes," I say, "we do." And having thus demonstrated our proficiency in English, we get our tickets. Reuniting with my wife, we board the train and begin our ride to Victoria Station, following a route through tenement housing heavily painted with graffiti much like that so common in San Diego: great chunky letters with colored shading to give the illusion of three-dimensionality, some of it indecipherable, much of it angry.

We have been told our hotel is only a two-minute walk from Victoria Station. Because, however, it is raining, we approach the taxi stand to ask about a ride. No need, says the driver, it's just a block or so around the corner. So we grab our bags—one per hand, and, in the case of my wife and I, one per shoulder—and set out in the indicated direction. I feel at this moment like a cross between a war refugee and the stereotypical middle-class American tourist that I am, obviously laden with far more stuff than I need.

The definition of a "block" can be somewhat arbitrary, and it is difficult here to see what one block might actually be, since the streets cross at myriad angles. Is the tip of a pie-shaped bit of land ending at a traffic circle a block? Before finding out, we are nearly killed as we look carefully in the wrong direction for cars before venturing across our first intersection. Despite the advantage of their high speed and our inexperience, they miss us, and once across the street, we put down our bags and again consult our map. Whether we've gotten any closer is uncertain. We select a course and resume our trudge. But in a moment my son complains—the bags are too heavy.

Yes, I know. And it's wet and we're tired and we're about to get lost, if we haven't already done so. So we find a covered doorway, and I leave my wife and son while I go to find the hotel—Pa Shepherd scouting ahead while his homeless family huddles on a street stoop. Luckily, this only takes a few minutes. I return to my wife and son, and we again hoist our bags—they're still too heavy, says my son—and set off.

After checking in, we shower and venture across the street for a sandwich. It is now 2 P.M. London time. We have been cautioned by everyone we know not to go to sleep upon our arrival, since it will only delay getting used to the time change and will leave us wide awake in the middle of the night. Nonetheless, my son is exhausted, as am I, and wants nothing but to sleep. In good conscience I can't make him stay awake. We are, after all, on vacation. So he and I return to our room, where I, being a good father, will go to sleep as well. My wife is stronger of both body and will, and elects to spend the afternoon sightseeing.

The next seventeen hours are spent in a stuporous delirium, a murky semiconsciousness of drifting in and out of sleep. As predicted, we awaken at midnight and then again . . . and again . . .

and again. We lie in bed and consider our options—we could see the sights at night or go find a bite to eat, but we decide it best to sleep on. Once I awaken and find myself thinking of Ronald Reagan, who was ridiculed for stopping a day in Hawaii to acclimate himself during a state trip to Tokyo. He was in his seventies at the time, and the maneuver now strikes me as well considered.

That I find wisdom in an act by Ronald Reagan is a clear sign of my disorientation, but eventually the morning comes.

## MAY 22

I am awakened by an intense white light. I think at first that perhaps I am hallucinating again, but this is real and the light fills the room as though we were on a stage. But before I can react, it begins to fade and then to go out, accompanied by a curse from my wife. The electrical plugs in England are big, industrial-strength affairs, and she has plugged her makeup mirror into the wall using the necessary U. S. to U. K. electric-socket adapter. But she has neglected to use the equally necessary voltage converter. For the briefest of moments the lights of the mirror had shone brighter than they had ever shone before, but then they had died, spent by the effort to exceed their limits.

Our first alert activity is to consume a "Traditional English Breakfast," which in this hotel consists of meat, eggs, potatoes, tomatoes (grilled whole), and various fruits, juices, and pastries. The word *tomato* appears half a dozen times on the menu, and not once is it spelled with an *e*. I begin to suspect that *tomatoe* is an acceptable English spelling only for Jackie and a handful of Quayle apologists. But the breakfast is wonderful.

In sound tourist tradition, we begin the day with a bus tour of central London. This takes us past the big biggies: Big Ben, Parliament, London Bridge, and the Tower of London. We pass also the stone foundation of the Temple of Mithras, a Roman place of worship that serves to reinforce this city's nearly two-thousand-year-old heritage. In fact, the city is even older than that, for the Romans took the name they gave the place, Londinium, from a Celtic name in use by settlers who had arrived before them.

At the conclusion of the tour we are deposited at Hyde Park, from whence we set out on foot, destination varying. We pass a pub with an ugly gash in its metalwork and over which a protective piece of acrylic has been placed; the gouge, says a sign, is damage from a German bomb. We come to Mount Street Park, a small pocket park with lush grass, London Planes (a large shade tree with maplelike leaves), and well-tended flower beds. Large buildings so surround the park that it is completely secluded from the outside world—a secret garden. Curiously, the park's paths are lined continuously with elegant teak benches, identical save some are new and some are weathered and upon which no more than two or three isolated people are sitting. There are many more benches than necessary, but on each one I find a plaque bearing the name of a benefactor or of a deceased loved one on whose behalf the bench was given and who had enjoyed the solitude and serenity of this park. A surprising number are American.

The reason for the American benches becomes clear a few blocks away when we stumble upon Grosvenor Square, and along one side of it the U. S. embassy—the first I have ever seen. On a corner of the square stands a statue of Dwight Eisenhower looking across the way towards the building that housed Supreme Headquarters Allied Expeditionary Forces; it is here that the invasion of Normandy, the fiftieth anniversary of which will occur in two weeks, was planned.

A few blocks from Grosvenor Square we find convincing evidence of the English ability to spell, despite their fondness for extra *u*'s. Here we arrive at Shepherd Market, a narrow pedestrian-only lane lined with shops. Shepherd Market parallels Shepherd Street, on which is Shepherd House (purveyor of miniature figurines) and Shepherd Tavern.

We would like to go into Shepherd Tavern, but it is closed. And so we make our way, at my son's urging, to Piccadilly Circus. "Circus" in this case is a linguistic derivation of *circle*, as in traffic circle, but the place is actually more a zoo than a circus, crammed with people and run through with unpredictable, high-speed traffic. Giant neon signs look down on us, and though the bus guide had told us proudly that the signs in Piccadilly were the precursors of those in Tokyo and Times Square, I am most reminded by them of *Blade Runner's* futuristic and decadent Los Angeles.

The cultural, as it were, center of Piccadilly, appears to be the Trocadero. This is a large, enclosed arcade and food fair filled with escalators, noise, and young people as varied in the languages they speak as they are uniform in the black clothing they wear. Naturally it holds a powerful appeal for my son. Inside is the Guinness World of Records exhibition hall. My son wants desperately to go in, and to my protests that it is bound to be tacky (an aesthetic that perhaps must be experienced to be learned) he accurately points out that this is something he cannot do at home. So a compromise is struck: he and my wife will go in, and I will meet them in an hour.

During the hour I wander the nearby streets and discover London's Chinatown, marked prominently at its entrance by an iron gate adorned with dragons and Chinese characters. Only two blocks long, Gerrard Street is lined end-to-end with Chinese restaurants, their windows filled with sausages, roast ducks, and slabs of pinkish barbecued pork ribs. A dense mixture of Oriental natives and Occidental tourists mills the street, all embraced by the smell of Chinese cookery. Interspersed among the restaurants are numerous small produce markets, their goods displayed on stands set out on the brick pavement. The variety is staggering: there are two-foot-long Chinese radishes, bok choy, cilantro, onions of all sizes, and greens of all sorts. There are fruits I know—mangoes, melons, oranges, sweet pears, apples, cherries, apricots—and those I do not: a great spiked thing called a durian, the size and shape of a football, and a rambutan, which looks like a strawberry with long green hairs—a botanic version of a sea anemone.

And there are tomatoes. They are small and pale, and the boxes they are in are marked Holland or Spain. This doesn't much surprise me, as this is clearly not the best of climates for tomato growing. But it does occur to me as I stand pondering their origins that to arrive at this place, these fruits and I, we have traveled the globe: they are descendants of a plant from South

America, grown by Continental farmers in countries that once struggled with England for world dominion, displayed in a market catering to immigrants from Asia, in the heart of the remnants of the British Empire, on a street that reminds me of San Francisco.

I am further impressed with the "broadening effect" of travel when I rendezvous with my wife and son. The Guinness Exhibition, they report, features a replica of a $7\frac{3}{4}$-pound tomato grown in 1987 by Gordon Graham, of Edmond, Oklahoma. This is the current world-record holder, and it exceeds by a pound and a half the stated record in the radiation-produce catalog. Had we stayed home, I would forever have remained ignorant of the true potential of the Supersteaks I gave away.

Graham, I later discover, also holds the record for "tallest tomato," a $53\frac{1}{2}$-foot-tall plant grown in 1985. One record he does *not* hold is that for most fruits per plant (16,897), a mark set in 1989 by a cherry.

And so it goes in our first full day as innocents abroad.

## MAY 23

Today is Monday and my wife has business obligations. Accordingly, my son and I decide to do "guy things." At his request we visit the Imperial War Museum.

This museum, at which we arrive by taking some of the same Undergrounds used as air-raid shelters during the London Blitz, was created in 1920 to depict the history of the Great War. Of course, the war that would end all wars did no such thing, and the museum has had the opportunity since to expand its collection considerably, so that it now includes such treats as a production prototype of Little Boy and a Polaris nuclear missile.

The front entrance to the museum, which is surrounded by an idyllic, wooded lawn, is marked by two fifteen-inch naval guns that independently saw service on two different battleships in both world wars and could easily be fifty feet long. Inside is a stupendous array of twentieth-century military hardware ranging from an Italian two-man submarine to a Sherman tank to the cockpit of a British bomber, all restored to original condition. My son is fascinated by all this powerful machinery, and we spend hours poring over the displays.

Eventually, though, we make our way to the basement, where we find a gallery of enlarged, sepia-toned photographs. One photo near the beginning of the hall is of a man leading to safety—if such exists—a boy my son's age who is bleeding from the face, arms, and legs. Fear and anguish are on both their faces; behind them a town lies in rubble. The picture was taken in Germany in 1945 and is accompanied by a caption from the British writer V. S. Pritchett: "One does not pity the people of the town, nor does one hate them. One says, 'They did it to us.' But one is just left staring. The scene has gone beyond argument." Across from this is a picture of an emaciated, lone Buchenwald survivor, with words from Edward R. Murrow: "I pray you to believe what I have said. I reported what I saw and heard, but only part of it. For most of it I have no words."

Barely do we enter this exhibit before my son grasps my hand and pulls me away. He does not want to go in. He does not articulate it, and most likely he can't, but he seems to know intuitively that here is the end to which the machinery upstairs has been put; that here in the basement it can be seen that the weapons above are little to be admired.

Naturally there are tomatoes in the war museum. They are here in a presentation entitled the Wartime Kitchen and Garden, part of a series documenting life on the British home front from 1939 to 1945.

During the war, Britain had an extensive supplementary food production program similar to that of the American Victory Gardens. Organized and promoted under the slogan "Dig for Victory," the British public was urged in every conceivable way to boost its domestic food production, the government noting that home-grown foods were "ship-saving." As noted in Jennifer Davies's excellent companion book, also called *The Wartime Kitchen and Garden*, British municipal authorities were empowered to confiscate unused lands and to divide them into "allotments" of thirty by ninety feet, which were then turned over to

## TOMATO BASKETS

4 firm English tomatoes
2 oz. cooked macaroni
1 teaspoon chopped capers
salt and pepper
mayonnaise or cream salad dressing
mustard and cress
a few parsley stalks

*Dip the tomatoes quickly in boiling water and remove the skins. Allow to become quite cold. Cut a slice off the top of each tomato. Hollow out the inside. Add some of the tomato pulp to the macaroni. Mix in the capers and season lightly. Bind with mayonnaise, and fill the tomatoes with this mixture. Cover the tops with bouquets of fine cress. Add "handles" made with parsley stalks. Chill thoroughly, and serve on a bed of mustard and cress.*

From *New Wartime Recipes for English Tomatoes* (1940).
Reprinted in *The Wartime Kitchen and Garden*

individuals for cultivation. By 1943 nearly a million and a half allotments were being tended by anyone who could wield a hoe. Regular radio series were broadcast to provide gardening tips. Garden layouts and crop-rotation schemes were distributed to maximize production, and pamphlets were given out to provide tips on everything from the building of compost piles to the use of "catch crops" (plants such as spinach and lettuce that are sown between the rows of other vegetables—a technique used routinely by my Italian neighbors). In addition, the government especially promoted the growing of some crops and forbade the growing of others.

## THE RIGHT WAY
## TO GATHER TOMATOES

Early morning or late evening, when the plants are full of sap, is the best time for gathering. After gathering stand the tomatoes in a cool pantry for twelve hours before you eat them. This gives the "flesh" an opportunity to set, and greatly improves the flavour.

From *The Smallholder and Home Gardening*, 10 July 1942.
Reprinted in *The Wartime Kitchen and Garden*

Because of their relative lack of nutritional value, cucumbers were one crop so frowned upon and their cultivation in greenhouses was banned. Tomatoes, on the other hand, were favored for exactly the opposite reason, and the government *required* greenhouse owners, most of whom had previously been growing flowers, to devote 90 percent of their greenhouse space to tomato production for six months each year. Amateurs, too, were urged to grow tomatoes, and the effort was supported through publication of the government pamphlet *How to Grow Tomatoes Outdoors and Under Glass*.

In a total war—a war Churchill called a war for survival— every resource, everyone and everything, had to be mobilized, and tomatoes were no exception.

### MAY 31

Jennifer Davies's book recounts the wartime food and gardening experiences of several elderly Britons. One is Harry, who was wounded in France and afterwards became a gardener for the British Admiralty. For the benefit of the book and a companion BBC television series, Harry re-created a wartime garden and in it he raised two popular tomato varieties of the time: Ailsa Craig and Best of All. In a small glass house, writes Davies, he also

grew a fine crop of "Potentate," a wartime variety suited
to a low house. Its rather "boxy-looking" fruit is now out
of fashion, but for years its earliness and heavy cropping
made it a favourite with tomato growers in the Channel
Isles. In fact Harry obtained his "Potentate" seed through
the kindness of the Guernsey Tomato Museum.

A tomato museum.

The thought of it has captivated me for days. In Scotland
(where my wife's job took us for several days), my son and I
passed a Carnegie Library and I went so far as to look up the
museum's location. Not surprisingly, it's on Guernsey, the largest
of several small islands clustered off the coast of Normandy and
known previously to me only as the name of a breed of cow. The
thought of going there is an excess I find hard to countenance,
but my wife has been urging me on. "When will you be this close
again?" she asks.

She is right of course, and so I begin the day (the last before
we return home to San Diego) at London's Gatwick Airport,
where the weather is beautiful ("A superb day for flying," says the
pilot), and I climb aboard an airplane that looks like a shoebox
with wings. From London we fly first over the quilt of greens
textured with threads and patches of forest that is the British
countryside. Then we head out over the Channel. As we approach
Guernsey we pass rock outcroppings topped with lighthouses, and
then the tapestry of greens we left in England reappears, but with
a difference. Here, in every field, behind every house, there are
greenhouses. Uncountable greenhouses, large and small. Greenhouses hundreds of feet long and a dozen abreast. Greenhouses at
angles to each other and spraying splinters of light in all directions, like a huge crystalline micrograph. Guernsey greenhouses.
Filled, says my guidebook, with tomatoes.

Tomatoes were first grown under glass in Guernsey about a
hundred years ago. A medical journal of the day reported that
tomatoes could cure liver disease, and demand in England surged.
The tomatoes supplanted grapes, which had been grown in
Guernsey greenhouses as far back as 1840, and because of their

original function as grape houses, the greenhouses here are still known as "vineries."

From the airport I walk to the museum. It is three miles, and the walk alone is worth the trip. The road from the airport is two-laned, and, with its painted stripe down the middle, is a main thoroughfare. It takes me past old stone houses and new stucco homes. Many have goods set out along the roadway for sale, accompanied by tin collection cans: flowers, eggs, parsley, and horse manure (30 pence a bag). Green farm tractors pass by frequently, as do stainless-steel tanker trucks labeled "Guernsey Dairy."

The road takes me also past a turnoff to the Occupation Museum. Germany captured the Channel Isles in 1940 and incorporated them into its "Atlantic Wall." Tunnels were dug throughout the island's rock core, and scores of concrete bunkers and gun batteries were built—the latter now looming above the beaches like squat stands of mushrooms.

From the main road I turn onto a winding and narrow lane, barely the width of a car and bordered by rock walls. Purple, white, orange, and yellow wildflowers grow from crevices in the rock, and hedges top the walls. The hedges mostly block the view, and the effect is of walking in a maze. When I can see out, I am treated to the sight of green fields sprinkled with tan-and-white cows—Guernseys—and the blue ocean in the distance.

Along the way I pass a thousand-year-old church (St. Saviour's—in fine repair and used daily), spring-fed glades, and many a greenhouse. Most of the greenhouses are too far away to see into, but I can make out the contents of a few. One, a personal-sized model adjoining an elegant old home, houses a gnarled and twisted grape vine that rises to and spreads out in a plane just below the roof. Another features a clothesline strung with washing. A third is filled with rosebushes.

Tomatoes, I discover later, are still grown commercially in Guernsey, but in nowhere near the numbers suggested by my guidebook. As tomatoes once displaced grapes, so flowers have replaced tomatoes. Rising fuel prices in the 1970s increased the production costs of the growers, whose greenhouses must be heated. To compound the problem, countries of the European

Community, particularly Holland, began paying subsidies to their tomato growers. Guernsey, a self-governing bailiwick that prints its own money and makes its own laws, can't afford such subsidies, and as a result many of the growers have converted to flowers or, in some cases, simply abandoned their greenhouses.

Finally I arrive at the Guernsey Tomato Centre, to which I am directed from the road by two large hand-painted signs made to look like red tomatoes. Outside, the parking lot is empty but for a gold Rolls-Royce convertible. Inside, the first thing I see is . . . oysters. They reside in a basin on a counter next to the door, and if I am so inclined I can buy one and have it shucked right there. Perhaps they come from the waters off Guernsey and are in this way related to tomatoes. But there is no indication one way or another, and, bypassing the oysters, I step to the admission desk and pay my entry fee: £1.50.

There are two halves to the Tomato Centre: one housing the museum, the other a restaurant. Because it is lunchtime and I am hungry, I decide first to visit the restaurant. A corridor leads the way, and through it I pass a line of sales counters, racks, and alcoves. These have postcards, jewelry, and assorted curios for sale, but few make even the most distant reference to the Centre's erstwhile subject. There is a rack of secondhand mystery novels, but no books on gardening, horticulture, or tomatoes. There are no cookbooks. No sauces. No pastes. No preserves. No tomato wine (which is advertised but not available). No tomatoes. It is the strangest of feelings, as if the books at the War Museum gift shop had made no mention of weapons or war.

They do at least have a cart bearing packets of tomato seeds. Seventeen varieties are available, and among them is Potentate, the greenhouse variety grown by Harry and called here "the original Guernsey Tom." Other offerings range from the familiar—Sweet 100 and Big Boy—to the new: Eurocross, Dogham X, Money Maker, and Potato Leaf. My yard at home full, and my enthusiasm for starting from seed temporarily diminished, I refrain from making a purchase, but still I savor the names.

Eventually I make my way to the restaurant, where I am the only customer. This could be due to environmental considerations:

the seating area is inside a converted greenhouse and is incredibly hot and bright—ideal for tomatoes but less so for people. The menu consists primarily of "something plus chips," as in beef burger and chips, Cornish pastie and chips, and sausage roll and chips. They do have tomato soup, but I elect instead for a "crab salad."

The restaurant is apparently operated by two young teenage boys, and though there are no other customers to delay them, it is a long and sweltering time before my salad is served. It comes on two plates: On one are cubed chunks of crab—in the shell. On the other is the "salad": slices of ham, cheese, and tomato, the latter pale, unripe, and tasteless. In the way of utensils, I am provided with a pewter crab cracker and a metal pick. Uncertain what to do, I proceed to fracture and poke at my crab until I have before me a small pile of meat. Just as I am ready to eat it, one of the servers reappears, says something unintelligible, and takes my plate away. A few minutes later my crab returns, reincarnated as a small English tea sandwich, cut into triangles and with the crust removed. I eat it quickly before it can be removed again.

The people who work here are friendly and well meaning. Upon my inquiry, the ticket taker at the front entrance offered to ship me some tomato wine when it becomes available. But they seem as bewildered as I. Two years ago the Centre went bankrupt and closed its doors, reopening only last month after it was purchased by a new owner—a hotel mogul and owner of the gold Rolls-Royce. Whether he bought the place out of an abiding love of tomatoes or for tax reasons, I cannot say. But clearly he has skimped on staff training. Nor has he sought employees with a keen interest in tomatoes.

The exception is Marian Le Prevost, of whom I catch sight soon after entering one of the five greenhouses that make up the Centre's museum. She is carrying two buckets. One is filled with all-purpose fertilizer, and as she works her way down a row of tomatoes, this is what she uses most often—"for general plant growth and to help swell the fruit," she says. The other contains a powdered mixture of "blood, fish, and bones," and this she applies selectively to those plants whose growth is lagging and that she feels need an extra boost.

She is, I would guess, in her fifties. Her hair is wrapped in a scarf, and over the scarf she wears a straw hat. Her hands are strong and thick from work, nails cut short, caked with dirt—the hands of someone who plies the soil, but the hands, too, of a spry and spirited woman whose bluish fuchsia lipstick hints at a touch of flamboyance. She tells me that her mother and father grew Guernsey tomatoes in greenhouses for decades, and that after her father died, she became her mother's principal assistant. Together they cared for four thousand plants in 590 feet of greenhouse. In the late eighties Marian took a break from tomatoes and went to work tending roses. But the roses, she says, are housed under sodium lights, and the yellowish light didn't agree with her. ("I didn't feel well in there. It took all my energy away.") So when the job at the museum opened, she took it.

I walk with her through the greenhouses, each representing a different era of Guernsey tomato culture. The first represents a turn-of-the-century greenhouse and is given over largely to grapes. We begin in the second, this one representing the 1920s and distinguished by rows of cast-iron pipes laid out on the surface of the soil and through which steam is forced to provide heat. "We have a boiler in the parking lot," says Marian.

The plants are laid out in rows, one per heating pipe, that run the length of the greenhouse. In the rows, each plant is growing from a precisely excavated square hole eighteen inches on a side and six inches deep; their purpose is to allow for the optimal hand-watering and feeding of each plant. The hundreds of holes, each one sculpted with a flat spade, must have taken an enormous amount of work—and all of it provided by Marian.

In contrast to the pale seedlings I so recently parceled out at home, these plants are lush almost beyond description. All are of the deepest green and have stems an inch and a half in diameter at the base and thick throughout their full four feet of height. Each has been trained to a single stem held erect by a string that rises to a rafter overhead, a system Ortho calls the Sky Hook. Countless clusters of golfball-sized fruits hang from the vines. I am overwhelmed by the plants' vigor. Here is the work of a master.

She doesn't say who chose them, but the selection of varieties here is clearly a disappointment to Marian. Predominantly, the plants in this greenhouse are Spectra and Turbo—varieties that Marian says would not have been grown in Guernsey greenhouses in the 1920s. Had the collection been more authentic, it would have consisted of Alicante, Pagham Cross, Money Maker, Potentate, and Ailsa Craig. There is, though, an extraordinary surprise here, no matter how inauthentic. Midway along one wall of the greenhouse, at the end of a row of tall, regimented plants, are a half dozen multistemmed tomato plants twelve to eighteen inches in height. These have not been trained, and their stems and leaves are smooth; they have, Marian points out, no "tomato hairs." Over them hangs a sign that reads "Wild." They are *Lycopersicon esculentum* var. *cerasiforme*—the original tomato. The mother tomato. Progenitor of the Spectras and Turbos and all the varieties Marian would have liked to have grown; forebear of the Champions, Lemon Boys, and all the varieties I have in my yard. I have stumbled upon a shrine, and it is here at Marian's insistence, for "It wouldn't have been a museum without them."

Together we continue our tour, moving next to a greenhouse filled with equipment used for the growing of Guernsey tomatoes during different historical periods. The early growers faced the same problem I have in my patch at home—soil infections due to the repeated planting of tomatoes in the same location—and the most interesting devices here are the sterilizers, great gangly affairs made of curved pipe and used to inject pressurized steam into the soil.

Eventually Marian must leave me—she has errands to run— and I am left to wander on my own into the 1960s-era greenhouse. Here dramatic changes are evident, wrought by the effort and expense associated with the early growers' incessant need to steam the soil. The construction is more modern, and the heating system is now forced air, but the biggest difference is that the tomatoes are no longer growing in the ground. Instead, the plants rise out of peat moss "propagation pods" inserted into plastic bags of potting soil. The bags themselves lie in rows on heavy plastic sheeting that covers the ground completely.

The plants appear healthy. They are as big and laden with fruit as those in the 1920s house. The problem of infected soil has been dealt with. But the place is eerie. With its bright light, white walls, white bags, white ground coverings, and loops of black irrigation tubing snaking into each propagation pod, I am reminded more of a hospital room than of a plant nursery.

This transformation is complete in the final greenhouse, the one depicting the modern era. It reminds me of an intensive-care room. A pump quietly cycles on and off, and from it water and liquid nutrients are automatically fed to the plants through a maze of tubing. Having dispensed with the ground in the 1960s, the very soil itself has been eliminated in this stage of development. The tomatoes are growing in long plastic-covered rectangular blocks of rock wool—the same material in which my son's baby-sitter had grown his hydroponic tomato. And that indeed is what is happening—the tomatoes are being grown hydroponically.

Near the door of this "modern" greenhouse is a sign describing the developments inside. It tells of the propagation pods, the rock wool, and the feeding technology. And it concludes with the statement that although the growing method shown here "gives an excellent sellable shape and color for supermarkets and shops to sell, the traditional Guernsey sweet flavor of yesteryear is lost."

Whether Marian wrote this I do not know. But whoever the author, he or she was too polite to suggest that this bland finale of the Guernsey tomato growers' horticultural progression might have had as much to do with their demise as the fuel subsidies of their Dutch competitors.

The plane in which I leave Guernsey flies out over the east coast of the island. We pass more fields and greenhouses and the town of St. Peter Port, which has winding streets, whitewashed houses, and a picturesque harbor. Near the harbor I spy a large rectangular hole cut into a shelf of rock just slightly above sea level. It is filled with water, which I presume it catches and recatches at every high tide. From this height it looks to be a swimming pool, and its location and apparent method of filling strike me as ingenious.

Perhaps, though, this is common in some parts of the world, and I've just never seen it before. On the other hand, my map tells me I could be looking at a model yacht pond. The truth from here I cannot know; tomatoes have led me to Guernsey, but I've pursued them single-mindedly, making a narrow trek across this beautiful island, and that to which I've been introduced I've largely missed. I will have to return.

# JUNE

### JUNE 1

WE LEAVE LONDON TODAY, to return most likely to a yard in need of watering, pantries in need of stocking, a cat in need of loving, mail in need of answering, clothes in need of washing. Tomorrow I'll go back to work, and the day after so will my wife. Such thoughts would be wearying were it not for the memories we carry and the knowledge that all these things mean also a return to home: to John, Albert, and Vito, and to our pink sidewalks; to my wife's father and sister; and to our routines—to trips to the bus stop and early-morning scrambles, to coffee made the way we like it, to our fuchsias, citrus, irises, and to our tomatoes.

The ride to Gatwick we make now like seasoned travelers. Clear weather helps. But we've learned also that the two-pound cab fare to the train station is a bargain, even if it is only two blocks away.

As before, the train takes us over the Thames, through bleak and depressed areas not included in our first day's sightseeing tour. The flight back is less debilitating than the flight to, probably because we regain as we go the hours lost at the beginning of our trip. When we arrive, the skies are blue and cloudless and the temperature is in the low seventies. "First clear day in weeks," says the taxi driver.

At home, things are much as I'd expected: the lawn is shaggy, the iris have died, and there is to the yard a general look of overgrowth and neglect. One unexpected development is the coming into bloom of the melaleucas, which are so covered in white cottony flowers that the trees look as if covered with snow—a rare sight in San Diego.

The tomatoes, too, have grown. Easily they've doubled in size and are well over two feet tall. But as I step from the taxi, my attention is drawn to the plant farthest from the street, the Lemon Boy. A snail is climbing its cage—an enormous snail, over a foot in diameter and with eight-inch orange antennae. A scrawled note is affixed to its papier-mâché body:

> WE DID OUR BEST TO PROTECT YOUR GARDEN.
> UNFORTUNATELY, SOME GIANT SNAILS GOT THROUGH. SORRY.

Such are the risks when one's passions become public. The identity of the prankster is a mystery, but will have to remain so for now. We are too tired for detective work, and we carry in our suitcases—too heavy to the bitter end—set them on the floor, and go to bed.

## JUNE 3

Late this afternoon I go for a walk, and when I return, I spot John in his front yard—in his garden. I wander over and he greets me with a huge, twinkling smile and a two-handed handshake. "Steve," he says, "we missed you! I didn't know you would be gone for so long."

I tell him about our trip, and he sympathizes with my jet-lag woes—when he and Rose fly to Sicily, they go yet another time zone to the east. We review his garden: His tomatoes are belt-high and have thick stems. The thick stems, says John, mean they will have big tomatoes. His parsley, garlic, onion, basil, radishes, and eggplant are all healthy and vigorous, and they give his yard a look of great abundance.

I do not tell John of my trip to the Tomato Museum, thinking he might think it excessive. But even with the omission we talk easily for an hour—my wife tells me this pointedly when I come in to a dinner already in progress. She is irritated that I have stayed out so long, but despite her reproach, the glow of my conversation with John suffuses my meal. It is the glow of a simple conversation about simple things; the glow of friendship building.

## JUNE 6

This evening as I am out working in the yard, a neighborhood couple stroll by with visitors in tow. The visitors are mother and sister and I discover later that they are here from out of town on a possible home-buying expedition, thinking that perhaps they might like to bring their family closer together.

As people often do now, they stop to look at the tomatoes, which are beginning to form an impressive stand by the sidewalk. We chat for a bit and the sister says she has tomatoes in her yard, "But they don't look as good as these." Her plants, she says, are turning yellow. We discuss her watering regimen and the fertilizer she uses, and after a few more pleasantries they continue on their way.

The couple escorting this mother and daughter are gay, one of many such couples—male and female—in our neighborhood. A few months ago the house between John and Vito changed hands. The old woman who had lived there for nearly three-quarters of a century died late this winter. A young woman bought the place and has been working on it tirelessly ever since, trimming plants, painting, installing new wiring and plumbing, and generally addressing the myriad parts of the house that had fallen into disrepair.

In addition to being competent, industrious, and single, she has short hair and favors men's work clothes. So do many of the women who visit her, and shortly after she moved in, John asked me if she was a "How you say? Leessbean?"

I didn't know, I had said, but my guess was that, yes, it seemed possible. He nodded in thought and then moved the talk to the next subject.

If he has needed it (and I don't know that he has), John has had a lot of time to get used to this. For the last dozen years his neighbors on the opposite side have been a middle-aged gay couple and one of the men's aging mother. Their house, too, is always well kept, and they and John share lemons from John's tree, as well as compliments about each other's house and yard. One of the men, who was once married, had a teenage son who died in an accident, and so he and John share also the terrible knowledge of what it is to lose a son on the cusp of manhood.

I have had many a conversation with these two men and never has the subject of homosexuality come up. This, I suspect, is due more to my reticence than to theirs. But then, the subject has never been relevant. They are simply neighbors whose cares and concerns about the neighborhood are the same as mine. Indeed, I have often thought that we are fortunate to have them as neighbors. In a form different than I and my wife can provide, they set an example for my son—of responsible people leading ordinary lives of commitment—to each other and to the people around them. And along with our new neighbor across the street, the many Italians, and the many mixed-race families in our neighborhood, they serve as daily reminders that there are more varieties of people than there are even of tomatoes.

## JUNE 9

On the radio I hear that today is the anniversary of Cole Porter's birthday. Porter, says the announcer, began his career in 1928 when five of his songs were used in the Broadway musical *Let's Do It*, and he went on to write such hits as "Anything Goes" and "You're the Top." Today also marks the ninety-sixth anniversary of the British lease of Hong Kong; in three years the lease will expire, and the former colony will revert to Chinese rule.

Both these occasions are listed in a fascinating book called *Chase's Annual Events.* Indeed, the radio announcements match the print descriptions almost word for word. *Chase's* is a storehouse of trivia, and from it I learn also that today is the birthday of Robert McNamara, Les Paul, and Donald Duck (who joined the world on June 9, 1934). A new moon will begin today, as will the Napa

Valley Wine Auction and the Glenn Miller Birthplace Society Festival. (Miller has been in the news this week for other reasons as well: President Clinton has been in Europe to help mark the fiftieth anniversary of D-day, and among his stops was a U. S. military cemetery in Cambridge, England. Along with the bodies of 3,812 U. S. fliers, the cemetery has a wall with the names of 5,126 servicemen missing in action, including that of Major Alton G. Miller, who disappeared in 1944 on his way to a Christmas concert in France.)

Besides birthdays, historical dates, and municipal booster days, one of the staples of *Chase's* is food festivals. Among the many are the Mushroom Festival (held in Richmond, Virginia), the Rhubarb Festival (Intercourse, Pennsylvania), the Luling, Texas, Watermelon Thump (with World Champion Seed-Spitting Contest), and the Bradley County Pink Tomato Festival, which is today.

As many as sixty-five thousand people are expected to attend. According to Gina Craig, at the Bradley County Chamber of Commerce, in Warren, Arkansas, the festival was started thirty-eight years ago to help promote the tomato industry in Bradley County. Named after the Bradley Pink, a lightly colored variety favored by local growers, the three-day festival features music, square dancing, fireworks, and a Miss Pink Tomato beauty pageant. Other events include a tomato-eating contest (the winner, says Ms. Craig, usually eats about three pounds of whole tomatoes in the allotted three minutes), a charity auction (previous years' prices having reached two thousand dollars per lug of Bradley County Pinks), and an all-tomato luncheon.

The luncheon will be held in a church, with open seating and tickets selling for seven dollars. On the menu will be "to-marinated" carrots, green-tomato beans, ham with Bradley County sauce (made from chili sauce, tomatoes, brown sugar, mustard, pineapple, and soy sauce), heavenly tomato cake (chocolate cake made with tomato juice), tomato breadsticks, tomato juice, and iced tea— sans tomatoes.

In the wake of my trip to the Tomato Museum, my tomato travel budget is now depleted. But I do wish I could be there. Who knows? I might have caught a tune by Cole Porter.

## JUNE 11

This evening my son is invited to spend the night at his best friend's house. He has been asked to bring his saxophone, and as we arrive we are greeted at curbside by the exuberant strains of a clarinet from inside the house. The boys will have a concert. And though I am pleased the two will have fun, I am equally pleased that the venue will be their house and not ours.

My son also takes his goalie equipment. His soccer team has practice tomorrow and he will go directly from his friend's house. He and his friend are a year and a half apart in age and necessarily play on different teams, but his friend is also a goalie and he too has practice tomorrow.

These parallel interests and activities are no coincidence. My son has had the same best friend for half his lifetime. They have similar tastes and temperaments, and the interests of one stimulate the interests of the other. The two can play side-by-side for hours without speaking, surrounded in my son's room by buckets of Legos and emerging only occasionally to show off a constantly evolving array of space stations and fantastic flying machines. Or they can lose themselves in an art project, or the building and testing of a toy racetrack.

Sometimes I forget, and I take the nature of their play for granted. But then a child from school or elsewhere spends a few hours at our house, and the time is all squabbling and rambunctiousness and thirty seconds of this and thirty seconds of that. And then I realize anew that theirs is more than a friendship of convenience. Theirs is that most precious of treasures: a childhood friendship with the chance to grow and deepen over the course of a lifetime. I have a few such friendships, begun in Davis and nurtured through the years, and they remain today among the most important parts of my life.

At the front door, my son's friend bursts out and there is a rapid and excited exchange of questions and answers about our trip. The two are all about and abustle, and I am overwhelmed by their intensity, until the other boy turns and asks me mischievously if I found any snails on our tomatoes when we came home. So it was he who was perpetrator and creator of the giant snail. He says he had planned a whole army of the monstrous mollusks, but we returned sooner than he expected, and he was only able to unleash the one.

My son's friend has taken a special interest in our tomatoes this year. He monitors their progress each time he comes over. And though it would be too great a conceit for any one person to take credit for the undertaking by another of an endeavor so grand as the creation of a garden, my son's friend has indeed put in his own plantings, and I do believe I have had an influence. In each corner of his family's front lawn, like sentries, he has planted a tomato—each a foot high now and topped with a cage. He shows us these eagerly, and then he takes us to the backyard, where he has commandeered a once-neglected area and planted squash, radish, lettuce, peppers, basil, parsley, carrots, and another half dozen tomatoes, all healthy and engaged in riotous growth. All this—from planning to weeding to watering—he has done himself; his parents have acted only as chauffeurs. And of this he is justly proud.

## JUNE 12

The sex life of a tomato is a private affair. Each flower has both male and female parts and is self-pollinating; it needs only itself to satisfy its reproductive imperative. It does not need other tomatoes. It does not need bees. It does not need people.

Nonetheless, people have long intruded themselves into this most intimate aspect of the tomato's life. Indeed, it was we who brought about their current self-sufficiency. The original South American wild tomato was pollinated by insects, and the transfer of pollen was primarily between, rather than within, flowers. This was so because the female pistil extended beyond the mouth of the flower and away from the flower's own pollen-bearing anthers. Only through the visitations and wanderings of insects could pollen reach the pistil's end.

When the tomato arrived in Europe, its native pollinators were no longer available, and the plants most likely to reproduce were those that were self-pollinating, meaning those with pistils short enough to capture their own pollen. The result was the selection of plants with ever-shorter pistils, a trend culminating in today's hybrids, wherein the pistil is entirely ensheathed within a fused cone of anthers and is no longer accessible to the outside world. Thus have we altered the tomato's very sexual anatomy.

More recently, of course, the genetic engineers at Calgene have involved themselves in the tomato's reproductive affairs. And this afternoon so do I. My tools are more basic than Calgene's; I use only my hands, stepping outside just after lunch to tap, shake, and bang the wire cage around each plant. I do this in hopes of improving the rate of pollination among my flowers and thereby increasing the size of my harvest. The shaking will help loosen and transfer pollen within the flower. There are more high-tech ways of doing this—Ortho suggests attending to each individual flower with an electric vibrator; but this seems to me entirely too intimate.

It was for this same purpose—increasing my yield—that I bought the Tomato Bloom Spray. The spray acts as a substitute for a natural plant hormone that triggers the growth of the flower's ovary into a fruit. But the stuff is a little off-putting. The resulting fruit are said to be puffy and hollow, the directions are laced with cautions, and the resulting fruit are said to be puffy and hollow. Moreover, the spray is only useful when the flowers have failed to pollinate because of cool nighttime temperatures. Only once in the last six weeks has it dropped below fifty-five degrees. On my plants, I now see small fruit and abundant flowers. And so I decide to forgo the spray and content myself instead with the provender now accruing from the interactions of nature, the doings of the generations before me, and the efforts of my own hands.

## JUNE 13

This evening we have friends to dinner. These are my wife's oldest and truest friends, her counterparts to my childhood friends from Davis and to my son's best friend. They and my wife went to school together and have since stayed in touch. As girls they played together. As teenagers they traded stories of boyfriends—and perhaps the boyfriends as well. As adults they have traded complaints about men in general and husbands in particular. And along the way they have grieved, as each in turn lost her mother.

There is an air of anticipation as we ready the house for their arrival, and when they do come, my son rushes out to greet them. Because the tomatoes are growing right next to the sidewalk and have become quite conspicuous, they form almost the first subject of conversation. Both women are growing their own and are eager to trade tips and stories. One has grown tomatoes before, but this year has only two plants—she is unmarried and without children, and these should be ample.

My wife's other friend bought a house this year for the first time. Previously she had lived in a condominium; there her and her husband's tomato-growing experiences were disappointing more often than not—they would buy pots and potting soil, stakes, sprays, and potions, only to return after a weekend away to find the plants drooped over and dead. At season's end they would never have much to show for their effort "but a single forty-dollar tomato." This year they have tried again, but for the first time they have sown their crop in the earth.

Now she has tomato fever and is eager to see the methods of other growers. After scrutinizing my plants, she and her husband join me in a quick round of the neighborhood; we review Albert's Beefsteaks and cross the street to look at John's plants. Then we examine the foursome in the front yard of the owners of Dan the Dog. The plants are spindly, stunted, and yellowish, each bearing but a single, large green fruit. They are starved for light, living as they do in the shade of my melaleucas. But our guest looks thoughtfully and in silence at the plants for some time, and when finally she speaks, it is not of the plants or their emaciation, but of the cages that stand above them.

"Is that," she asks, "how they are supposed to be used?"

I have never thought about this. My neighbor's cages are the conventional store-bought variety: wire cones flaring up and out from prongs that stick in the ground.

"Yes," I reply, "that's how they're used."

"Oh," she says, "I didn't know that."

Curious, I ask how she thought they should be used.

"Well," she says slowly, "I put mine the other way."

We learn by example. But until now our friend had never seen tomato cages in use. Those she had seen were upside down in stacks at the nursery—on a concrete floor this is how they are the most stable—and that was her example.

Basking each in our own revelation, we file inside the house. My wife has filled the table with food, and as we settle around, her other friend—she of the two plants—begins to tell of her recent trip to New York—a trip she won while working at home one afternoon, tending to paperwork and watching a TV game show.

Normally, she declares (more than a little defensively), she doesn't watch TV while working ("And certainly not game shows!"). But she came home for lunch one day, found nothing to read, turned on the TV, surfed the channels, and found a trivia contest. "Trivia," she says, "is one of my greatest skills." And for $4.99, viewers could play, punching in answers on their telephone and competing against contestants nationwide.

The first time she played, she won: "A lovely cherrywood TV stand." And from that point on, she was hooked. She began to organize her days around the show, growing nervous as the time to play approached, and, while playing, slipping into a "Zen-like lizard state" of concentration. When she wasn't playing, she found herself practicing lightning-quick entries on her telephone keypad.

Her next win was a recliner chair. After that, a kitchen mixer. Finally, she made it to "the finals" and keypunched her way to the top, winning the all-expenses paid trip for two. Her destination was to be an upstate dude ranch, and in the visitor's brochure she read that she would be pampered; she dreamed of spas, saunas, and foot massages.

Her traveling companion was a friend with whom she had been planning to go to Paris. But in April the pair flew instead to New York and were met at the airport by the ranch owner's son. He drove a "filthy old Toyota," and for two hours smoked cigars and spoke nonstop of sex, driving them deep into the woods. After a time, the two women began to get worried at the resort's remoteness, their driver's frankness, and his casual mention that they "might be the only guests this weekend."

At the resort, where they finally did arrive, "Spring had not yet arrived, and it was not pretty. No green, no leaves." Their host dropped their bags at the foot of a barrackslike building, pointed to a distant, upper-floor room, and told them, "The key is in the door." Inside were three double beds and a crib, dirty shag carpeting, a broken sink, fake wood paneling, and an original painting of an Indian straddling a freshly scalped cowboy.

That night they ate at the ranch. The dining room, she says, "could easily have sat six hundred people. But it was empty, save far, far in the corner, where there were two white paper place mats, two white paper plates, and two plastic glasses of water." Dinner was turkey, potatoes, and cream pie—the latter still frozen.

Because it was twenty-five degrees outside, they declined the after-dinner hayride, choosing instead to spend the evening watching a six-hour television series about cats. "Now," she says, "we know everything about cats."

The next day, and contrary to their driver's belief, the ranch did have new guests: two hundred boy scouts. They dined that night with the scouts: "Fried fish, fried chicken, sliced ham, and meatballs. And water." But the day after, they asked to be taken to the train station.

They spent the rest of the week in New York City. This cost them each a thousand dollars, on top of the taxes they owed on the trip's prize value. "My free trip," she says, "cost me a fortune." But it did have its good side—she's been to the Bates Motel and survived, and she never played the game show again.

Of course, she got more from the trip than that. She tells the story with animation and hilarity, and more than once we are in tears as the narration proceeds. And while none of us would have chosen to go in her stead, we are all glad she went. Paris wouldn't have been nearly as much fun in the retelling.

After dinner it is our turn to tell of trips and adventures, and we show our pictures of England and Scotland, and the Guernsey Tomato Museum. There is throughout the evening an air of comfort and gaiety, and when finally our friends leave my son goes to bed and my wife and I do the dishes.

When my wife and I were married, we held the wedding in a park. It was a do-it-yourself affair, put on without benefit of caterer or take-charge relative, and when the organized festivities were over a group of us returned for further celebration to our apartment (the same apartment where later I grew my first tomato). Among that very welcome but unplanned gathering were these same friends, and as even this group eventually dwindled, it was they who stayed and cleaned the kitchen. Tonight we do not need such help, and our rhythm is easy and practiced. But though I cannot now recall what material gifts they gave us that day, for that perfect bit of help those many years ago, I will always remember and always be thankful.

### JUNE 17

Standing behind our paired tomato patches, Albert hails me as I walk into my front yard. "Look!" he says. And with a big grin, he shows me that his tomatoes are now as big as mine.

Ever since we returned from England the weather has been wonderful, both for people and for tomatoes. High and low temperatures have ranged from the low sixties to the mid-seventies, and the days have been sunny; June gloom this year occurred mostly in May. The tomatoes have been responding with an astounding rate of growth. My Champions are now climbing out the top of their cages, and soon I will have to decide what to do with their excess: clip their tops, jury-rig a new support, or let them sprawl. Albert's Beefsteaks, which started life as pale and leggy rejects, are also racing and now match my plants in height.

But, he says, "No fruit."

No, I tell him, I bet there are fruit. And I begin rummaging through his plants, among which I quickly find a half dozen marble- and pea-sized fruit. He is satisfied, and both of us are happy.

### JUNE 19

The counting and quantifying of plants, of their height, width, girth, and general prodigiousness, can become an engrossing activity. I have been drawn into this since I first began tracking the growth of my seedlings in March, and I now find myself measuring my tomatoes' height with a tape measure and crawling about on all fours to count their flowers and fruits—an imprecise business given the density of their foliage and the increasingly large numbers of countable objects, some of which I no doubt miss and others of which I no doubt count twice, if not thrice. As to why I do this, the simplest answer is the one I give today to an inquiring passerby: curiosity. It is, for instance, how I learn that my plants are now growing an inch a day, that I have 368 open flowers, and 122 green fruit.

It can feel a little ridiculous—peering and probing intently under plant leaves, scribbling on paper with green-stained hands. But I am not the only person so engaged. Along with his fellow world-record holders (the grower of an 816½-pound pumpkin, for instance), I suspect that Gordon Graham was a counter. And today I find that so is Albert.

He appears as I am out front with the tomatoes, counting and measuring. After watching me quietly for a while, he points to his patio and says, "Look. One hundred thirty-five inches!"

A wall surrounds his patio, and so I have not previously noticed the half dozen spindly sunflower plants to which he now directs my attention. These, with their yellow faces and long shadows, are the by-product of my April's gift to Albert. He did plant his sunflowers, but not in the way of my tomatoes. As to why Albert measures his sunflowers, I can only suppose his motives are similar to mine. Of course, the quantification of good results can also substantiate one's prowess as a gardener. And so it is my hope that Albert's sunflowers grow to twenty feet or more and affirm for him eternally his decision to grow them in this new location.

As I finish my inventory, my neighbor with the bad back, the cement contractor, passes by. His walk is still painfully slow and he is clearly far from recovered. Capitalizing on the chance for a rest, he stops and compliments me on the size and health of my tomatoes. Although he and I exchange greetings, we have never talked extensively. His English is limited, and the old and leaking trucks that line the street in front of his house, along with a brood of troubled and rebellious children—grown but still at home—have left him something of an outcast in the neighborhood. In turn, he keeps mostly to himself.

Nonetheless, he seems today to want to talk. In return for his compliment, I tell him his tomatoes, the thirteen amongst his rose-bushes, also look good. "Psshhh," he says, waving his hand in disdain, "those are nothing." In his backyard, he says, he has his real crop and those are . . .

Momentarily he is at a loss for words and he casts about, searching, until his eyes land on one of the palm trees bordering my sidewalk. Inspired, he finishes his sentence, raising his eyes and his hands in a great upward gesture from the ground to the sky and proclaiming that the tomatoes in his backyard are

. . . "like trees!"

They are, he says, eight or nine feet tall—so tall he can't reach their tops and must support them with wooden two-by-fours. He speaks of them animatedly and with passion, as if he has been waiting a long time to tell of these plants he has raised.

He tells me that each year he saves seeds from the biggest of the plants he grew the preceding year, and as he talks, his hands and fingers form first an imaginary orb and then fly through air, selecting the big tomatoes, cutting them in half, and squeezing out their seeds on paper towels to dry. In textbook fashion, he is telling me how an heirloom tomato variety is created and perpetuated.

I ask what he does with his fruit, imagining that like John and Rose, he too makes sauce. But instead, his answer surprises me—he dries them.

Again his hands take flight as he describes his method. He forms another imaginary tomato, cuts it in half, squeezes it gently to remove the juice, salts the top, and places it on a wooden board in the sun. Morning and night, for a week, he shuttles the tomatoes back and forth from indoors to out.

This, he says, is the best way, with the best flavor. But sometimes he uses a dehydrator, which his children gave him one year for Christmas. With the dehydrator, he says, he can dry the tomatoes in a day, but the finished fruit are "too dry." Either way, he bottles the end product in olive oil.

Tomatoes have led me to many things, but this is a conversation I would not have expected. Over the past few years, dried tomatoes have acquired an aura of gourmet chic; trendy magazines feature them in spreads with glossy photographs and recipes that tend to call for goat cheese and pine nuts. I, myself, love them. I put them on pizza, and I eat them plain. But when purchased in a store they are expensive, and their image is definitely upscale.

I tend often to pigeonhole people, taking a snapshot and putting them in a box, expecting them ever after to be this way or that, this thing or that. It is, I suppose, a way to get by without engaging in the time-consuming, messy work of really getting to know a person. Or perhaps it is just another form of yuppie arrogance: there are in our neighborhood doctors and lawyers aplenty, and of any of them I would readily have believed they had acquired a taste for dried tomatoes and a penchant for making their own. But of the cement contractor—a man with halting English and a ruined back for a diploma—I would last have had such suspicion.

Without warning, he has sprung from the box into which I had put him. Reflexively, I seek to restore him to the place in which I know him, and I change subjects. I ask him if he is working.

"No," he says, "I can no longer work. Mostly now I take care of my granddaughter. And I study tomato."

And at that, he hobbles away, and I am left to wonder: Should I fashion for him a new box? Or need I do more than revel in the discovery of our shared passions?

## JUNE 20

My sister joins us this evening for dinner. She is in town visiting a friend, a woman who works on the boats in San Diego's fishing fleet. My sister and her friend have known each other since high school. At times they have lived together, and more than once they have come to each other's side in times of need. It is for this reason that they are now spending time together, for both have had difficulties in their personal lives of late.

During dinner my sister tells us she has had a chance to taste a Flavr Savr. She says the tomato (purchased in Davis, and one of the first available in the nation) did not have the explosive, full flavor of a vine-ripened backyard tomato. But it was much better than a typical store-bought. She believes the fruit she tasted was not completely ripe, and that its flavor would have improved had she kept it a while longer. But in the main, her judgment is strikingly similar to that of a taster for the *New York Times*, who found the Flavr Savr "a welcome addition to the produce department"—equal to a top-of-the-line gourmet grocery-store tomato, but no rival of a fully ripe homegrown.

### JUNE 21

Today is the first day of summer and all that it is supposed to be: temperatures in the mid-seventies, sunny, and the sky (in the words of John Dos Passos) a robin's-egg blue. My son goes to the beach with his new baby-sitter, and despite repeated reminders and the provision of two bottles of sunscreen, he comes home with tomato red feet and face. He moves very slowly and speaks not a word, and after dinner he asks to take a cool bath. Bedtime will come early. But, he assures us, he had fun.

Outside, I see John in his front yard, and I tell him of the cement contractor's nine-foot tomato plants. Has he ever seen them?

No, says John, he and the contractor don't talk.

The contractor's backyard, John explains, borders the yard of the home in which John's father-in-law lived for more than thirty years. Long ago the contractor and the father-in-law had an argument—about what John does not say—and from then on the contractor began to ignore John. "He started not to see me," says John. "And so I said, 'Who needs him?'"

The two of them—fellow immigrants and *paesani*, neighbors, fathers, and growers of tomatoes—have no relationship. Rather, they cultivate a nonrelationship. It is, I suppose, a feud.

Two years ago John's father-in-law died. From the vantage of the uninvolved, such an occasion might have presented an opportunity for a rapprochement. But apparently the chance was lost, for still they do not speak. Whether the thought even occurred to either of them, I cannot say.

### JUNE 22

The interest shown this year in tomatoes by my son's best friend has been spurred in part by a school assignment. In his class there are only fifteen students, all high achievers. It is a class unlike any I have ever seen in a public school. The children help teach each other (chess is popular); musicians, dancers, and scientists are frequent visitors; and not too long ago the class spent a week in Colorado excavating dinosaur bones.

This spring my son's friend and his classmates were each given planter boxes and seeds for a selection of miniature vegetable varieties: radishes, lettuce, onion, and tomato. He sowed the seeds and tended after them (for a time placing the seedlings on his parents' garage roof), and today he and his class took their crops to the county fair for judging and display. The basis for judging was unclear, he says. Whether points were awarded for the biggest plants, or the healthiest, or for their overall aesthetic cohesiveness, he doesn't know. But whatever the criteria, he came in second and is happy.

He is happy, too, because today is his last day of school before summer vacation and he is bound now for seventh grade. Catapulted in part by tomatoes.

### JUNE 25

Today I have helpers in the tomato patch and am relieved of the chore of tapping on my cages to aid in the tomatoes' reproductive success. A colony of bumblebees has discovered my and Albert's tomatoes, and is swarming about them with great interest. What has attracted them so suddenly and in such great numbers I have no idea, but there is no mistaking their presence.

In theory, the fused anther cones of my hybrids (which lock each flower's pollen tightly inside itself) should render them unappealing to insects bent on gathering pollen. But oblivious to theory, the bumblebees visit flower after flower, seeking those in which the central floral structure is loose or loosening and through which they can insert their mouths to forage for pollen. A great deal of jostling, groping, clawing, and leg rubbing accompanies this activity, and pollen clearly gets carried from flower to flower and plant to plant. Intermittently, a bee zooms off and visits the flowers on my nearby lemon tree, mixing, I suppose, tomato and lemon pollen. The resulting pollination is at once random, incongruous, and miraculous. It is also superfluous, but what I am witnessing is yet another example of nature's propensity for redundancy: the plants are self-pollinating but are equipped all the same to take advantage of the wind, insects, . . . and me.

This evening my wife and I go to a movie, leaving my son and his best friend home alone. Our son's friend has previously been left alone by his parents under similar circumstances, but this is the first time we will have done so. The fact that there are two of them is the deciding factor, but still my wife and I are slightly apprehensive. On the other hand, it has to happen sometime.

When we return, there is a phone message from the wife of the neighbor who sang in Mendelssohn's *Oratorio:* Would we like to go see the grunion run?

Grunion are silvery, sardine-sized fish that spawn on Southern California beaches during the highest of summer's nocturnal high tides. It is past our bedtimes, and my wife and I have long since passed the stage when spontaneous, late-night excursions tend to sound even remotely enjoyable; but my son has never seen the grunion, and so we accept.

We drive to a wide and gently sloping beach that in the daytime is one of San Diego's most popular. At eleven-thirty at night it is virtually deserted, however, and we have our pick of parking spots. With our neighbors and their seven-year-old son, we walk to the beach and then string out along the shore, fourteen eyes looking for grunion. It is nearly a full moon, and the sky and the sand are well lighted—as they must inevitably be when the grunion go to the beach.

The kids romp and splash, and the adults talk and walk, and the half hour that elapses before we spot our first grunion goes quickly. This sighting occurs just after high tide. The fish is a loner and comes and goes so quickly that I fail to see it. Minutes pass and then another is sighted (I miss this one too), and shortly thereafter a pair. A sense of anticipation builds with each new sighting, but among the parents so does a fear of letdown: What if we have raised our children's expectations, and this is all it amounts to?

Soon, however, the pace of the landings picks up. The grunion come in on the highest waves—those that will bring them farthest ashore—and we quickly learn to look most intently in the wake of the very waves that catch us unexpectedly and drench our shoes. By twelve-thirty the miracle is in full swing. As each wave recedes, the sand is covered with thousands upon thousands of writhing fish, their bodies glinting in the moonlight.

They have but seconds to fulfill their reproductive mandate. The females, when they are cast ashore, dig their bodies into the sand, head up, tail down, and deposit their eggs. This done, they evacuate the hole and begin wriggling back towards the water, struggling to catch the next wave out. Behind they leave a finger-sized hole in the sand with their red roe at the bottom. Almost immediately, waves splash over the hole and bury the eggs. The males' job is to eject their semen onto the eggs so they are fertilized, and when things go well, each upright female in the sand is surrounded by a mass of males coiling their bodies around the female in what has the appearance of a miniature rugby scrum.

Often though, things don't go well. Each wave leaves behind scores of females head up in the sand, laying their eggs alone before scrambling desperately for the water. They cannot wait; to do so would be to perish. Similarly, the beach is covered with males who squirm in their frenzy, deplete themselves, and flip back towards the sea never having been near a female.

These nonmeetings probably occur more often than the scrums, and from the vantage of a single fish, it appears a highly inefficient system. But for the grunion as a species it clearly works—the evidence is all around us. In its way, it is little different than this morning's visitation of the bumblebees to my tomatoes, or of the once-rampant proliferation of nutsedge in my yard. It is but another of life's improbable means of ensuring its own continuance.

## JUNE 26

The insects giveth and the insects taketh away. For the past week, holes have been appearing in the lower leaves of my potted tomatoes. This morning the damage has increased substantially. The California Suns are particularly affected; their lower leaves now resemble wafer-thin slices of green sponge and their fruit, too, have been attacked, with holes and tunnels throughout.

I pick the hole-ridden fruit and toss them—four California Suns permanently eclipsed. Then I search the plants. The perpetrators are green caterpillar-like worms that range in length from three-eighths of an inch to an inch. Consulting Ortho, I find no exact match. One possibility is tomato fruitworms: the damage to my fruit matches the illustration, but my worms are green rather than brownish. Moreover, the fruitworms' name is inconsistent with the destruction to my plants' leaves.

I think it unlikely because of their small size, but another possibility is hornworms. These are among the most disgusting creatures on earth—the size of a finger and filled with green ooze. As kids, we called them tomato bugs, and one of the worst tortures I or my friends could inflict on each other was to find one of the horrid things and flick it on an unsuspecting companion, whereupon its discovery would be followed by horrified shrieks ("Get it off me!"), a generalized flailing about by the victim, and howls of laughter by everyone else.

Regardless of their exact identity, the recommended treatment is to dust with Sevin. On close inspection, though, I find I can spot a good many of the worms and simply pluck them off. This is a method of pest control much recommended in organic forums, and—mostly in the hopes of avoiding a trip to the nursery—I think for the moment I'll give it a try. If the nibbling continues, however, I'll go for the Sevin.

## JUNE 27

It doesn't take long to learn that handpicking worms is less than effective. Today I find another two dozen, some an inch or more long—and this after I thought I had cleaned them thoroughly yesterday.

The problem is the worms' camouflage: their green coloration matches perfectly that of the tomatoes' foliage and renders them virtually undetectable. Indeed, I wouldn't be surprised to learn that their coloring is actually provided by the plants they eat and that were they not filled with tomato leaves their bodies would be colorless. Hopefully, though, I can at least stave them off until I make it to the nursery.

Summer is now truly upon us. In the harbor this evening there is a fireworks show. The display is sponsored by a downtown tourist and shopping consortium, and from our house we can hear the distant booms. If we stand in the street and look over the rooftops and between the palm trees, we can even see the highest of the explosions. For the rest of the summer, the displays will punctuate the night sky, and on occasion I or my wife or my son will call to each other and say, "Come outside and look at the fireworks."

We are in the midst of a heat wave. High temperatures the last several days have been in the mid- to high eighties, and to the north of us in Pasadena, the on-field temperature in yesterday's U. S. versus Romania World Cup soccer game was one hundred and twenty degrees.

Throughout the neighborhood, tomatoes are beginning to ripen. John, the owners of Dan the Dog, and the contractor all have fruit in the last stages of ripening. On the Internet, too, announcements of first harvests are appearing:

It happened last night. I picked a half-pounder and sliced it for dinner. Lightly seasoned with salt and pepper . . . the juice ran redly down my chin. Aaahhhhhhh, they're back!

It will be weeks before I share in such pleasure, and so I sympathize with the respondent who pleaded for restraint:

Please sir . . . no more of this madness. Do not discuss the eating of fresh tomato flesh in this group again. Not unless you have one for each of us. It is just too much to bear.

JUNE 28

Sitting on the low brick wall that borders his driveway, John asks me today if I have yet seen the contractor's nine-foot tomato plants. I suspect he thinks the contractor is exaggerating. No, I tell him, I haven't seen them, although I would like to. As an aside, however, I add that among the plants in the contractor's front yard, I have noticed that several are paste-type tomatoes, with elongated fruits.

My guess is that these are for drying, but John's assumption is otherwise. Many Italian people, he says, grow Romas for sauce. "But they are not really too good for sauce, because they are too thick. The sauce they make is too thick. The big tomato," and he makes a globe with his hands to show that he is talking about a spherical tomato, "makes better sauce. It is thinner, but has more flavor." He goes on to say that if you have both kinds—Romas and "the big tomato"—you can mix them together. But if you don't, "What are you going to do?"

Engaged now in his own Socratic dialogue, he answers his own question: "You use the big tomato and cook it a little longer."

Their specialties differ—sauce for one, drying for the other. But the contractor is clearly not my only neighbor to have applied himself to the study of the tomato.

We talk also about today's big soccer match. Italy and Mexico played in the final game of the first round and tied 1–1. Ireland and Norway, the other two teams in the same group, also tied, 0–0, and the result is a grand, four-way tie. How this will be unraveled and the teams ranked is a mystery to me, and John, too, professes ignorance. But for clarification he suggests we ask his son, Jerry.

John, I discover, was an avid soccer fan when he was a young man in Italy. When he came to the United States he found it hard to follow the game and his interest waned. But his sons, Jerry and Luciano, played in high school and, says John, "were quite good." Jerry was offered a chance to play goalkeeper professionally. "But then Luciano died." And after that, Rose began wearing black, and Jerry put away his goalie gloves.

This is one of the few times John has mentioned Luciano to me. Millions of Americans have been watching the World Cup games this past week, reading of the tournament's progress in the papers, and cheering the exploits of Team USA—the first American team in sixty-four years to advance to the second round. Most of these new fans are temporary, drawn by spectacle and the sudden rocket of success. But for John, the games' arrival is different. With it he has allowed himself, perhaps, a rekindling of a passion he has long kept dampened.

## JUNE 30

Early this morning as I leave the house, I see John in his front yard. In his hand are two tomatoes—his first of the season. I am in a hurry and I haven't much time, but I wander over nonetheless for a look-see. The tomatoes are not particularly impressive—smallish and a bit on the pale side, and they appear to have come from the two volunteers growing next to his orange tree—they are too large for the Sweet 100s I gave him, and too small for the Champions.

Unlike the hyperbolic Interneters, John takes the event in stride. Instead, he shows me with great pride his Ichiban eggplants, handsome plants with purplish stems, purple morning-glory-like flowers, broad purple-veined leaves, and—the objects of John's immediate interest—long, pendant-shaped purple fruit. Several of the latter look utterly delectable, and I suspect they will be in Rose's kitchen by dinnertime.

When I am done admiring these beauties, he points with a note of dismay to several nearby eggplants of the fatter, more traditional variety. Their leaves are broader and without the purple veins of the Ichiban. They look healthy but have no fruit. The spot they are in, says John, doesn't have enough sun, and the temperatures here are too cool. "So whatever they do, we going to be happy. What do you expect? This isn't a farm."

# J U L Y

WE ARE AWAKENED this morning by deep sonorous booms interspersed by flashes of light. Together they fill the room and their frequency and intensity build as we lay in bed, marveling. A storm. In July.

July is the driest of months in San Diego. This time of year the mere appearance of a clouded sky is reason for comment, and as the sound grows in volume and proximity, our delight is multiplied as we begin to hear the faint falling of rain.

The drops grow fatter and gain company—as do we. Our son joins us in bed, and together the three of us listen as the rain's crescendo builds, steadies, and tapers away, all within minutes. Later we learn that it leaves behind three-hundredths of an inch of water. Not much, but even so, it is the first measurable rain on July 1 in the recorded history of San Diego. It is enough, too, to leave the day charmed, for throughout the rest of the day people speak of the storm and how it woke them—this summer storm that in many places would be too ordinary for comment.

## JULY 2

This morning John tells me that the supplier from whom he normally buys the tomatoes he and Rose use to make their annual supply of sauce has gone out of business. I tell him there are certainly others from whom he could buy tomatoes. Yes, he says, there are, but their prices are too high. He needs thirty lugs and doesn't want to pay more than three dollars a lug. We talk about alternatives, and he finishes by saying that one way or another, he'll get his tomatoes.

He lingers a moment, then adds a curious comment. "I can take care of this problem," he says, "if other problems don't get in the way." He begins to walk away, then returns. He has just been diagnosed, he says, with prostate cancer.

Cancer of the prostate is not one of the more deadly cancers. Unlike, say, liver cancer, which has a five-year survival rate of 5 percent, the comparable figure for prostate cancer is more than 75 percent. But this information is of no help now. What can you tell someone? "Gee, that's not the worst cancer you could get." Instead, I am dumbstruck, washed in a wave of sadness.

Finally, I mutter the obvious—"I'm sorry to hear that"—thinking all the while that this is the second time his family has been through this. He has been offered two treatment options—surgery versus radiation therapy—and he has chosen radiation. It will weaken and make him sick, but he says it is not as bad as chemotherapy. His son had both, and the chemo was worse than the radiation.

The irradiation will start next week. I can only imagine how unsettling this must be. And though I offer to help in any way I can, John already has what he really needs—a close, capable family—and what I can offer is trivial in comparison. All I can really do is watch, listen, and hope.

## JULY 3

The caterpillars are still chewing at the potted tomatoes. Moreover, holes have begun appearing on the leaves of the main tomatoes. Accordingly, I go this morning to Anderson's nursery. I have in mind to purchase some Sevin, but I am not wholly convinced this is the best solution.

My reservation centers on the bumblebees. They are no longer around in the numbers in which they first appeared, but there is still a steady stream of visitors, with up to a half dozen probing the tomato flowers at any one time. I doubt they make a significant difference in the tomatoes' pollination; but I like having them around and am loathe to wipe them out.

As I stand before the insecticides, before row upon row of brown bottles and cylindrical boxes, my attention is caught by an "organic" caterpillar spray. The product is a solution of *Bacillus thuringiensis,* a bacteria lethal to caterpillars but safe for bees and earthworms. It is labeled for use on tomatoes and appears to be just what I am after. I don't much care about its organicity, but caterpillars are my only problem, and it would be fine with me if caterpillars are all it kills.

Along with the *Bt* spray, I pick up a new box of fertilizer and stakes for the potted tomatoes. The bill is $19.12. Back home, I mix the spray and apply it carefully to the tomatoes, inserting the spray nozzle into the plants' interiors and spraying upwards to cover the underside of their leaves. I work up from the lowest leaves, plant by plant, and when I reach the top I reverse the process to cover the leaves' topsides.

Shortly after I have finished, I am called to the front door by our new neighbor from across the street. Am I aware of what's going on down the block? she asks. I am not, so she leads me out to where I can see two just-arrived police cars in front of the cement contractor's house. An enraged daughter-in-law has taken to one of the family cars with an ax.

Thank God the police are here. It is best to stay out of such altercations—although we might not have had such a luxury had the police not arrived so quickly and the ax-wielder's fury been directed at an object more animate. I learned this years ago when we lived in the apartment where I grew my first tomato. One couple in the building had a stormy relationship, and one night we heard screams and thuds reverberating through the walls. I was on good terms with the man and knew the history of the relationship, so I gathered my courage and knocked on their door. "Was everything all right?"

My appearance afforded the besieged woman the chance she needed, and she fled the moment the door was opened, screaming that the man had gone crazy. It happened with lightning suddenness, and when she'd gone, he stood in the doorway and looked at me, his eyes a mixture of rage, sadness, and relief.

Whether my action was more foolish than heroic is hard for me to say. The situation I had stepped into was extraordinarily dangerous, and there were many outcomes possible other than the favorable one we had experienced. Later, the couple got married. We have since lost touch, but my guess is that their relationship still harbors the possibility for a recurrence of that sad night's conflagration.

Similarly, the ax attack is but the latest in a long series of public flare-ups between the contractor's son and daughter-in-law. I can only imagine that the marriage is a source of great pain to the contractor. For whatever the immediate cause of their arguments, it is clear the pair have made bad choices for themselves. Only in the young granddaughter, who accompanies the contractor on his slow walks around the block, might he seem to have hope for a bit of redemption from this union.

We go this afternoon for a Fourth of July weekend swim and barbecue to the house of the TV game-show winner. We are joined as well by my wife's other good friend, she of the upside-down tomato cages, and by my son's best friend. Among us, then, are two great sets of friendships.

We spend the afternoon in conversation and the pool. The recent storm is on everyone's mind. Near the home of our hostess, an electric power transformer was hit by lightning and exploded. My wife's other friend tells of a co-worker in whose front yard a palm tree was hit by lightning and burst into flames. The incident so frightened the woman's Saint Bernard that the dog ran back and forth outside the house, desperately scratching and clawing at the doors and shredding the screens in the process. Reluctant at first to let the dog in for fear he would rampage through the house, she eventually yielded, only to discover the frantic animal had bloodied his paws and was tracking blood on her white carpets. Whether such damage is covered by home-owner's insurance none of us knows.

During the afternoon I examine our host's tomato plants. Both are on the east side of the house and have the same light-starved appearance as the melaleuca-shaded plants in my neighbor's front lawn. They have as well an abandoned, derelict look, and their owner confesses that she stopped tending them soon after her return from the debacle at the dude ranch.

Her vindication comes at dinner, which includes salmon, fresh sweet corn, fruit salad, and tomatoes from a seasonal vegetable stand. She has sliced the tomatoes into slabs, marinated them in balsamic vinegar and olive oil, and sprinkled over their tops salt, pepper, chopped fresh basil, and chunks of feta cheese. They are exquisite, as is the whole meal, and I am in heaven.

## JULY 4

My wife this week will be hosting a colleague from her company's London office, and our job today is to show her the sights. Conveniently, this is Independence Day, and the entertainment has been planned well in advance.

We retrieve our guest and wend our way through the city, driving through the university and stopping to show off the library from which I once watched the fog break the Santa Ana. We visit the hang-glider port, where souls more intrepid than I run off a cliff overlooking the ocean and are borne aloft on the incoming breeze. We watch sea lions play and pelicans skim. And we drive to the top of Mount Soledad, with its full-circle view of city, ocean, bays, and mountains. Descending, we make our way to the home of my sister-in-law, whose house sits on a hillside with a panoramic view of the Pacific. From here we will watch fireworks.

Our guest has seen U. S.-style fireworks before, but not on the Fourth. She has eaten barbecue, although it rained that day in London and the grill had to be brought inside. And she has eaten watermelon—once. And so we are pleased to be able to share with her these American traditions.

Before we eat dinner, however, I am escorted across the street. My sister-in-law has found an unusual tomato plant and I am to see it. The plant is a volunteer that sprang from a pot on a neighbor's patio. It belongs to a woman who has lived more than forty years in a beautiful house with a view that looks down on the community of La Jolla—down on a curve in the shore that provides a resting place in January for migrating whales, and out on a curving bluff-edged coastline that fades from sight thirty miles to the north.

It would be a fine place to grow old, but the woman's husband died some years ago, and I gather she is lonely. Apparently, this tomato has become a source of great interest for her. She has no idea how it got there, but once it decided to stay, she began to tend the plant daily. She keeps a handheld mister at the ready, and has espaliered the stem almost to her roof. It now rises a good seven feet from its pot . . . and she wants it identified.

Fortunately, the plant has unmistakable yellow fruit, each shaped like a tiny rugby ball. They are yellow plum tomatoes, twins to those my wife brought home from the store a few months back. Had the variety been among the multitude with big, red, round fruit, I would have been unable to identify it, and my status as "expert" would have withered on the spot.

Pleased at the discovery of her tomato's identity, the woman brings forth a dish of samples. In it are four rinsed and polished tomatoes, and she offers us one each. Eating this tomato is like eating a piece of sushi—it forms a perfect single bite. The fruit is sweeter than any I have tasted since last summer. It explodes in my mouth, brings a spasm of pleasure . . . and is gone. Furtively, I glance at the plant itself, on which are several dozen more ripe fruit. But we are to get only the one. We exchange a few more pleasantries and then tell the woman we must rejoin our party. As we leave, she invites us to come back after dinner to watch the fireworks from her house. The offer is genuine, almost an entreaty, but we decline, having plans already to watch from my sister-in-law's balcony.

The dinner is wonderful and the fireworks predictably spectacular. They are shot out over the ocean from a point just below us, and our view is sensational—during the performance we can see six other shows up and down the coast. The grand finale consists of a flurry of rapidly exploding low-altitude white bursts over which arc expanding dandelions of red and green. It's an impressive display, and though our British guest is not effusive in her praise, I believe she has enjoyed herself.

Whether the same is true of the woman across the street is less certain. Whether, alone, she even watched the fireworks is also uncertain. What is certain, in hindsight, is that we should have reversed her invitation and asked her to join us, to have offered to share with her our company. But we often fail to recognize our chances to do such a simple good, and I suppose it is of no use to berate oneself for vision that is less than perfect and only human.

## JULY 6

This evening while I am mowing the lawn I spot the contractor out hoeing his tomatoes. Because of his back, he works slowly and deliberately, gingerly working the hoe between his roses and tomatoes. The hoe he uses has a triangular head and reminds me of the instrument with which I spent many a childhood hour tending the corn, tomatoes, and melons in my parents' backyard.

I am drawn by the hoe. But in truth I am also fishing for an invitation: I want to see the nine-foot tomatoes in his backyard. And so I mosey down for a chat.

In his front yard are the Romas of which I spoke to John, and I ask if these are the ones he dries.

No, he says, not just these. He dries them all.

Does this mean the tall ones in his backyard, too?

Yes, he says, those, too. And he adds that they are now "ten feet tall."

"Here," he says, "come see."

He leads me through a side gate and along a walkway bordered with dense vegetation. We pass corn, borage, zucchini, and peppers; flats of basil, and fig, apple, and apricot trees. At the end of the walk we come to the tomatoes, a whole row of them. Here I see that he has not been exaggerating. The plants are by far the tallest tomatoes I have ever seen, and they are easily ten feet tall, towering over the path below. And, yes, they are supported by two-by-fours.

I was, I suppose, expecting a uniform stand of supertomatoes, made so by the contractor's years of careful culling. But instead I find a more diverse collection. There are his "big" ones—tall where the sun is full, and with baseball-sized green fruit. Belt-high are several plum-type tomatoes, loaded with strikingly beautiful ripe fruit and vaguely reminiscent of pepper plants. And sprinkled throughout are red and yellow cherries.

Nearby is a grape arbor, and both the grapes and the tomatoes are covered with bluish gray drops and splotches. This, he says, is a sulfur preparation he applies with a paintbrush. Its purpose is to prevent disease, and it seems to work, for the whole of the yard seems in exuberant good health, with an almost junglelike green and denseness.

I could spend hours in this garden. But one of the contractor's sons is here also, and he seems unsettled by my sudden appearance. Our stay is brief, and within minutes I am ushered back out to the street, expelled after an-all-too-fleeting glimpse of this unexpected Eden.

### JULY 9

The *Bt* spray seems to have worked. The day I sprayed I found one of the caterpillars and out of curiosity put it in a jar with a freshly sprayed leaf. Within a day the caterpillar had quit moving, and in another it had grown flaccid and died. Since then I have found no other caterpillars. Failing to find them, however, does not mean they are not there—they are too well camouflaged. And so today I spray again, heeding the warning on the label to reapply "before extensive feeding damage has occurred."

While I am doing so, Albert appears. He asks what I am doing, and I explain about the caterpillars, first wriggling my finger through the air, and then holding up thumb and forefinger to indicate a creature half an inch long. He nods in understanding. Since his plants are leaf-to-leaf with mine and no doubt harbor their own caterpillars, this is another reason to repeat the spray—and to continue doing so for the rest of the season.

While we are talking, he shows me his plants. The tallest is now more than six feet. He bends down and parts their leaves, revealing big clusters of green fruit. Already, he says, he has had a red one.

This is interesting, given that Albert and I planted on the same day, and I don't expect ripe fruit for another week. Whether his plants are early, or mine late—or whether the difference is due to anything other than statistical variability—is open to question. But with Albert I refrain from such speculation and merely continue our review, and when we are done we both conclude, with satisfaction, that things are going well. He goes back inside, and after a time John stops by on his bicycle, a great clunker of a thing he rides around the neighborhood. He has been watching Italy versus Spain in the World Cup quarterfinal, and I have been able to follow the action by way of the groans and cheers from his home. It is now halftime and Italy leads 1-0. Before the game, his son called their relatives in Sicily, and everyone there had their TVs on in anticipation. If Italy wins, says John, they will all get in their cars and drive around honking their horns. "They are really crazy there."

John began his radiation treatments this week. He has been going every day and will continue to do so for at least the next month. His spirits seem good, and at the moment the process is mostly an inconvenience—driving every day to the hospital. But I fear that with time things will change. In the newspaper today is an obituary for Dick Sargent, the actor who played the husband in *Bewitched*. Sargent died at sixty-four of prostate cancer, five years after it was diagnosed. His cancer spread despite treatment and, says the article, towards the end of his life, not only was the disease making him ill but he was "further weakened by daily radiation treatments."

Of course, every case is different, and the way things turned out for Sargent aren't necessarily the way they will for John. But still I worry.

## JULY 13

Growing tomatoes ought to be a cure for the affliction of striving for perfection, but it is not. Every year since the first that I have grown tomatoes here in our home, I have tried for a bigger and better crop. Or, as my aspirations have become more modest, at least for a respectable yield with plants free from glaring disease.

The first year I had nothing on which to base my expectations. I was naive, and so naturally the yield was tremendous, the growing was trouble-free, and nothing has been quite like it since. Other experiences in my life have had similar characteristics.

Try as I might, my tomatoes now have problems every year. The caterpillars, I believe, are under control. I have seen no new damage since I began spraying. But tonight I discover that I have lost five good-sized tomatoes, one almost ripe, to blossom-end rot.

My plants have had this before; it was blossom-end rot that once spurred me to fill my soil with eggshells. But the disorder has never made much sense to me. It is easy to diagnose: ugly, round brownish craters on the blossom end of the fruits. But how to make sense of the myriad book and magazine descriptions as to its cause? Calcium deficiency compounded by water stress, says one. Sudden changes in soil moisture, says another. Uneven watering, says a third, particularly during periods of rapid plant growth and high or varying temperatures.

I water my tomatoes regularly, which should be the same as "evenly," using the same once-a-week-deep-soaking schedule I have used for years. I've got calcium in my soil. And daily high temperatures the past two weeks have ranged from seventy-one to seventy-six degrees, which is neither high nor variable. So why do I have blossom-end rot?

Finally, this evening, I may have begun to understand. As I am removing the affected fruit, I look at Albert's plants. His plants, of course, have the same weather exposure as mine. But he waters more liberally—soaking them every two or three days. Perhaps he waters less deeply than I, but unquestionably he waters more often. And his plants do not have blossom-end rot. Nor do John's across the street, or for that matter, the container tomatoes in my patio, which I water almost daily.

Clearly, the blossom-end rot is my own doing—I have not been watering my tomatoes enough. Probably this has been true for years. Always I have hewn to the less-frequent-but-deep school of watering. But what I have failed to appreciate is that less-frequent-but-deep still requires enough. In its simplicity, the insight both startles and embarrasses me.

As a consolation prize, I am able to salvage one of the larger green tomatoes. After trimming off the bad end, I cut it in slices. I toss these in flour, salt and pepper the tops, and set them to fry. Over the years we have followed an increasingly "health conscious" diet, so the pan I use is nonstick and I use only a tablespoon of canola oil. When I was a kid, my mother used to cook fried green tomatoes in a cast-iron skillet with a deep pool of bacon fat. The house would fill with a glorious smell, and beside her a platter would grow tall with layer upon layer of crisp, brown slices, hot and succulent inside. It was one of my favorite dishes, and as I look down at the hissing dry pan below me, I realize that what I am seeing is a sad excuse for the real thing.

Next time, I vow, I'll use bacon fat.

### JULY 14

I see John briefly today and we talk tomatoes. He has lots of fruit, but the vines themselves are beginning to show signs of senescence—dying and yellowing lower foliage. Already he has pulled one up, a volunteer that he says "was done."

We also talk soccer. Italy beat Bulgaria 2-1 in the World Cup yesterday and has now won the right to play for the championship. I did not see the game, but the description in the paper was of high drama: Italy down by a goal until the last two minutes, when their star forward, Roberto Baggio, scored. Later, in overtime, it was Baggio again who scored the winning goal.

I mention to John that one of our neighbors, a lawyer, will be going to the Rose Bowl this coming Sunday for the final game, and I ask if he has ever been to a World Cup game.

No, he says, but twenty years ago he went to Los Angeles to see the Italian national team on tour. "That," he says wistfully and without elaboration, "was when I was young and happy."

### JULY 16

This evening we go out for dinner. The restaurant for which we are bound is new to us, chosen on the strength of a newspaper review. But we are drawn also by the restaurant's name: Tomatoes Plus. Why it bears such a name the review does not say, but it is only one of several San Diego eateries with similar titles. We also have Tomato's Ristorante, and in Carlsbad, a few miles to the north, Branci's Caldo Pomodoro—a. k. a. The Hot Tomato. Indeed, tomato-named restaurants can be found across the land, from Phoenix's Ripe Tomato Cafe to the Tomato Palace, in Columbia, Maryland. Nor are purveyors of food the only establishments so named. In San Diego you can buy a car from Tomato Auto. Los Angeles hosts Tomato Art, Tomato Inc., and Tomato's Bail Bonds. Sarah Tomato will paint your face in San Francisco. And in Sacramento you can play your hand at the Big Tomato Card Club.

But my favorite tomato-named business is Tomato Records. Now virtually defunct, Tomato is the publisher of a classic two-CD collection featuring such artists as Louis Armstrong ("St. Louis Blues"), Koko Taylor ("Wang Dang Doodle"), and Jerry Lee Lewis ("Whole Lotta Shakin' Goin' On"). I have spent many an hour with *The Great Tomato Blues Package*, and each time I open its case, I am cheered by the silver discs' red round logo with the stylized green leaf.

One reason we have not heard previously of Tomatoes Plus is its location in an unfamiliar part of town. My wife therefore studies the map as we drive. But after a time I notice that she is peering not at the map but at me.

"Dear," she says with a grin, "you have a gray hair in your moustache."

This is news to me, both unexpected and unwanted. More-over, the timing of the message is unfair given that I cannot run to a mirror to confirm or refute her report. Accordingly, I do the only logical thing: tell her she must be wrong.

## JULY 17

Early this morning I pick my first ripe tomato—a perfect, oblate-shaped Champion, deep red, and blemish free. I cut it in three sections so we can all share, and it is . . . wonderful. A dozen or more other fruit are just beginning to turn pink, and soon the flood will begin in earnest. I can hardly wait.

John is also full of anticipation, but for another reason. The final game of the World Cup will begin at noon: Italy versus

Brazil. Italy, he says, *must* win. But his voice is tinged with concern—Roberto Baggio, Italy's great forward, has injured his leg and may be unfit to play.

The tournament's official concert was televised last night from Dodger Stadium. John watched all three hours, and his eyes take on a beatific, faraway look as he tells me about it. The Three Tenors—Plácido Domingo, José Carreras, and Luciano Pavarotti—sang in a reprise of their famous 1990 concert. They sang, John says, mostly in Italian: operatic arias and popular traditionals. But they also included a few hits in English for selected audience members—all, says John, "big people": "I'll Do It My Way" for Frank Sinatra ("When they sang that, he stood up and he had tears in his eyes") and "Singin' in the Rain" for Gene Kelly.

"Music like that," says John, "it is so good that if you are sick, it can make you better."

John has his whole family over to watch the game—sons, daughters-in-law, and grandchildren. The street outside is filled with cars, and afterwards, when all have left, John walks over to me as I am watering my tomatoes.

"Don't talk to me," he says. "I am mad."

For two hours—ninety minutes of regulation play and thirty of overtime—Italy and Brazil fought it out, neither team scoring a knockout, neither scoring at all. The tie forced a shootout, and on the last shot, with Italy trailing 3–2, the great Baggio, who played lame, missed. Italy lost.

To me, Italy looked tired. They had a multitude of injured players, Baggio only one among them, and the weight of carrying those players simply took its toll. The game ebbed and flowed, but they could never mount a sustained attack.

John's analysis is harsher and more incisive: "They play lousy. They start lousy and they finish lousy. They play defense. All defense. And if you play all defense you can't win."

To divert him from his disappointment, I ask if he has found tomatoes yet for their sauce. Yes, he says, a wholesaler downtown sold him half of what he needed—eighteen lugs. The tomatoes were red and starting to soften, so he got them for half price. Already Rose has cooked them into sauce.

In addition to watering my tomatoes (the second installment of their new twice-weekly-deep-soaking schedule), I give them a general tending. I fertilize and spray, and I count and measure.

The latter reveals an interesting finding. Two weeks ago I had more than seven hundred flowers; today I have less than two hundred—and virtually none on my main plants. Yet during that time, my count of green fruit has increased only slightly. Most of that plenitude of flowers never bore fruit, and the buds now hang brown and desiccated, dropping to the ground at the merest of touches.

Why this should be, I can only speculate. But it may be that the plants have crossed some hormonal threshold and have now stopped gambling on the production of new offspring and shifted their energies instead towards the successful development of those fruit already fertilized and under way.

If this is so, it represents a point of demarcation—a shift from youthful exuberance to mature conservatorship. The plants are beginning to age. It is surprising to me how early in their lives this has happened. But not nearly as surprising as the discovery of a lone gray hair in my moustache—about which my wife was not wrong.

## JULY 19

This evening as my son and I are kicking a soccer ball in our front yard, the cement contractor comes by on his daily walk. He asks if we saw *the* game, and then he goes over to inspect the tomatoes, both mine and Albert's. He hefts a few of the exposed fruit in his hands and pulls aside leaves to peer inside the plants' depths, and as he does, there is a touch of jealousy in his voice. His plants, he says, are now "twelve feet tall. But not much fruit."

He passes slowly down the row, and at each stop I tell him the name of that variety. The Beefsteak, I tell him, is the same kind Albert has; the Lemon Boy will have yellow fruit.

Do I like yellow tomatoes? he asks.

I don't know, I tell him, it's an experiment.

He nods in approval and repeats what I have said: "An experiment."

Experimenting is one of the great joys of gardening, a means with which to indulge one's curiosity, and a source of grist on which to think, ponder, and observe. It is clear he is no stranger to this satisfaction.

He asks if I have any cherries, and in reply I show him the potted plants inside our patio. Here he looks around and tells me that once he had an opportunity to buy our house. They couldn't agree on a price, however, and the deal was never struck. One reason he wouldn't up his offer was the house's lack of yard space, and by way of explanation he casts his arm about my patio now crowded with tomatoes.

As we return to the sidewalk, a car passes us by on the street and we both wave. The driver once lived only a few houses away. He moved recently, after his marriage of nearly twenty years ended in divorce, and he left behind both home and children. "Poor man," says the contractor, "he lost everything. His wife changed him for another man."

### JULY 22

A tomato has been stolen, a small one off the Champion from which I have already harvested two fruit. I know to expect this, for it cannot be avoided. But still it annoys me.

This theft particularly irritates me because the fruit was not large and was not readily visible, having been relatively well covered by leaves. Moreover, it happened at night. All of which suggests that my plants are under surveillance—and *that* is what annoys me. I expect to lose a few fruit to the occasional passerby who succumbs to temptation: the inventory shrinkage thing. But to have some vulture watching my crop with the intention of picking tomatoes just before I do is another matter entirely. It takes considerable joy out of the growing.

### JULY 23

If life gives you green tomatoes, make green tomato pie.

For some reason unknown, three large green tomatoes have dropped from the vine the last few days. Because we have not yet acquired any bacon fat, I am seeking some use for these fruit other than simply to let them ripen on my windowsill, by which time I should have scads of true vine-ripened tomatoes.

There are marmalades, chutneys, relishes, pickles, and countless other uses that have been devised for green tomatoes. Most, however, appear in newspaper articles with titles like "Too Many Tomatoes" and whose underlying premise is that the reader is awash in fruit and desperate to dispose of them. Accordingly, they tend to call for dozens of tomatoes rather than three. Since I am not inclined to sacrifice future ripe tomatoes in order to use the few unripe ones that I have, I look for a recipe more modest in its requirements. *Tomatoes! 365 Healthy Recipes for Year-Round Enjoyment* has an entire chapter on green tomatoes, and in it I find a recipe that calls for exactly three green tomatoes.

## GREEN-TOMATO PIE

pastry for two 9-inch pie crusts
3 large green tomatoes, cut into ½-inch cubes or thinly sliced
pinch salt
1 tablespoon unbleached all-purpose flour
1 cup sugar
1 tablespoon fresh lemon juice
1 tablespoon butter
1 teaspoon ground cinnamon
¼ teaspoon ground nutmeg

*Preheat oven to 350°F. Line a 9-inch pie pan with half the pastry. Roll out the remaining pastry for the top, and cut four 1-inch slits in the center.*

*In a medium-size bowl, combine the remaining ingredients and fill the pie crust. Top with the rolled-out pastry and crimp the edges to seal. Bake for 45 minutes. Serve warm.*

I have neither made nor eaten a green tomato pie before. Nor has my son, and he declines to participate in the endeavor, stating vociferously that the proposed pastry is "weird." But undeterred, I decide to proceed. Such a creation, I figure, couldn't continue to flourish were it entirely unpalatable. And flourish it has.

Ortho has a recipe similar to the one I plan to use. In *Tomatoes*, Lee Baily has a recipe for "Green Tomato and Apple Pie." And Jesse Cool, in *Tomatoes—A Country Garden Cookbook*, provides instructions for a "Green Tomato Raspberry Pie." Both sound scrumptious, but at the moment I have neither apples nor raspberries. A newspaper version I have collected calls for raisins, but this is an elaboration I forgo voluntarily.

In their multitude and variation, these recipes suggest the underlying presence of a classic combination, and I unexpectedly extend the tradition when I find that the only flour in the house suitable for making pie crust is whole-wheat pastry flour. Accordingly, I dig up a recipe for whole-wheat piecrust and carry on with what is now "Steve's Green Tomato Pie with Whole-Wheat Crust."

The actual making of the pie is a decidedly amateurish affair. It has been a long time since I have made a pie crust, and I spend a considerable amount of time rolling and flailing at the dough to get it flat and round. The latter requires a little cut-and-paste work, but eventually the crust is in the pan, the filling is in the crust, and the pie is in the oven.

The problem with platitudes is that they oversimplify. This becomes apparent when the pie is ready to eat. In Diane Wakoski's poem "Pamela's Green Tomato Pie," the protagonist (who, unlike me, is ethereal and competent in her pie-making) manages to make a pie so "exceptional" it entices her ten-year-old son to eat two helpings. In contrast, *my* ten-year-old remains entrenched in his conviction that a green tomato pie is an unnatural thing and refuses to try so much as a bite.

Not until my wife comes home do I sample my work. Then—the howlings of my junior gourmand notwithstanding—she joins with me in confirming that the pie is good. It is spicy and flavorful, and the whole-wheat flour lends nutlike overtones to the taste of the crust. Definitely it bears repeating, and perhaps even a venture into an apple or raspberry permutation. My son, I believe, will eventually come 'round.

## JULY 24

I am standing on the front porch this afternoon when my neighbor the newspaper reporter passes by on the sidewalk towing his young son in a small wagon. He stops to say hi and soon comments on my tomatoes, noting that the plants I gave him in May are considerably smaller than those in my front yard. Nonetheless, he says he is having fun in their growing and that of the two six-packs I gave him, he in turn gave one to his next-door neighbor, an elderly woman with whom he now compares notes.

As we talk, he attends constantly to his son, at one point lifting him high in the air and administering a "belly buzzer"—burying his face in the child's tummy and blowing wetly, side to side. This elicits the sound of fluttering flesh and shrieks of laughter. The boy has just begun to walk, and as we step into our living room he takes no more than a few steps at a time before collapsing on crossed legs and diapered rump and beginning to investigate whatever is nearby.

One such object is our cat, and the father asks if he scratches. "No," I say, "not . . . "

And I am about to say, "Not unless you stroke him repeatedly or too vigorously in the same place." No, I am about to say, not unless you pull his whiskers. And I am about to tell the story of the time years ago when my son interrupted me on the phone with a tremendous wail and a burst of tears—the cat had scratched him. Why? I had asked. No reason, said my son. Well, he had said, the cat had been "taking a bath"—grooming himself—and he had . . . What, exactly, my son had done we never learned, but the incident had not been repeated, and we had given it little further mind.

Yes, I am about to relate these amusing aspects of our cat's behavior when there is a low hiss, followed by a piercing scream. It happens fast, so fast neither of us sees the actual encounter, but as we rush to the boy, we find a flaming welt rising across his cheek.

The father scoops the boy up in his arms, checks for blood, and holds him tightly to his chest, rocking him back and forth.

No, I was about to say, not as long as he doesn't poke him.

I apologize profusely, but this is of no help. "We have to go," says the agitated father. And I open the door for him, his exit preceded by that of the culprit slinking underfoot.

In a flurry they are gone, and I am left alone. The power of tomatoes to help forge human links is strong, but they cannot transcend the quirks of a cat and a parent's protective instincts.

### JULY 25

My son today begins a new school year with a new school schedule—"year-round." He is just beginning sixth grade. The class he is entering is the class from which his best friend just graduated.

Results from a standardized test are the magic that have granted him entry to this class. I have mixed feelings about this. Kids who are already high achievers will be lavished with advantage—a small class, special books, engaging classmates, a gifted teacher—and they will do well. There's little to argue with in this, but the formula is self-fulfilling, and the question arising is: Why shouldn't kids who are less advantaged at the outset be treated this same way? Wouldn't the kids in the class my son just left—the class and the school we are fleeing—also succeed if they were treated in this manner?

Still, the cliché is true: I am not about to let larger social concerns get in the way of *my* son's education. I am grateful for the opportunity he has received and the resources to which he now has access. Besides, how can I have misgivings about his acceptance into a class whose students grow tomatoes?

### JULY 26

I pick today three tomatoes, all from the Celebrity closest to the street. They are red, but a few days shy of their peak. I know this as I pick them—they lack the deep ruby-orange coloring of a fully ripe tomato. But I figure it's now or never: If I don't pick them, the thief will. I could put them on the windowsill to finish ripening, but instead I cave in to the desire for immediate gratification and cut up two for salad.

At dinner, my wife points out tactfully that the tomatoes I've picked are not especially tasty. And they are mealy. She is right about this, and it occurs to me that even though the thief did not get these tomatoes, I have been robbed all the same. But what has happened is worse, for I have done it to myself.

The only solution to this dilemma, as far as I can see, is a change of attitude. There is no practical way to catch the thief or discover his identity. I could put up a sign. But this could do more harm than good, as in the apocryphal story of the New Yorker who leaves a placard on his dash: THERE IS NO RADIO IN THIS CAR, PLEASE DO NOT BREAK IN. Only to find his windows smashed and an angry written response: WELL GET ONE!

Or I could continue to try and out-anticipate the thief, but that way lies a tomato-grower's version of the arms race: He would try to out-out-anticipate me, and I would have to out-out-out-anticipate him, leaving me with an ever-lengthening windowsill of ever-paler tomatoes. This is pretty much contrary to what growing your own tomatoes is all about, and down that path I see naught but frustration and self-reproach.

No, the only thing to do is make peace with the devil. The toll I pay for growing tomatoes in the front yard is going up. But dwelling on it further is only going to cause a greater diminution of my tomato-growing pleasure than the stolen fruit are worth. I shall worry this no more.

## JULY 27

Much as I love it, our neighborhood is not perfect. I am reminded of this while working in my front yard this evening as I am approached by a trio of older women.

All are longtime residents, and they are making their way door-to-door through the neighborhood distributing a flyer. I glance briefly at the sheet and see that it concerns a neighborhood house in which a small daycare center for children has recently begun operation. I have heard already of this issue, having been given accounts of it by a neighbor who takes her baby to the center while she goes to work. The people who run the center, says the woman, are loving and responsible, and they spend time with the children rather than planting them in front of a television. They have been, she says, a real salvation.

Ostensibly, the residents who have come calling are concerned both with the procession of cars that pick up and deliver the kids and with the noise of the children playing. And though my wife and I have been through the endless headaches of trying to find decent childcare, I can sympathize with these women's complaints of traffic and noise. But on looking at their handout, I see that these are not the issues at all.

The flyer is crudely composed, consisting of handwritten annotations scrawled upon an advertising circular prepared by the daycare operators. The couple who run the day care also teach yoga; they are Sikhs and have unconventional names, and this is my neighbors' true point of objection. In front of an arrow pointing to a drawing of the Yogi wearing his robes and headdress, they have written, "This is unacceptable!" Near his address they ask, "Wonder why he moved to our neighborhood?" And throughout their tone is venomous and ugly. I am both saddened and dismayed to have received such a thing. But I don't see that a debate will do much other than antagonize the holders of these views, and so I am quiet.

Sensing their failure to enlist me, one of the women asks instead if I have "gotten any tomatoes yet?" Yes, I tell her, a few red ones and a few green ones. In years past, this woman has knocked on my door and asked for tomatoes, and I have given them to her. But this evening I am not so inclined, and she does not ask. She does, however, ask what I did with my green tomatoes.

Made a pie, I say, and fried some.

At the mention of fried green tomatoes all three of the women join the conversation simultaneously. How do I make mine? asks one. "I use cornmeal," says another. And the third uses cracker crumbs. I roll them in flour and fry them in bacon grease, I tell them. And on hearing this, they want to know where I learned my technique. From my mother, I say, who learned from my father's mother, who lived in Oklahoma. This seems to satisfy them, and they move on to problems they've been having with bugs. But for me, the conversation has been tainted by the flyer and the purpose of their visit, and I find no joy in it.

Eventually they leave, and when they do, I take the flyer inside and show it to my wife. And, along with Rodney King, I wonder: "Why can't everybody just get along?"

## JULY 30

My son leaves the house early this morning in the company of his best friend's family. They are going on a thirty-mile bicycle ride sponsored by a bike club to which the family belongs.

The parents of my son's friend are passionate bicyclists, having raced for many years and being owners of a custom-built tandem. But they cultivate as well an aura of elitism about their two-wheeled doings. Many times they have invited my son on these rides, and always before he has refused, feeling, I believe, a bit intimidated. He and I ride similar distances, and he is a strong, confident rider. But our rides are for fun, while his friend's are "serious." This distinction, artificial though it is, has left him hesitant about going along. And so I am pleased at his decision today to go, pleased at his decision to give it a try.

In truth, I am pleased also at the hours his outing will give me alone, for I have innumerable chores—from putting up shelves to grocery shopping. I have just begun the first of these when the telephone rings.

"Is this Gabe Shepherd's dad?" asks the caller.

"Yes," I reply. And as I do, I know that this is not going to be a pleasant call and that the chores I'd planned are not going to get done. This, I know, is the call that every parent dreads.

My son has had an accident, says the caller. It is not life-threatening, but he has cut his finger badly, and I had better come get him. I speak also to the mother of my son's friend, and she says she has put a tourniquet on it, but, yes, it is bad and I should come. It is 8:30 A.M.

My wife is just getting out of the shower as I find her. Our son, I tell her, has had an accident. Immediately I follow this with the statement that he is all right, but as soon as I speak I see that I have erred in my delivery, for she both slumps and recoils as if struck. I hold her for a few moments before telling her what I know and repeating that he is basically okay.

When we arrive, we find a group of cyclists standing around my son, who is lying on the road. He is on his back, legs bent and knees raised. The forearm of his uninjured hand is crossed over his eyes and forehead; his injured hand is upright, elbow on the pavement. A T-shirt has been wrapped around the hand. We decide to take him directly to the emergency room, and my wife takes him to the car while I collect his bicycle.

Inside the car, he cries for the first time since we have arrived. My wife sits next to him, comforting him, and he tearfully asks the question we always ask, but which rarely has an answer: "Why did this happen to me?"

Our decision now is where to take him. The most competent medical care is generally to be found at large, teaching hospitals. However, such hospitals tend also to be busy and impersonal, and since it appears that he will mostly need to be cleaned and stitched, we decide simply to take him to the closest emergency room, which is at a small community hospital two miles away.

Here, it is as I suspected. Only one other party is waiting, and their attentions are fixed on a loud television set mounted overhead. This is an inevitable feature of all modern hospitals, as if the medical community had determined that in the twentieth century healing cannot begin, or death or grieving proceed, without the accompaniment of professional wrestling or soft-drink songsters cooing "Uh-huh." While I sit with my son, his head on my shoulder, my wife registers and affirms our ability to pay.

Eventually, we are led to an examination room, where my son is placed upon a gurney. A nurse unwraps his finger and I see the wound for the first time: a fat, nasty gash arcs from the very tip to the first joint of his middle finger. Blood wells from the wound, and the nail is turned to one side; apparently he caught his finger in the bicycle's spokes, and the turning wheel cut, tore, and twisted the finger all at one time. The nurse begins to examine him, followed by a doctor. They conclude that his nerves and tendons are intact, but X rays and a tetanus shot are ordered.

The needle for the tetanus shot is both thick and long; the reason for its sturdiness is to facilitate injection deep into the muscle. My son turns his head to avoid looking as the nurse swabs his arm, but as she inserts the needle and buries its one-inch length, he does not even flinch. Indeed, except for his tears in the car, he has not uttered a single complaint.

As my wife tracks down coffee and doughnuts, I walk alongside my son as he is wheeled to the X-ray room. Here he begins to assess the implications of his injury. Will he be able to hold a pencil so he can write at school? I don't know, I say, it will probably be difficult. But he'll adjust, people usually do. Saxophone will be out for the immediate future, as will soccer, or at least goaltending.

The X rays show that my son has fractured his fingertip. They suggest further that the bone's growth plate has been wrenched from the shaft of the fingertip. If left as is, the finger will be permanently deformed. The emergency room physician feels at this point it would be prudent to contact our pediatrician—and to find a qualified hand surgeon.

The next few hours pass interminably. It is the weekend, and San Diego's doctors are all golfing or have their phones turned off. Or they "don't do hands." Finally, an orthopedic surgeon is located who will see our son. But only if we drive to a second emergency room at one of the big teaching hospitals—where it now seems we should have gone in the first place. In preparation, the nurse applies a temporary dressing to my son's finger, which is still oozing blood. Notes are typed, and the X rays packaged, and we leave. It is 1:30 P.M.

Conditions at the teaching hospital are as expected: dozens of sick and injured people fill the waiting area, and before we can register we must first preregister. Fortunately, the doctor is expecting us and our wait is short. The stereotype of orthopedic surgeons is of big burly men—"bonesetters"—who need immense strength to reposition joints and wrestle contracted muscles. But instead we are faced with a petite young woman, with red hair and freckles. I take this as a sign of progress.

We are led to a suite of curtained rooms and deposited in room *A*. Across from us is *M,* and around the corner are more lettered curtains—how many I cannot see. Through a gap in the curtain, I see a young man wheeled by on a gurney, his neck in a brace and his eyes straining to keep sight of a little boy who walks behind him. The sight fills me with anguish. Not because the man is injured, but because of the pain I know he feels for the worry he has caused his son.

The doctor looks at the X rays and begins an initial examination. Her opinion is that he definitely has a fracture, but that the growth plate has not been ruptured. Surgery will not be necessary.

What will be necessary, of course, is to sew him up. To prepare for this she must numb his finger. She explains to my son that this will be like the shots he gets at the dentist, but he has never had such a shot and this is no help in preparing him for what is to come. She fills a syringe—its barrel three inches long and half an inch in diameter—and explains to him that the nerves "look like spaghetti" and run up each side of the finger; she must numb both sides. She begins by inserting the needle into the back of his hand just to one side of the knuckle, a spot that still harbors a tiny pad of baby fat. She pushes the needle almost clear through his hand to the palm; that's where the nerves are, she says, but the skin of the palm is too thick to penetrate. Grasping the barrel of the syringe with all four fingers of one hand, she then presses the plunger with her thumb, exerting a great deal of pressure and swelling his flesh with the injected fluid.

This is an excruciatingly painful procedure. When I was just a few years older than my son, I cut my hand with a kitchen knife and required stitches and injections almost exactly like this, and I can still recall the incredible, searing pain. As she presses on the plunger, my son grimaces. His features tighten and his face reddens, and he lets out a low, agonized "Owww." My wife is holding his uninjured hand, and I cup his face in my hands, rubbing his cheeks with my thumbs. He does not cry. But I do. Tears, I discover, are making their way down my cheeks. She repeats the procedure on the other side of his finger, and it is every bit as wrenching.

When she has finished cleaning and stitching the wound, the surgeon bandages him. She leaves the final writing of notes and instructions to the nurses and departs, returning home for the remainder of this Saturday afternoon, perhaps to her garden. We are to see her again in five days. Eventually we are discharged, and on our way home we stop by a pharmacy. It is 4:00 P.M.

When we arrive home, my wife and son go directly inside. "All I want to do," he says, "is lie down in my own bed." I stay behind to unload the car, and as I am doing so Albert's wife appears on the sidewalk. She has seen my son's bandaged finger and asks what happened. For the first of what I expect will be many times, I tell the story of his accident. In this case I make liberal use of hand signals—rolling my extended forefingers in tight adjacent circles to indicate a bicycle, making an abrupt falling motion with one hand, then with my left thumb and forefinger (as if I were holding a razor blade), making a sharp slashing motion across my right middle fingertip. She nods in understanding.

Having exhausted this one thing we can talk about, she points to my tomatoes, which are directly behind us, and indicates with uplifted cupped palms that they are doing well. Albert's, I say, in the now familiar mutual exchange of compliments, also have ample fruit. Nodding in agreement, she says "Look" and leads me up their driveway and around to the end of their row of tomatoes. There, she shows me a cluster of a dozen Beefsteaks, each probably weighing three-quarters of a pound. It is an impressive display, and I respond with the one Italian word I know. "*Bella!*"

"Pasta," she says. "I make pasta."

In the nearly seven years we have been next-door neighbors, this is the first multiple-word conversation we have had. All that it took was my son's first serious accident and a healthy crop of tomatoes.

### JULY 31

An unfamiliar pair of cars make an appearance before Vito's house today. One is a new Jaguar convertible. When it has gone, I find Vito in his yard and ask him about it. The car, he says, belongs to his son, a chiropractor, and with a mixture of pride and incredulity, he tells me it cost seventy-two thousand dollars.

The second car is a champagne-and-ruby-colored Thunderbird. It was the son's previous car and is now to be Vito's. Polished and well kept, the car is undoubtedly the nicest car Vito has ever owned. Together, we admire it for a while, and then Vito sweeps his arm towards my side of the street and says to me heartily, "How are your tomatoes? Do you have any ripe ones?"

It is an expansive, magnanimous gesture. Having shared his good fortune, he now gives me the chance to share mine, and we cross the street to examine my bounty. There are now hundreds of green fruit and scores on the verge of readiness. Among the latter are several Lemon Boys—gorgeous half-pound fruit the shape of canoes and the color of egg yolks. Earlier this morning I showed these same fruit to John, parting the leaves so he could look inside; he gazed at them for a long time in silence, and then told me in a voice just above a whisper, "They're wonderful."

Vito is less affected by the fruit, and his examination is more cursory. He is complimentary, but his principal reaction is to tell me that he recently saw a pair of teenage boys walk by and stop to pick a few tomatoes. This is better news than he might have thought, for it suggests my surveillance theory was wrong—or at least that random passersby are also contributing to the problem. As such, when we are done I write out a sign, which I slip inside a plastic cover and wire to the cage of the Celebrity nearest the sidewalk:

PLEASE DO NOT PICK THESE TOMATOES. IT HAS TAKEN MUCH HARD WORK TO GROW THEM. IF YOU SIMPLY CANNOT AFFORD YOUR OWN, COME TO THE FRONT DOOR AND WE WILL HELP.

Whether this will work, or prove counterproductive, I have no idea. It is in its way yet another experiment—this one social rather than biologic.

# AUGUST

FROM THE LEMON BOY, I pick today a large ripe tomato. I now have nearly a dozen ripe tomatoes on my windowsill, and this fruit I convey instead across the street. John is sitting on the brick wall near his driveway, and at my approach he puts down the newspaper he is reading. He smiles at the sight of the tomato I am carrying, and when I give it to him he hefts it appreciatively in his hand.

Is it ripe? he asks.

Yes, I assure him, it is. He calls then to his wife. "Rosa!" And in Italian—come have a look. She appears, drying her hands on her apron, and breaks into a broad grin when she sees the tomato.

"What color sauce will this make?" she asks.

Yellow, I imagine, although I can't say for sure. She has seen, says Rose, small yellow pear tomatoes, but never a big one like this. And for some minutes the three of us stand just looking at it, seduced by this unfamiliar version of an object we otherwise know so well.

AUGUST 4

I spy John this evening out watering his lawn. Has he eaten the yellow tomato? I ask.

"Yes," he says. "It was delicious. I ate it the Italian way: with bread, a little salt, and cheese." The bread, naturally, was made by Rose.

A week ago John asked me if it was too late to put in tomatoes for a fall harvest. I have never had much luck with this strategy, but I told him that to do it he would need a variety like Early Girl, with a short maturation date. I ask him now if he has pursued the idea any further, and he says no, he has not. To put in new tomatoes he would first have to take out old tomatoes, and, he says, he gets too tired now to do such work. He does not say it, but this is the effect of the radiation therapy.

Several large and ever-reddening Champions have remained on the vine and prominently in view since I posted my sign. I cannot yet say whether the sign has dissuaded any would-be thieves, but it seems definitely to have affected honest passersby.

This evening we are interrupted twice by callers at the door—"tomato customers," my son now calls them. The first is a woman from outside the neighborhood. She is riding an old and heavy bicycle and looks as if she has lived a hard life. "The sign," she tells me, as I step out on the front porch, "I like what it says about not being able to afford your own."

I am confused, not knowing if she is asking for tomatoes or money. And so I offer the less costly alternative first. "Would you like some tomatoes?" I ask.

"No," she says, "I just like your sign and what you said."

"Well, here," I reply, "come have a tomato." I lead her over to the tomato patch, and as I do she comments that this is a nice neighborhood. Where she lives, she recently had to flee a man who tried to choke and molest her.

I pick out a fat Champion; a red one close to a pound and free of blemishes. She stows it in a plastic grocery bag and then pulls a quarter from her pocket and offers it in payment. It is an unexpected and humbling gesture. "No," I tell her, "but thank you. And enjoy your tomato." She lingers and seems to want to talk, but I tell her I must return to my dinner.

Less than ten minutes later I am greeted at the door by two women, one the elderly mother of the second. I do not know them, but they tell me they are neighbors and live just a block away. They grow daylilies in their front yard, and people take them. They want to know: Does our sign work?

I tell them it seems at least to have slowed the tomatoes' rate of disappearance. They seem heartened by this and tell me they too have thought of a sign, but didn't know if it was worth the trouble. As they are leaving, I ask if they would like a tomato. No, they say, they have their own in their backyard—they aren't so bold as to grow them in front.

It is lack of space, not boldness, that has driven me to front-yard tomato growing. But I am not so sure I don't benefit from the arrangement, for it brings me not only tomatoes but also visitors, conversations, and compliments.

## AUGUST 5

My wife and I both take off from work early this afternoon. We are going to Davis for the weekend. It has been five years since last we were there; five years since last I was home.

We are going for fun. Fun and a reunion. When I was in college in Davis, I lived for a year in a house located incongruously in the middle of a trailer court. There were five of us, each to a room, and the house was the site of a near-continual party interrupted only occasionally by schoolwork. Among our wider circle of friends, those of us who lived in that house enjoyed for a time a near-mythical status for a certain gonzo approach towards life— made manifest late one night in a tequila and peyote inspired telephone call to Hunter Thompson, father of all things gonzo.

Of the five, two were the friends I have known longer than any others. These are the friends I grew up with, played sports with, went to school with, and worked with. At various times and in places other than the big house, I lived with each of these two friends, and it is with the family of one of them that we will stay this weekend. The other two members of that household I met and befriended in college; it is one of them—now a doctor—who has organized the weekend's main event: a raft trip and barbecue.

Before we leave, I pick tomatoes. Many are ripe, and though the sign appears effective, there is no point in tempting fate. I pick two Celebrities, ten Beefsteaks, and thirteen Champions. All are handsome fruit. The Beefsteaks are shaped like flattened disks with fluted tops; they have an orangish tinge and average more than a half pound each. The Champions are redder and heavier, with the two biggest weighing well over a pound. It is a satisfying harvest, and as I bring them inside, our kitchen counter disappears under a mountain of tomatoes.

From our closet I retrieve a small cardboard box that once held tins of almonds. I layer the bottom with foam peanuts and on them I place six of the tomatoes I have just picked. All are perfect, scarlet orbs of summer, and over their tops I place another layer of peanuts before closing the lid. Now a gourmet pack of tomatoes, this will serve as our hostess gift. My wife suggests that bringing tomatoes *to* Davis is perhaps superfluous. But I bear them proudly nonetheless.

Our flight north is mostly over ocean and dry, brown hills. As we begin our descent, however, we pass the Sacramento River Delta, where myriad twisting strands of water form countless small islands, given an illusory durability through the building of levees. Many of the islands—connected by ancient drawbridges and on which are pear orchards and corn fields—are below water level and occasionally they flood. This happened three days ago when the levee around Little Mandeville Island collapsed and turned the island into a six-foot-deep lake. The Delta is the point of origin for the California Aqueduct, which carries northern water south and is the source of up to half the water I use on my tomatoes. It is also the source of considerable acrimony between the state's upper and lower halves, the north viewing with deep resentment the more populous south's "theft" of its most valuable natural resource.

Flying into Sacramento, it becomes clear just how much water there is here. It is an abundance I failed to appreciate when I lived in its midst. In San Diego there is virtually no fresh water to be seen; no streams or rivers worthy of the name, and few lakes—all reservoirs. In contrast, Sacramento and the lands around seem an agricultural Venice. From the river the water courses into a vast network of canals, slews, and irrigation ditches, and from these it runs into the furrows that thread the rows of crops. All this water makes the plants lush and verdant, and the play of green and blue is richest in the rice fields—by which Sacramento's airport is surrounded; these are covered completely with water, its shimmering surface broken only by rank after rank of green, young shoots. Parched southerner that I have become, I am dazzled by it all.

At the terminal we are met by my friend and his son, who is six months older and a head taller than my son; the two boys are amiable but, unlike their fathers, they have not spent enough time together to become close friends. Driving from the airport, we take first the interstate and then a two-lane country road. We pass through field after field of corn, tomatoes, melons, and safflower, the latter dried and brown and ready for harvest. We pass, too, through immense swaths of alfalfa, some green and growing, some cut to the stubble, the baled harvest piled in stacks twenty feet high and hundreds of feet long. The alfalfa fills the night air with a sweet, grassy smell, and in countless other ways our senses tell us that the earth here is rich and being worked.

Approaching Davis we see first the cannery, brightly lit and exhaling white plumes into the dark. In the parking lot are scores of double truck trailers mounded high with tomatoes, and here the scent of agriculture mixes with the smell of ketchup and paste in the making.

At the home of my friend we are greeted by his daughter and wife, and by my other childhood friend—fellow veteran of the wild house in the trailer court and he whom I have known since second grade. We convene in the kitchen and review our plans for the morrow. Kids have not been invited on the raft trip—the trip's organizer felt the spirit of our more youthful days would be kept most faithfully if we were unencumbered by parental duties. This is not the decision I would have made, but my son seems remarkably understanding, and grandparents have been obtained for child care. Other details are discussed, and afterwards my wife and I step out for a walk before retiring.

Our path takes us down streets I have traveled countless times. But the trees are bigger now, and the houses less new. There are stop signs where once there were none, and the family carpet shop of the first woman I loved has now changed hands and is looking rather seedy. Later, we pass an industrial research park where there used to be fields, and we find now the headquarters of Calgene—its windowsills lined not with tomatoes but with instruments and glassware. But despite the changes, the air is as warm as it always was on August nights, the streets are quiet, and I know that I have come home.

### AUGUST 6

I am awakened early this morning by the distant drone of a crop duster. Soon the others are roused as well, and preparations for the day begin. Not too long ago our host was treated for testicular cancer and he gave everyone he knew quite a fright. It is not surprising, therefore, when he says he is feeling tired and may not go with us. This would be a great disappointment, but no one feels it wise to pressure him. We do, however, make a run for coffee and pastries, and these—combined with a dose of loud Grateful Dead music—have a salubrious and invigorating effect, and soon our friend decrees himself fit to come along.

We rendezvous first with my friend from second grade, and then proceed *en train* to Sacramento and the home of our friend the doctor. It has been five years since I and the doctor have seen each other, and a considerable time as well since he has seen the others, and when we arrive there is a warm and extended exchange of greetings and embraces. Inside, our hosts have spread a table with coffee, juices, fruits, and scones, and here we congregate happily and noisily as we await the final pair in our party; later, we will return for dinner.

Soon all are present—the five housemates and our five wives—and we depart for the river. Sacramento was founded near the confluence of the Sacramento and American Rivers. The American drains the Sierra Nevada west of Lake Tahoe—it was on the river's south fork that John Marshall discovered gold—and as it falls from the mountains, the river foams, swirls, and tumbles to form some of the country's most challenging white water. We, however, are in search of nothing so adventurous, and we aim instead for a nearby stretch made placid by dams, lakes, and the flat valley floor.

At the public beach that is our destination, a half dozen entrepreneurs have set themselves up in the business of renting inflatable rafts. A few miles downstream they'll retrieve the rafts and shuttle their customers back to their cars. Already the day is warm and each vendor has a long line of customers. The river itself is equally crowded, and I am amazed to find hundreds of yellow rafts upon the surface of the water—amazed in part at the numbers, and in part because when we were in college so many years ago and I and my friends made our inaugural voyage here, we were virtually alone.

Nonetheless, we soon obtain a pair of eight-person behemoths and drag them and our provisions to the water's edge. The latter include large quantities of food, beer, and water. Unbeknownst to me, we are equipped also with a pair of fantastically huge toy water cannon. Each has a barrel a yard long and sucks up a gallon of water at a time. They take two hands to operate, and can propel a stream of water fifty feet or more. It takes no great sleuthing on my part to discover these items, for I learn of their existence when I turn from stowing some supplies and find myself getting drenched from head to foot.

Naturally these devices are of great interest to the men. Just as naturally, the women declare themselves off limits as targets. I, of course, have no desire but to honor the women's wishes, and so it is a great injustice when, just as we are set to embark, one of my friend's wives misperceives that I might be about to soak her, and she leaps across the raft, plants both hands on my chest, and pushes me overboard. I surface to the sounds of great laughter, and once I am back in place we finally push off and venture out into the armada, our craft spinning slowly as we attempt to coordinate our paddling.

During the next few hours we keep the water cannon in near constant use, both upon ourselves and on other parties drifting on the river. Generally, we are victorious in these latter encounters, as we are the more heavily armed. But we are at one point forced to defend ourselves vigorously against a raftful of tattoo-clad bikers whose strategy is to try to board and capsize us pirate-style. We spend as well an interlude with the men in one raft and the wives in the other, and during this time the eyes in our raft seem more freely to linger on the many swimsuited young women floating on courses parallel to our own. Our raft seems also to fill more rapidly with empty beer cans and bilge water during this time, and when finally we regroup and sort ourselves into couples— shortly thereafter to find ourselves at the landing sight—it is only after having laughed so hard and so long that our jaws hurt.

Later in the afternoon, when we have cleaned up and returned to the doctor's for dinner, I overhear in the kitchen a conversation among the women about the nature of their husbands' friendships. Why, they wonder, does our behavior "degenerate" when we are together? The layers of seeming maturity they have seen us acquire in the years since high school and college seem to peel away in each other's presence. Why, they ask, must our reunions be marked by belches and shenanigans?

The reason, I think, is that our friendships have passed the stage of being competitive. Among ourselves, we needn't wear the cloaks of restraint, detachment, and factual knowledge that pass for maturity in most daily adult relationships. We already know who has the money and how successful each has been at his career; we know who got the girl and how big each other's houses are; we know the kind of intelligence each has, and we know each other's smells, biases, conceits, and shortcomings. None of these things needs to be probed for, and we needn't butt heads to determine each other's places. These things have been done long ago, and the results proven largely irrelevant.

So what we are left with is play. Which is what the water cannon and joking are about, and which is something none of us gets enough of in our everyday grown-up lives. There is, too, a great caring, which I am not sure our wives have thought to notice beneath the banter and frivolity. My friend the doctor, for instance, has several times today put his hand gently on my shoulder or the small of my back. I have seen him do it with the others as well. It is a gesture that years ago he would never have made, and that had he done so would have made me immensely uncomfortable. But he does it now with confidence and ease, and in a manner that conveys silently an appreciation of our closeness. It bespeaks, I believe, not a peeling away of maturity but the very opposite.

Before the day ends, the doctor takes me on a tour of his house and yard. He lives in an old and elegant area of town, and he and his wife have recently remodeled. He leads me room to room, the walls and woodwork newly painted, the hardwood floors newly refinished; everywhere light streams in from large, open windows. We visit his wife's balconied studio, where she paints grand, exuberant pictures of mothers and children, and we pass through the kitchen, where the counters are topped with polished stone and the ceilings are high, and we end up in his backyard, with its black-bottomed pool. Here he shows me his tomato plants, which occupy a narrow strip between driveway and house.

To me, the plants look scrawny. None are more than three feet, and all are thin of foliage and few of fruit. Nonetheless, my friend speaks of them with as much enthusiasm as he does of the redo of his house. Amongst his tomatoes he has an equal number of pepper plants, and the pairing helps him sustain a passion. "I love," he says, "tomatoes and peppers and beer."

He has a friend, he tells me, also from college and now a lawyer, who also grows tomatoes and peppers. Once a summer the lawyer will visit the doctor, bringing with him the fruit of his garden, and together the two will sit on the patio and eat tomatoes and peppers and drink beer—savoring their harvest, and feeding their friendship.

## AUGUST 8

This evening, home again in San Diego, we have bacon and tomato sandwiches for dinner. Big fat things, with avocado and sprouts on French rolls. For accompaniment, my wife makes tabouli, using tomatoes, mint, and lemons from our garden. We do this only a few times a year, bacon being hard to work into a low-fat diet. But when we do, it is heaven. It is summer.

As we are so engaged, we are interrupted by the knocking at the door of a small boy. I do not know him. He is barefoot, with short, blond hair, and is wearing cutoffs. On the sidewalk near the tomatoes his bicycle has been lain on its side, and cradled in his outstretched hands is a large, ripe, perfect tomato. A Celebrity, I'd say. Close to a pound.

"Beep, beep," he says, through the screen. "I picked this tomato."

It is an inarguable statement. Clearly he has picked it. Clearly from our yard.

"I wanted it for my family," he adds. "But you can have it back."

My wife is faster than me in these situations, and she cheerily tells the boy, "No, that's okay. You can keep it. And thank you for asking."

It's my sign again. Perhaps it hasn't completely curtailed my tomatoes' migrations, but now at least I can see where they go. This one gets on a bicycle and disappears down the street, weaving from side to side.

## AUGUST 10

Two weeks ago John found the remaining eighteen lugs of tomatoes he needed for sauce. When Rose had finished their cooking, she was done making sauce for the year. But she had told me then that when I had enough tomatoes of my own she would show me how she did it. Ever since, I have been awaiting that moment, and today the time has come.

When I arrive home from work, Rose crosses the street to greet me at our door. I invite her in to show her the counterful of tomatoes I picked before our trip to Davis, and without hesitation, she sweeps them into a basket. Bounding out the door, she tells me to pick more red ones and to come over when I have changed my clothes.

I do as I am told, and proceed to pick another half dozen red tomatoes, a mixture of Champions and Beefsteaks. In addition, I pick six Lemon Boys, of which the largest weighs a pound. We are going to experiment and make yellow sauce, which Rose says she has "never, never" made before. Earlier I had purchased onions

and garlic, and for the final ingredient, I pick from our yard a bag
of basil leaves.

With all this in hand, I hurry across the street, where I find
Rose busily cutting tomatoes in chunks. She does so with a small
paring knife which she wields on whole fruit held in one hand,
letting the pieces fall directly into a large pot set on the table.
Some twenty to twenty-five large tomatoes from my plants go
into this pot, all cut without wasted motion. Two yellow onions
are cut in like manner and added to the pot, and from a small jar
of peeled garlic she removes eight cloves and adds them as well.
She then places the pot on her stove and sets it to a low boil. This
done, she repeats the process with the Lemon Boys, using this
time only one onion and four cloves of garlic.

## ROSE'S TOMATO SAUCE

6 pounds fresh, ripe globe-type tomatoes (approximately one
   dozen large tomatoes), cored and cut in large chunks
1 medium onion, cut in large chunks
4 whole, peeled cloves of garlic
½ tablespoon salt
1 handful of fresh, whole basil leaves
⅓ cup extra-virgin green olive oil

*In a large, uncovered heavy pot simmer tomatoes, onion, garlic, and
salt for 1 hour, stirring occasionally. Remove from heat and pass mixture through food mill, turning until seeds and tomato skins are virtually dry. Add basil and oil (and, if desired, 1 tablespoon sugar) to the
resulting purée and return sauce to heat. Simmer for 30 minutes,
uncovered, or until thickened.*

  *Serve over spaghetti and top with grated Romano cheese.*
*For 1½ quarts of sauce*

While the sauces cook, Rose shows me her freezer, which is full of frozen tomato sauce in plastic tubs. Next to it is a wallful of shelves filled end-to-end with bottles of tomato sauce. The bottles are of all sizes and shapes, and between the shelves and the freezer I am looking at her and John's entire store of sauce for the coming year.

The kitchen where Rose makes her sauce is in the garage. Her baking she does in the house. The use of two kitchens is apparently not uncommon among Italians, or at least among Italians who have emigrated to San Diego. The Italian family who once owned our house also had a second kitchen in the garage. And they too, I have learned, rarely entered through the front door, using instead a side entrance approached through what is now our bedroom—which is why the ground beneath our floor is paved with marble.

Next to the sauces, Rose is cooking an octopus. It will go into an antipasto. The trick to cooking an octopus, she tells me, is how you put it in the boiling water. Too quickly and the tentacles will coil; rather, you must dip it slowly, so the tentacles stay relaxed.

This octopus came from a local market. But while the sauces cook and we sit talking on the patio, John tells me that when he was younger, he used to swim in the waters offshore and catch his own. The octopi would hide in the rocks, and when he and his companions found a good spot, they would squirt bleach in the crevice. Irritated, the octopi would come bolting out, often wrapping themselves around the very arms of their captors. In the same waters, he harvested sea urchins and mussels—"Big ones!" he says of the latter. And to illustrate he touches together his thumbs and forefingers, forming a diamond six inches from end to end. Now, he sighs, the game wardens control what, when, and how many creatures you can catch, and mostly the only place you can get them are in the stores—where they are "expensive!"

After an hour, Rose removes the pot of yellow tomatoes. These at the outset were less juicy than the red, and they have taken less time to thicken. She sets a food mill across the top of a pan and empties the tomatoes into the mill. I then turn the crank, turning, turning, and turning until all that's left in the mill are seeds, skin, and the remnants of the onion and garlic. Rose tastes the sauce, testing for sweetness and the possible need for an added spoonful of sugar (it needs none), and she then throws in a handful of the basil leaves from my yard. The beauty of the sauce at this point is breathtaking, a smooth custard-colored purée with a suspension of bright green leaves. Finally, she pours in a partially filled tumbler of olive oil.

None of the ingredients are measured, but I suspect her proportions are exact, nonetheless. When I worked building houses, there were among the crew men who had been carpenters for decades; on request they could cut a one- or two-foot piece of two-by-four that, when measured on a tape, was always twelve or twenty-four inches long. Later, I worked as a bartender and I learned then to pour an ounce of alcohol without measuring; time after time, shot after shot, one ounce. This ability comes from familiarity with your task and materials, and I suspect people develop this skill in almost any endeavor they perform.

After the addition of the basil and the oil, Rose returns the sauce to the stove for a final thickening. As it cooks, we repeat the process with the red tomatoes, running them through the food mill, adding basil and oil (and this time a spoonful of sugar), and returning the purée to the stove. When Rose pronounces the sauces done, I return home for containers. The final result is a quart of yellow sauce and three quarts of red.

Previously, my wife and I had decided we would afterwards invite Rose and John to eat with us. Now, I tender the offer but both demur. John has already eaten his main meal of the day, and Rose says she must stay to cook for her son. But the real reason, I suspect, is that the act of sharing a meal suggests to them an intimacy with which they would feel uncomfortable—just as I feel uncomfortable approaching their house at the side entrance rather than the front door. Even with the best of intentions, these cultural differences are hard to surmount.

As a compromise I ask Rose to keep the yellow sauce. I, after all, can now make more. Again she says no, but on this I am more insistent and in the end she agrees to take half. Even in this battle of courtesies she wins, however, for while I was retrieving my containers she put on a pot for pasta and she now packs for us a platter of spaghetti, across the top of which she ladles some sauce, a side plate of thinly sliced fried eggplant, and a basket of homemade rolls topped with sesame seeds.

To be carrying home such booty after having received such a singular lesson in cooking is embarrassing, but my nose tells me not to argue. With a profusion of thanks, I trundle home with Rose's many gifts.

Shortly afterwards, my wife and son arrive home, and we sit down to our meal. The eggplant, from John's garden, is exquisite, both topping the pasta as intended and as finger food. And the sauces . . . the sauces are beyond description. The red contains within it the summer's sun, the gallons of water, and all the attention I have lavished on my tomatoes these many months. Its taste is light and delicate and is not overwhelmed by excess cooking, onions, garlic, or any of the other myriad additions so commonly found in American sauces. Its taste is unlike any to have emerged from any store-bought can or bottle, or from any pot ever in my kitchen. Its taste is pure tomato, complemented only by a hint of basil, as the viola complements the violin.

The yellow sauce has within it all these same qualities, but its taste is smoother than the red. For me, its taste is sublime, bordering on the illicit, and I find it the better of the two. On this, my wife and son disagree with me. But we will have many opportunities to consider the matter further.

## AUGUST 13

Today I pick seventeen ripe tomatoes. Of these, two weigh nearly a pound and a half each. Despite their size, both are slightly catfaced, and neither is the equal of that perfect Leviathan I once gave away. No, that one was unblemished, huge, and of textbook shape. Nevertheless, they are a pleasing pair, and I give one to John, who receives it with a soft exclamation of "Jesus Christ."

Giving away tomatoes is one of the joys of growing them. It is, I suppose, a cheap form of beneficence. Besides the big one I give to John, my wife takes a bag to her hairdresser and I take a foursome to a nearby neighbor who is pregnant and overdue. She is taking her prolonged maternity in good cheer, but the weather of late has been hot and humid, and though the summer has otherwise been cool, I imagine her condition is fast growing tiresome. Perhaps the tomatoes will provide a momentary diversion. Certainly, they can't hurt.

## AUGUST 15

This evening I tend the tomatoes. I fertilize, spray with *Bt,* and perform a census. Surprisingly, I find that the plants out front have begun to lose height. The Celebrities, with their self-pruning gene, may well have stopped growing by now. But mostly the shrinkage is due to my own laziness: long ago the plants outgrew their cages and I did nothing about it. Now, like octogenarians with osteoporosis, they are collapsing under their own weight.

There are, however, other signs of aging about which I could have done nothing. All the plants have stopped flowering, and the bottom leaves of the main plants are dying, with the lower third of their foliage now formed exclusively of crumbling brown leaves. Other plants in the neighborhood look much the same, only in most cases worse. Albert's Beefsteaks have begun to whither and topple to such a degree that they have now lost half their height.

As usual, these activities produce considerable interest from neighbors and passersby. A couple I have never seen before stop to remark that they, too, have tomatoes, but the fruit are still small: they only just moved to the neighborhood and were late in starting their garden.

As a welcoming present, I pick for them three large Celebrities. They are much appreciative of this and tell me that despite their recent arrival they have managed to grow zucchini and will bring me one. This causes me a smile, for when *we* first moved to the neighborhood my father-in-law brought an old friend of his, a realtor, to look at our purchase. He looked things over and concluded that we had chosen wisely. Among the neighborhood's positive attributes, he noted, was that there were Italians and that this was good because they would bring us lots of zucchinis. And now we are indeed to be given zucchinis, although our new neighbors are not Italian.

When they leave, Albert comes over. He has been mowing his lawn, but now he walks up my driveway, points to the Lemon Boy, and asks what kind of tomato it is. I tell him the name and point to my lemon tree for emphasis. But this only confuses matters, and he looks puzzled. What am I trying to tell him? That this tomato is related to a lemon tree?

In any case, he makes it clear that he would like seeds from this plant. I pick a large, perfect specimen and give it to him, trying at the same time to explain that, this being a hybrid, "the seeds are no good." But this is probably as confusing as the contorted relationship between the tomato and the lemon. For of course the seeds are "good"—they will produce tomato plants. They just won't reliably possess the same characteristics as their parent. There is, though, no way I can explain this to Albert.

Later, the parents of the baby scratched by our cat stroll by with their child. I greet them sheepishly and inquire about the infamous mauling. The child has emerged without long-term damage, although the same may not be true of the father. He, of course, had to explain to his wife how the cherub entrusted so briefly to his care had managed to get raked by a child-baiting cat. *My* wife joins us at this point and asserts that I was the bigger idiot for letting our cat anywhere near the unknowing child. Woe to the bumbling, dunderhead dads, say the moms.

But all is now well, and in further atonement for my cat's misdeeds, I pick for them three fat and crimson Champions. What, they ask, is my secret? Why are my tomatoes so much bigger than theirs? Clearly the answer is more nature than nurture: of the tomatoes I gave them, the ones they kept for themselves must have been the collection of dwarf and miniature cherries I so thoughtfully prepared in February.

But still they ply me for my "secrets." And so I tell them: I water and fertilize regularly, and I use a bacterial spray to control the caterpillars. At this last—that I spray the tomatoes with bacteria—the mother blanches, evincing a sudden disdain for the fruit I have just given her. I try to explain. ("It's organic!") But to no avail. I would have better luck pursuing hybrid genetics with Albert. Not only do I throw children to lions, but I dispense infected tomatoes to the neighborhood.

The tomatoes I gave them may never get eaten. But I have nonetheless incurred a debt and they tell me that when their grapefruits ripen in the fall, they will give us some. I will have then converted tomatoes to both squash and citrus, a bit of alchemy rivaling in its way that of Calgene.

## AUGUST 20

Today is the second day of my son's first soccer tournament this season. Yesterday, his team played and won; today they will play in the afternoon and, if successful, will advance and play again in the evening.

The tournament itself will last three days. Hundreds of teams from throughout Southern California are in attendance, and they will play at more than a dozen sites across the city. Just at the one school where my son will play, six fields have been laid out, and all will be in use from dawn to dusk. About these fields, players and families mill by the hundreds; brightly colored uniforms distinguish the teams, and in many cases the display of regalia is enhanced by matching sports bags, ice chests, water bottles, chairs, and banners. Often, these latter items are arranged in formation; this is done by slightly crazed and hyperventilating parents—for I have learned that the sport is different, but the Little League parent syndrome is alive and well in youth soccer. Indeed, as we navigate the field, we pass a game-in-progress that has been halted temporarily while the referee waits for a belligerent spectator to leave the premises. If he dawdles or refuses, the game will be awarded to the opponents of the team on the sideline from whence he came. The officiators know well that if they tolerate such behavior, they will be inundated by it.

Amid the swirl, we find our son's team and he joins them in pre-game drills. Earlier this week, his doctor cleared him to play; the broken bone in his fingertip has mended and the cut closed and healed. It has been three weeks since his accident, and aside from the scar he will bear for life, the only remaining evidence of the mishap is a lingering swelling and a discoloration of his fingernail, which soon he will lose.

The bulk of the early game is played on our opponent's half of the field, and my son, the goalie, sees little action. This is a merciful circumstance for his nervous parents. Eventually his team scores, and the players' confidence surges—as does that of their parents. Perhaps they become too confident, for minutes later the other team scores as well. This occurs when players flood the goalie box and my son's vision is blocked—he never saw the ball. Momentarily his spirits sag, but he has several good saves during the remainder of the game and the contest ends in a draw, ensuring that the kids will play again later this evening.

Our dilemma now is what to do in the intervening hours. Making use of these fragments of time is a common problem during tournaments, and we decide to eat and to visit a nearby cooking-utensil store so that I might look for a food mill like Rose's, with which I can make my own sauce.

Every year Miramar Naval Air Station, home of the navy's "Top Gun" fighter school, holds a hugely popular air show featuring the Blue Angels. Hundreds of thousands of people attend these performances, and the surrounding roads are clogged for hours before and after the event. Naturally, Miramar lies between us and the shopping center we have chosen to go to, and lest we had forgotten this was the day of the show, a great white corkscrew of smoke spirals up from the air base as we stand deliberating. Nonetheless, we decide to make the trip, figuring the show is now in progress and the road should be clear.

When we reach the freeway, the planes are looping and twisting overhead, and it is difficult to concentrate on driving. Nor am I not alone in this. Seemingly every other driver's face is craned skyward and pressed to the windshield. Local lore has it that the accident rate on this stretch of road goes up dramatically during the air show, and, reminded of this, I redouble my efforts to concentrate. But just as I do, I look to my left. In the distance I see a small speck just over the horizon, and before I truly have time to register its presence, it grows enormous in my window, explodes to fill my field of view, and then thunders past, leaving in its wash a tremendous, screaming roar that rends the air and rocks the car. We have been buzzed by an F-18. After I collect myself, I have no trouble at all paying attention to the road.

Rose's food mill was a simple metal device with a wooden-knobbed handle and a wide mouth. It was less elegant than functional, but functional it was. In the culinary store they have bottled walnut oils, electric bread machines, and heavy-bottomed "professional" pans, but they have only two models of food mill. One is of a design similar to Rose's, but is small and made of plastic. The other is not literally a food mill, but is called instead a tomato press. It too is plastic (tomato red), but is made primarily for tomatoes and comes from Italy; it has a funnel-like top and a handle mounted to the side, like a sausage grinder, which rotates a pair of paddles across the curved surface of a sieve. The purée comes out the bottom, the seeds and skins out a separate chute.

Neither device is expensive, but I agonize over the choice nonetheless. The mill is what Rose uses, but this one is cheaply made. The press has the dual virtues of being specific for tomatoes and Italian in origin. But whether it will re-create Rose's sauce I do not know. On the other hand, I suppose I needn't find an exact replica of Rose's mill; either of these will probably serve the purpose, and swayed by the redness of its plastic and the authenticity of its heritage, I buy the tomato press. As I leave the store, the staff—relieved to have seen my indecision expurgated—wish me luck with my tomatoes.

After eating, we return to the tournament. Here we repeat the afternoon's routine: hunting for parking, finding the team, and congregating with parents while the kids practice. My son again plays goalie, and after just a few minutes, it is apparent that his is to be a thankless job. The opposing team keeps the play in our half of the field, repeatedly working the ball down the sides and to the corners and then crossing it to the center for a shot on goal. It is a textbook attack. When foiled, they simply cycle the ball around for another shot. For the first five or ten minutes, my son blocks these shots, my heart beating wildly at each attempt, but then there is a penalty kick. From twenty yards out, a striker hammers the ball high and to the corner of the net. It is a remarkable shot, and my son has no chance to stop it. More of the same soon follows: high, hard shots, over my son's reach but under the top bar and into the net. Each one scoring a point. Each one causing me pain. The assault is relentless, and the fifth or sixth such goal is accompanied by tears in the goalie box.

My son does succeed at blocking many goals, and once he even manages to reach and deflect one of the high shots, after which a teammate turns and shakes his hand. But our kids are clearly outmatched; the other team is playing at a level we are yet years away from. This is painfully obvious; the only disagreement on our side is whether the final score is seven, eight, or nine to zero.

I have at these tournaments seen parents ruthlessly berate their children for failing to perform to expectations. Once I saw a father slap his son for some supposed ineptitude. The children of these parents, as is natural, deride each other, and I have seen teams on which the children had nothing but criticism for the other children with whom they played. But today I see something I have never seen before.

When the game ends, I walk to my son on the field. He is inconsolable—his head is downcast, and he refuses to let me put my arm around his shoulder. Silently, we walk to the sidelines, where his teammates have gathered. As we approach, they suddenly rush towards us, mobbing and congratulating my son. There are cheers and handshakes and many a "Good job!" I am overwhelmed by the display, and I drop back, a lump rising in my throat, as the kids perform magic and my son's spirits come back from the abyss. Overpowered on the field, these children are as capable of exceeding expectations as those by whom they were vanquished, and they too are winners.

## AUGUST 21

After the soccer tournament last night, I put my new tomato press to the test. I had to, because I couldn't wait. I figured the easiest thing I could make would be tomato juice, so I grabbed a flashlight and hunted up four good-sized tomatoes. I searched also for a little guidance on technique, but most tomato cookbook authors apparently consider juice too simple to warrant a recipe. Ortho, a compendium of all things tomato and not strictly a cookbook, is less assuming and does provide some instruction: heat cut-up tomatoes until soft and run them through a food mill. Or, in my case, a tomato press.

I did just that, and the press worked perfectly, generating from four tomatoes over a quart of juice and a neat little bowl of pulp-free skins and seeds. Having taken the press for a sea trial, I plan today to apply it to the task for which it was purchased: the making of Rose's sauce. For this I select two dozen ripe Celebrities, of which several weigh more than a pound. Carrying the tomatoes inside, I plop them in a sinkful of water. The fruit are neutrally buoyant, and some bob on the surface while others float suspended or rest lightly on the white sink bottom, all depths of the medium populated, as in a Magritte painting. I have picked enough to make two batches of sauce, and as I remove them from the rinse, I begin the steps Rose taught me: coring and chunking the tomatoes and tossing them into a large pot, to which I add onions and garlic. As the juices are released and the pot starts to boil, the house fills with the delicious and distinctive aroma of cooking tomatoes. Unabashedly the smell makes its way outside and announces to the neighborhood that my tomatoes are being transformed. At the midway point, I run the tomatoes through the press, and it performs flawlessly—as its Italian designers no doubt knew that it would.

My son is absent as I rend the sauce from its origins. Instead, he has chosen to spend the afternoon at the local circus. Three years ago San Diego's Fern Street Circus sprang from the imagination of a local university professor—a man who, more than anything, had always wanted to run a circus. It has no animals and no arena, and relies instead on an outdoor spot in the park, donations from the community, and the talent and enthusiasm of local clowns, contortionists, comedians—and willing children. Among the latter is my son's best friend, who serves as both juggler and acrobat. Two weekends a year the troupe assembles amidst hand-painted sets, wearing handmade costumes, and performs a loose and zany script written by the professor. The audience—composed largely of friends, family, and neighbors—is forgiving, and inevitably a good time is had by all.

And so, given the choice between watching me make tomato sauce and going to the circus, my son is gone. Our plans, however, are to have his friend's family join us for dinner upon their return—they will have spent the entire day at the circus, and a ready-cooked meal will be much appreciated.

When they arrive, my wife and I put the finishing touches on dinner and we are regaled with reenactments of the performance and with stories of the circus and the lives of its actors. We serve the sauce over mounds of spaghetti, accompanied by salad and bread. To my mind, the sauce I have made lacks some indefinable magic of Rose's. It is a respectable reproduction, but a reproduction only. Others are less critical, however, and in the meal's wake, the mother of my son's friend asks for the recipe.

And so it is that having come from Italy, where Rose learned it from her mother, who learned it from *her* mother, and having crossed the ocean and a continent, and having spent a long hiatus in the house across the street from me, Rose's recipe resumes its journey.

## AUGUST 24

Though they do not talk, the cycles of their lives run parallel, and today both John and the cement contractor uproot their tomatoes. In both cases their plants were scraggly and more dead than alive, having stopped producing weeks ago. Albert's will be next, and then the potted Better Boys at the end of the street—whether their grower indeed needed help with their harvest I have never learned. The plants in the yard of Dan the Dog are also, I suspect, not long for this earth. My plants—those in the planter box out front may last a few more weeks. Mid-September at the latest.

## AUGUST 25

If truly we are what we eat, then we have become tomatoes. Or, as my wife says, "Tomatoes R Us." Despite the vines' growing emaciation, the fruit themselves are ripening faster than we can pick, eat, or give them away.

Though mightily we try.

Today I pick forty-one tomatoes, a harvest contributed to by virtually all my plants: red and yellow, large and small. Of these I ply several bags upon my neighbors. I give half a dozen to Vito, whom I catch walking home with an empty bucket and a large cucumber—the result, no doubt, of a just-concluded food exchange with some other neighbor. For lunch I pack a fresh tomato, as I have every day this week. For dinner we grill fresh tuna and tomato halves topped with Parmesan and pepper. And after dinner I begin my first-ever batch of dried tomatoes, following the directions in an inspired new cookbook.

*Tomato Imperative!* is the collaborative work of Sharon Nimtz and Ruth Cousineau, friends and neighbors from Vermont who share an obvious passion for food, cooking, and tomatoes. They offer up more than one hundred and thirty recipes, beginning, properly enough, with "Fried Green Tomatoes and Variations." Later, they offer a recipe for juice, and at the end they include a bibliography—in which I find note of a newsletter on tomatoes that I know I must have.

As for drying tomatoes, their directions couldn't be easier: cut the tomatoes in pieces, put the pieces on a rack in a gas oven using only the pilot light for heat, prop open the door, and wait sixteen hours. This, of course, is a far cry from the more practiced methods of the cement contractor; but I have at the moment more tomatoes than dehydrators, and the method of Nimtz and Cousineau has the great virtue of being something I am prompted now to do.

## AUGUST 26

A cool wind blows through our house. The doors and windows are all open, and the wind carries with it a touch of moisture. Indeed, it has been overcast today and raindrops have fallen—the first in nearly two months. In total, they bring one one-hundredth of an inch of rain.

Meteorologically, the rain is an anomaly. In San Diego, rain in August is nearly as rare as in July. But somehow today the weather seems right. Along with my and my neighbor's dying plants, it hints at fall, at the slow tapering away of spring's exuberance and summer's ripening.

### AUGUST 27

The weather today reveals that yesterday's rain and coolness were but a catnap in summer's afternoon. There are no clouds, and the sunshine brings with it temperatures in the eighties and humidity in the nineties. Our son is spending the afternoon and night at his best friend's, and to escape the heat, my wife and I go to a movie in the afternoon. This strategy is not completely effective, since the movie we see is a Harrison Ford thriller, and my shirt is as drenched at its conclusion as if I'd spent the time outdoors in the sun.

Near the theater is a small Italian grocery store recommended to us by Rose, and we stop here on our way home. Neither my wife nor I have ever been here, and we wander the aisles amazed at the countless brands and shapes of pasta, the myriad tomato products, the row after row of cans, jugs, and bottles of olive oil, and the many foil-wrapped liqueur-filled candies. A restaurant is attached to the store, but we decide instead to buy a few items and prepare our own meal at home, unharried and in shared parental solitude. Accordingly, we buy fresh bread, fresh-grated Parmesan, spinach-and-egg fettuccine, an eggplant, and a bottle of Italian Merlot.

At home, I pick a half dozen Lemon Boys and begin a small batch of Rose's sauce, in yellow. My wife follows Nimtz and Cousineau's directions for *bruschetta*—slicing and grilling the bread we have purchased and smearing the slices with olive oil, garlic, and a just-picked California Sun. To round out the meal, I prepare a platter of sliced tomatoes. As we work, we sip on the Merlot, and in the background Louis Armstrong and Ella Fitzgerald ask, "Isn't This a Lovely Day?"

We dine in our patio, where it is cool, and we eat slowly and without rush, refilling our glasses from the bottle of Merlot. We have used eight tomatoes in our meal. Counting the two I had for lunch and the four I added to those in the oven, we have used fourteen tomatoes today. And there are scores more on the vine.

After dinner we implore the cleanup fairies to come to our aid. But they are never around when we need them, and eventually we must clean the kitchen ourselves. When we are done, we make coffee and move to the steps of our front porch, where it is also cool and from where we can see the fireworks over the bay. As we sit and sip our coffee, Dan the Dog walks by with his owner and a dog I've not seen before.

Dan's owner likes to talk. As is his wont, he stops for a chat, telling us the new dog is named Lucy and that she belongs to his daughter, who is visiting. Lucy is small and all white save a patch of black that covers half her face, beginning at the tip of her nose to a spot midway between her eyebrows and sweeping across her right cheek to a point just behind her ear. The patch, says my wife, gives her the look of a harlequin.

Encouraged by the feedback from my wife, Dan's owner ventures from Lucy's markings to scratching and fleas, from there to veterinarians, and from veterinarians to Orange County, where once he lived and where the best vet he ever knew had worked. And then he tells us the story of Stinky.

Two and a half million people now live in Orange County, but when he lived there, "There weren't nothing but cow fields and tomato patches." Even then, long before Dan, he had had pets, and one day he came home to find his cat trying to nurse a baby bobcat. Having been spayed, the cat had no milk and my neighbor taught the bobcat to eat by dipping its face in a bowl of warm milk. He named him Stinky.

Soon Stinky grew up. He reached twenty-two pounds, and my neighbor kept him on a chain in his backyard—"So he wouldn't terrorize the neighborhood." He built a perch for Stinky in a shade tree, but the big cat preferred instead to spread full length on a branch and let his legs dangle beneath him. Every day when he came home from work—home, I imagine, from the shipyard where he got asbestosis—Stinky would come down from the tree and wrap himself around the man's legs in affection. He had a welder's mitt—"And you know how heavy those are. And I'd put it on and bat him around. He'd sink his jaws into that mitt, and I'd get black and blue from the force of it."

When he left Orange County, my neighbor gave Stinky to a man with two female bobcats, so he could breed them. "And he was successful. He raised nine litters of bobcats and took them all out into the wild and freed them." Five years later my neighbor was visiting in Orange County and stopped by Stinky's new home. The cat was in the yard, and when he walked in and called, "Stinky," he bolted up and wrapped himself around his legs, just like old times. "But I didn't have no mitt, so I couldn't bat him." A few years after that, he got the news that Stinky had died.

He is quiet for a few minutes when he finishes. Then he says, "I'd best be going. Good night." And lightly he jostles the dogs' leashes and heads for home.

This is, perhaps, the first time I have ever been party to a conversation my neighbor has ended on his own. Yes, says my wife, but it may also be the first time I wasn't in a hurry and didn't have to be somewhere else. Hurriedness changes entirely the balance between pleasure and irritation. Certainly, too, a bottle of Merlot can help. And as we continue to sit doing nothing, the air cool and the tomatoes growing in the starlight, I think to myself, along with Satchmo, what a wonderful world.

### AUGUST 28

This morning my wife and son visit the newborn baby across the street, whose arrival followed by three days my gift to his grateful mother of tomatoes from our garden. While they are out, I take a shower, and when I emerge I am surprised to discover a fresh-baked lemon meringue pie upon our kitchen table. This is curious, given that no one in our house had been making such a pie when I entered the shower.

The mystery is solved when I learn that the pie has been left by the mother of my son's best friend. She made it in thanks for the recent pasta dinner and for the receipt of a loaf of zucchini bread made by my wife from the zucchini received by us for the tomatoes we had given our new neighbors. Thus does our neighborhood food chain work: tomatoes become zucchini, which becomes bread, which becomes pie.

{♥ {♥ {♥

Perhaps pilot lights are kept hotter in Vermont than in San Diego, for the sixteen hours Nimtz and Cousineau said it would take to oven-dry my tomatoes has now stretched to sixty-four. Nevertheless, the results appear promising, and today at noon I remove the first of my efforts. To avoid devouring them all immediately, which I am inclined to do, I dutifully place them in an eight-ounce canning jar which I then fill with olive oil. Packed away thus they are safe, but still I hold the jar in my hand for a long time and gaze at this vessel of golden liquid filled with floating brownish red wrinkles from my garden.

I also attempt today to tend cosmetically to the tomatoes out front. The plants are beginning to look embarrassingly ragged, and I feel compelled to do something about this; by default they are part of my landscaping, and suburban etiquette requires they be kept tidy, just as I must mow my lawn and trim my bougainvillea. I begin therefore by pruning off the dead lower leaves from the Celebrity closest to the sidewalk. Quickly, though, it is apparent that this is time I could better spend on something else—anything else. The plant looks worse when I am done than when I began—like the old Babe Ruth: top heavy, and with exposed, skinny legs—and I leave the rest alone.

But what I cannot avoid is to scrutinize them. The Beefsteak and adjacent Champion look particularly bad. Their uppermost leaves are stunted and bushy looking and have from a distance the visual texture of broccoli. The other plants don't look bad in quite this same way; moreover, the affected branches are brittle, and when snapped open, reveal a brownish ring just inside the surface. More than just being old, I think these plants may now be diseased.

In contrast, the plants in the patio appear healthy and even robust. Unlike those out front, the patio plants are still producing large and well-formed leaves. The California Suns, in particular, are especially handsome, with each plant now bearing half a dozen clusters of deep red, medium-sized fruit. Of course, the patio plants were transplanted later than those out front, and so in a sense are younger. But whether that is the explanation for their better condition is hard to say. Certainly the plants out front have been more productive, so perhaps they have simply exhausted themselves, and thereby lost their looks.

## AUGUST 31

Attempting to resolve the issue of whether my broccoli-topped plants are diseased or merely old—and if diseased, what it might be—I call today for a plant pathology consult. That is, I call my father.

After a meandering discussion of the local housing market, recent movies, and cat deaths (his much adored Manx died recently at the age of fourteen), I lay out the facts: vigorous-looking plants in the patio; seven plants in the ground out front, all close together; good yields up to now; dying lower leaves on all seven. Two of these seven have severe stunting on the top leaves, plus aphids and a brownish ring just inside the stems' outer surface. I tell him, too, that my preliminary diagnosis based on the pictures and descriptions at my disposal is cucumber mosaic virus.

On the Internet, where there is no penalty for being wrong, people are not hesitant about diagnosing other people's problems—tomato or otherwise. My father, though, is a more experienced clinician, and he tells me first that it is hard to identify a plant disease without seeing it. He adds too that he has never seen cucumber mosaic on tomatoes, "although it is possible."

But to make me happy, he leads me through a brief differential diagnosis, asking first if there are yellowing, downward-curled leaves, and then if there is ringed spotting on the leaves or fruit. The former is suggestive of Western Blight, the latter of Tomato Spotted Wilt. But Tomato Spotted Wilt is carried by thrips, which I've not seen. Nor do my plants have rings or downward-curled leaves. And so I am left where I started: with an uncertain self-diagnosis of cucumber mosaic.

But whatever it is, my father agrees that it sounds like a disease rather than aging alone. The best method of control, he says, is probably to "rogue" the affected plants—that is, to pull them out and throw them away. The usefulness of this technique is predicated on the assumption that there is more to be gained by removing sick plants and losing whatever fruit they might yet produce than by gambling that the whole of the remaining potential harvest can be collected before the now-healthy plants become infected and lose their vitality.

It is, in other words, a cost-benefit decision. It is also a harsh and irreversible decision, and one I am not yet prepared to make. And so I decide instead to procrastinate.

# SEPTEMBER

### SEPTEMBER 2

O N THE RADIO TODAY it is announced that Gordon Graham's record is under assault. In his elliptic, staccato delivery, unchanged since my childhood, Paul Harvey intones that

> Miracle-Gro is offering $100,000 to the grower of the largest tomato. In southeast Ohio, Robert Ehigh is standing guard over his tomato with a rifle. It now weighs 6¼ pounds and is still growing an ounce a day.

Obviously this is no ordinary tomato. But protecting it with a lethal weapon would seem to be taking to extremes Keillor's notion of gardening as a competitive activity. Would the man shoot someone in defense of his fruit?

Later I learn that the Miracle-Gro company, hoping not to find out, has hired a twenty-four-hour security guard to protect the tomato, thereby freeing Ehigh from the need to do aught but tend to its growth. The company is indeed offering cash to the first person to grow a tomato heavier than seven and three-quarters pounds. But the contest was no doubt conceived as a good-natured competition, and I think it unlikely its sponsors contemplated the spilling of blood by overenthusiastic contestants.

At midmorning Albert hails me and asks if I like figs. Yes, I say, I love figs. He disappears for a moment and returns with a paper plate laden with figs so fresh they are still oozing from their stems. All are a deep purple, and the first I pop in my mouth is intensely sweet. These, I tell him, are fantastic! Never has he given us figs, and until now I had not even realized he had a tree, which he shows me is tucked away on the far side of his patio.

We are standing, as I lick the juice from my fingers, next to the tomatoes. Albert has already uprooted most of his plants, replacing them with peppers and basil, and he has cut back severely the two that remain, leaving only their drooping stalks and a handful of lonely fruit. Recognizing his impending impoverishment, I ask if he needs any tomatoes. No, he says, he still has some. But I tell him all the same that if he would like more, he should help himself. I would trade surplus tomatoes for fresh figs any day.

Soon afterwards, my neighbor the reporter (and fellow fatherly dunderhead) strolls by with his son. As we talk, he eyes my tomatoes. His wife has apparently overcome her squeamishness about my bacterial spray, for she now wants to know the names of the varieties I have planted. Their crop this year has been modest, composed as it was solely of dwarf cherries, but their thoughts are of next year. It is clear I did them a misdeed when I gave them the seedlings in May, for they have become tomato fiends. Recently, he says, they have virtually been living on tomato sandwiches. His technique is to toast two slices of French bread, smear each with mayonnaise, and to put between them a thick slice of tomato. His passion for these is undiminished despite his reliance for tomatoes on a roadside stand twenty miles distant.

In truth, I am not responsible for this. My neighbor grew up in Michigan and says he ate tomatoes "all day" as a youth. The tomato sandwich, he says, was his first recipe. All that I have done is to help rekindle a fire that had long been dormant. At the mention of recipes, I tell him of Rose's sauce, and eventually I bring him inside for a taste of the leftovers from the night my wife and I drank Merlot and ate of our plants.

He is wondrous at the sight of the yellow sauce. ("I never imagined such a thing could exist.") And when he closes his eyes and tastes a spoonful, I can almost feel the shock and glee that race from tongue to brain. He is quite tall, and I believe he may even have swooned.

Out of compassion, I give him Rose's recipe. I also lend him the tomato press: he and his wife are having guests for dinner, and the menu has suddenly changed. I give him a half dozen red tomatoes as well, but I have no Lemon Boys to spare. This is no problem, though, for he has just made plans for an emergency run to the vegetable stand.

## SEPTEMBER 3

My son's new class is holding a potluck social this afternoon. Each child will present a short autobiographical talk and for the last few weeks my son has been practicing his speech. ("My name is . . . I live in North Park with my parents, my cat Herbert, and my dad's tomato plants. He is obsessed. . . .")

Despite my son's filial jab, he shares a certain pride in the household's tomato-growing activities, and it has been decided that our contribution to the potluck will be a platter of tomatoes. The two of us go out to the tomato patch and from the Lemon Boy he picks the last three ripe fruit, saved especially for this occasion. Then we go to the patio, where he picks four large California Suns, now the best-looking and tastiest of my red tomatoes. He also picks an assortment of cherries, including eighteen marble-sized yellow Floragolds, each covered with a peachlike fuzz; this will be the main harvest of the season for these tiny plants.

We bring the fruit inside, and my son washes them in a sinkful of cold water. I slice the big ones into quarter-inch slabs and lay them in a ring on a clear glass platter, overlapping the slices and alternating red with yellow. In the center of the ring I place a sliced White Wonder, purchased for this purpose by my son's aunt from the same vegetable stand visited yesterday by my neighbor. Untrue to its name, the White Wonder is the palest of greens, but it adds to the visual diversity of the platter all the same. Over the top we sprinkle basil and black pepper, and over this we drizzle olive oil and vinegar. The cherries we put in a clear glass side bowl. The whole makes a handsome presentation with which we both are pleased.

The potluck is held in the backyard of one of my son's classmates. Chairs are set up under a shade tree, and as the children prepare, I wander the yard, curious. Our hosts have an outdoor aviary filled with parakeets and a small garden planted with a purple bell pepper, carrots, basil, and a single cornstalk. Two tomatoes sprawl uncaged, and the whole of the plot suggests its owners are firm adherents of the laissez-faire school of gardening.

Eventually the speeches begin. This one class includes children in third through sixth grades. They are from many different backgrounds. One is, as she says, "ABC" (American-born Chinese); her parents are professional musicians, and her grandparents still live in China. Many children have parents in the navy; one lives with her family "and nine other people" in half of a duplex; many play musical instruments; many have pets. Roald Dahl, author of *Matilda* and *Charlie and the Chocolate Factory*, is the favorite writer of many. They are bright, composed, and well prepared—none flub their lines, and all are engaging.

After the presentations we line up for the potluck and as we do, I find that amid the bowls and the plates my tomatoes have cloned themselves. There, immediately next to the platter we brought from home, is an identical glass platter covered with sliced red and yellow tomatoes, topped with basil, olive oil, and vinegar. The only variation is the replacement of the White Wonder with a mound of red cherries.

Never in my life have I grown yellow tomatoes. Never have I seen them sliced and layered with their red mates. Never have I taken them to a party. But when I do, someone else does so as well. It is an uncanny coincidence—as if Cinderella had gone to the ball and found she had a twin.

Naturally I seek out the creator of this dish. From him I learn that the yellow tomatoes are Lemon Boys; the reds, Supersteaks; the cherries, Sweet Millions—the elusive Sweet Millions. I sample the Millions and am confirmed in my belief that I erred in not having more patience in the spring and holding a space to accommodate a seedling. Their taste is far superior to any of the "jumbo" cherries I grew in my patio.

Unlike myself, the man who grew these tomatoes is lucky enough to have a full-sized garden. In fact, he has two. The second is at a house he keeps as a rental property. He says that he tells each new renter the garden comes with the house; they needn't do any work, but they must eat half the yield. Then, every August, he is forced to remind them, "You're not keeping up your end of the bargain"—for the garden is spilling over.

I doubt whether he has evicted anyone on this count, but he has had to resort to additional tactics to dispense of his bounty. Some he gives to shelters, some to neighbors. Recently he had such plenty that he sent his children door-to-door giving away Millions packed in baskets.

He tells me he makes four kinds of sauce, which he freezes. He makes *bruschetta*. And every five days he makes Tuscan tomato bread soup. ("That's about how long it takes the bread to dry out before you can make the soup.") He has, he says, between twenty and twenty-five plants, and clearly they are working him hard.

But just as clearly, he loves it. We talk easily for an hour. And though we are here because of our children and their education, they do not enter our conversation. Nor do we talk of our jobs or careers. We do not speak of politics or sports or real estate. Rather, we exchange watering schedules, fertilizer recommendations, and plans for next year. Without design, tomatoes have freed us of the need to define ourselves by what we've accomplished and what we own, and in this way our conversation is like that that I have with my oldest friends.

When we return home it is early evening, and I spend some time tending our yard. I trim the bougainvillea. I water plants. And I rogue the Beefsteak. I have been putting this off, both because of its finality and because it seems such an inglorious end to at least part of my tomato growing season. But this evening I cease procrastinating and strip the plant of its fruit. Its final yield consists of nine reddish orange fruit, the largest less than eight ounces and all quite hard; all had been on the vine for weeks, neither growing nor ripening. I also pick thirty-six very hard green fruit, most weighing less than an ounce.

Through the plant's cage, I then snip at its stems with my pruning shears, yanking out the stunted and wilted foliage as I go. When I have removed all but a stub of the main stem, I grab it and pull out the roots.

My row of tomatoes looks a little gap-toothed when I have finished. But its overall health appears much improved. The Champion next to the Beefsteak has some stunting of its own, but much of the misshapen growth I was seeing earlier seems to have belonged to the Beefsteak. Because the affected Champion has lots of large green tomatoes and isn't nearly as bad as the Beefsteak—and because I am tired—I decide to put off roguing this plant until later. For now, I retire for the night and ponder what to do with three dozen tiny green tomatoes.

### SEPTEMBER 5

The newspaper reporter has made Rose's sauce, and he is effusive in its praise. "You've made me a hero," he says, with reference to the dinner party for which he made the sauce. Rose plainly deserves the bulk of this credit, but she is not here and I do not argue.

We are at his home as he tells me of his heroics, and as we are talking, he invites me eagerly into his backyard. He shows me the plants I gave him—the Floragolds in their pots no taller than six to eight inches and each with a dozen or so tiny fruit. He shows me the sunlit patch of grass where next year "I'm going to put my tomatoes"—big ones. And he tells me I have got to see the tomato plant his neighbor received as a gift this summer. "You will not believe it."

His neighbor is an eighty-nine-year-old woman who has lived in the neighborhood since childhood, having grown up in the house next door. After several unsuccessful attempts to call to her over the back fence ("She wears a hearing aid"), we knock on her door and are greeted warmly. She invites us in—myself, the reporter, his wife, and his son—and our entrance creates an inordinate amount of excitement for the small black terrier who is the home's lone other occupant. The dog barks noisily and scurries about the bare feet of the reporter. And just as its owner is telling us he won't bite, he latches onto the reporter's leg. It takes no more time than it did for my cat to swipe at his son, but when the dog lets go, he leaves a bruised patch marked at the corners by dots of blood.

All the same, the reporter is unfazed, and once the dog is shunted to a side room, we proceed to the backyard to see the mystery tomato. Here, I glance quickly around; the yard is pleasant, with shade trees and a lath house. But I have no chance to explore, for my attention is directed towards the tomato I will not believe. "This is it," they all say, and then await my reaction.

I am dumbstruck. The plant is about five feet tall and has heart-shaped leaves more than a foot across. More than anything, it looks like a cross between a rubber plant and a fiddle-leaf fig. For a long while I stare in amazement, and then the words jump forth almost before they have formed: "It's a tree tomato," I say. I have never seen a tree tomato, but that is all it can be.

Tree tomatoes *(Cyphomandra betacea)*, like regular tomatoes, are members of the family Solanaceae. But the plants are otherwise unrelated. According to Ortho, tree tomatoes are native to the Andes; other sources say the plant can reach as tall as twenty-five feet and will regrow rapidly after pruning—this being necessary so they can be brought indoors and protected from the winter cold. Their fruit is called a tamarillo; and though red and egg-shaped, the plant's name comes not from any visual similarity of its fruit with that of tomatoes, but from a reported slight likeness in taste. According to a recent Internet correspondence, "The fruits have a vaguely tomato-ish flavor and are best eaten cooked (often with a small amount of sugar)."

How to eat the fruit of the plant we are looking at is not an issue, however, for there are none. But fruit or no, the plant's owner is clearly pleased with its exotic nature and proven ability to lure visitors.

### SEPTEMBER 10

My wife today goes to the hairdresser to have her hair "done," and upon her return, she asks the inevitable: "Dear, do you notice anything different?"

This is a question dreaded by all husbands. If the change is substantial enough to be truly noticeable—purple dreadlocks or a pink bouffant—it is apt to provoke a spontaneous—and harshly punished—negative reaction from the male spouse. But if the new coiffure is less than cataclysmic, it is likely to go unnoticed, which in my experience can lead even to worse consequences.

After I fail this test miserably (the correct response having been "My, what an attractive *light frosting*"), my wife proceeds to tell me that while she was there, one of the salon's hairdressers talked nonstop about her trip last month to the Pittston, Pennsylvania, Tomato Festival.

According to the hairdresser's T-shirt, Pittston is "The Tomato Capital of the World." The shirtmakers are wrong, clearly having never been to Davis. But even so, the tomatoes of Pittston are reputed to possess a unique and spectacular flavor due, it is said, to percolating chemicals from underground coal mines.

"The tomatoes there are the best I've ever tasted," said the hairdresser. "They're great, excellent, really delicious. And they're everywhere. They're like weeds. Everyone grows them."

The hairdresser's partiality is forgivable, I suppose, for she is a native of Pittston, and the Pittston tomato is the tomato of her youth. Twenty years ago she left home, and the festival marked the first occasion in many years for which she had returned. There was a parade with marching bands, fire trucks, a contest for the biggest tomato, and a Little Mr. and Ms. Tomato pageant for children.

The festival and its events had helped draw the hairdresser, but she had gone as well to visit the people she had known growing up. The combination of friends, family, tomatoes, and home had worked magic, and she was, she said, "very happy." But how could it have been otherwise?

❧   ❧   ❧

Later in the day I learn of yet another tomato festival, this one in Reynoldsburg, Ohio, a town which calls itself "Birthplace of the Tomato" by virtue of Alexander Livingston's work on the Paragon. The source of this information is the newsletter I found listed in the *Tomato Imperative!* and to which I mailed promptly for a subscription. Today my first issue arrives, and it reveals itself an amazing compendium of tomato fact, fiction, and surprise.

*The Tomato Club* newsletter is eight pages and two colors. The July/August issue I have received contains an extensive article by a horticulturist at Rutgers on the watering of tomatoes. Elsewhere are a pair of "weird science" articles, one on the use of diluted salt water for irrigation ("Researchers in Israel . . ."). And there is a nineteenth-century poem, introduced by the editor and publisher as a "short but excellent rhyme."

## THE TRYST

Potato was deep in the dark underground,
Tomato above in the light.
The little tomato was ruddy and round
The little potato was white.

And redder and redder she rounded above
And paler and paler he grew
And neither suspected a mutual love
Til they met in a Brunswick Stew.

—John B. Tabb
late nineteenth century

But the piece that most intrigues me is a biographical feature on one Kenneth Harper, of Columbus, Ohio.

Harper is what the newsletter dubs a Super-Grower. Each year he grows 20 to 25 different varieties and 350 to 400 individual plants—all from seed. He devotes to the endeavor more than five thousand square feet of backyard. And he reaps an incredible haul. A photograph of a daily harvest shows Harper standing beside a tomato-covered picnic table while cradling in his arms a trio of fruit, each the size of a boccie ball.

Surely this is phenomenal excess. Harper—who is *not* a commercial grower—grows over two tons of tomatoes each year. Mostly he gives them away—some to colleagues, some to friends, and some to charity.

The suggested motivation for this is that Harper is stricken with tomato fever. But I believe there is more to it than that. Harper has a wife and three grown children, in-laws, and grandchildren, and all participate in the family's tomato growing. Together they till and plant and harvest. Together they enter contests. Together they cook and together they can. Together they share a passion. Tomatoes help bind this family, and were it not so, I doubt that Harper would have let himself become so consumed.

Unfortunately, along with the newsletter comes a letter:

Dear Tomato Gardener,

    Due to limited interest, The Tomato Club has very recently ceased operations. . . .

    We are saddened by this development and hope we can serve you at a future time.

Cordially,
Robert D. Ambrose
Publisher

The issue I have received, the fourteenth, is the last.

Wondering what went wrong, I give Ambrose a call. As many as fifty million Americans are thought to have a home garden, and 85 percent of these contain tomatoes. This was the inspiration for the founder of the Tomato Club. There were, he says, newsletters for the lovers of sweet peas and newsletters for lovers of azaleas; newsletters for those who grew potatoes and for those who grew violets; for the fans of raisins and for the tenders of palms. But none for the tomato. There was, it seemed, a vast market waiting to be filled. Ambrose figures he could have made sixty thousand dollars a year if *The Tomato Club* had garnered one hundred thousand subscribers. "I'm ten years away from retirement," he says, "and it would have made a great retirement vehicle."

I once wrote for a monthly health newsletter, and I learned then that there are two main types of newsletters: not-for-profits and profits. The first survive on the heart and soul of their publishers, the second on marketing. Commercial newsletters require constant and enormous infusions of cash, which are used to feed and maintain their mailing lists. The large health letters, which have readerships in the millions, devote half their budgets to a relentless solicitation of new readers; the moment a publisher stops trolling, its subscription list begins to dwindle and its demise is in sight. Ambrose tried to build *The Tomato Club* without spending on direct marketing and by relying instead on word of mouth and favorable coverage in magazines, newspapers, and radio. But it didn't work. The newsletter never had a circulation of more than seven hundred, and it never broke even. "I have consumed oodles and oodles of debt," he says, "and it got to the point where I had to say enough is enough."

There is no mistaking the bitterness in Ambrose's voice. But it is equally clear that along the way this man—who may or may not have cared much about tomatoes—did acquire a passion for his endeavor. "*The Tomato Club*," he says, "had some of the best gardening articles I have seen. It was well done. Creative. We gave people science and horticulture and botany. One issue had an article about photosynthesis—that's what makes the world go around. We invented words: *tomatology*—the study of the science, art, and history of tomato growing. One issue had an "Ode to a Home Grown Tomato," written by a reader. There was lots of stuff in there, and good stuff. I miss it."

And so will I.

## SEPTEMBER 11

Today is the day of our annual neighborhood block party, and we will be taking salsa and chips. Salsa is a great weakness of mine. My first exposure came when I was in college and working in a Mexican restaurant—the same restaurant where I met my wife. A highly popular hot *salsa cocida* was prepared here and served with a basket of chips to all customers. I worked as a bartender, and when the salsa bowls at the bar were empty, I would have to refill them. This involved a trip to the walk-in cooler where the salsa was kept on the floor in the enormous aluminum vats in which it was cooked. These vats were so large it took two men to carry them, and when one was low, it was emptied by consolidating its contents with the other. This meant the contents of a vat could develop an extensive history, and it was not unusual to walk in and find one of the pots bubbling gently. The staff would avoid eating the salsa at these times, but I don't recall that it was ever wasted—rather, it simply acquired an added mystique.

I am not alone in my love of salsa. It is now the most popular condiment in America, more so even than ketchup. It exists, of course, in infinite variety and degrees of heat, and there seems an equal number of glossy picture books filled with instructions for highly complex mixtures. I am sure that virtually all of these are good. But when I am the chef, I tend towards the simple, and so for the block party I make a basic *salsa cruda*. Considerable chopping is required, and I spend a good part of the morning cutting up onions, peppers, cilantro, and several dozen tomatoes.

When I have finished, I venture briefly to the party site—as always, the block party is to be held on a short cross-street around the corner from our home. Here I help set up chairs, tables, and volleyball net, and then I return home and shower. My wife makes similar preparations, and as the final step in our readiment, we don our neighborhood association T-shirts, which feature woodcuts of several of the more prominent bungalows interspersed with palm trees and underscored by a pink line representing our pink sidewalks. Every year these shirts are made and offered for sale in a new combination of colors, and we have in our closet a considerable assortment—as do most of our neighbors.

## FRESH SALSA

5 medium to large ripe tomatoes, seeded
1/2 red onion
2 cloves garlic
3 to 4 serrano peppers
juice of 1 lime
1/2 bunch cilantro

*Chop all ingredients. The onion and peppers should be cut particularly fine. Mix and serve.*
  *Excellent with chips and superb on scrambled eggs.*

The party is well under way by the time we arrive. Tables have been arranged to receive the potluck contributions, and already a line has formed as people work their way along the platters and dishes, piling high their plates. We place the chips and salsa in the correct gastronomical order dictated by the placement of other items (that is, somewhere before the desserts) and then wander off for name tags and hellos.

The air is filled with the smell of hamburgers and hot dogs, and on a nearby front lawn a bluegrass band is playing, courtesy of a dulcimer-playing neighbor. Elsewhere on the street, firemen are giving tours of their truck. Children, now including my son, are bouncing raucously inside a giant inflatable Astrojump. And milling through the crowd is a U. S. congressman. The congressman lives just outside our neighborhood (we know this because his sidewalks are white instead of pink), and we in turn live just outside his district. But he has friends among us, and on this basis he is welcome.

When my wife and I were married, all of our friends and family were at the wedding. Never before had I been in such a concentration of the people who were important to me, and intermixed with the joy the assemblage gave me were unexpected twinges of guilt and regret, for on no one person could I bestow the depth of attention they warranted and that I would liked to have given. It is, I suppose, a favorable sign of the degree to which we have become a part of our neighborhood—and it of us—that the block parties now arouse in me similar feelings.

John and Rose are here of course, and I talk briefly with John. He has just finished his radiation treatments. His doctor has told him he will feel tired for another month, but he will then begin to regain his strength. By three months he should be back to normal. This is welcome news, and John is clearly relieved. I too am gladdened, and hope only that it comes to pass as the doctor says.

Before we can talk more, I catch sight of a neighbor who has just returned with her husband from a vacation in England. Outrageously, they went sans children, and I am eager to hear of their trip. I excuse myself and make my way to her side, soon to begin comparing notes on our respective adventures. We are frequently interrupted, however, by a constant stream of neighbors who pass us by. Among these are the newcomers who gave us the zucchini and the woman who lives across from me in the house where the 104-year-old once lived. For both of them it is their first block party, and the effusion of goodwill has fixed great smiles on their faces.

My wife engages herself in a similar round of greetings and conversations, and eventually she signals me that we should eat. We rendezvous in the food line, and begin to acquire hamburgers, hot dishes, and samples of myriad salads: fruit, green, bean, macaroni, and gelatin. Rose has brought a bowl of her pasta and sauce, but by the time we pass by it is almost gone, and I feel an obligation to let others behind me taste of her magic. It is, though, a wicked thing to do—to introduce them to the sublime when the bowl is near empty.

We emerge with our plates piled high. Indeed, my wife has two plates, for my son is too busy to serve himself. We find seats and are soon joined on one side by the Sikh woman who runs the daycare center that caused such a hubbub earlier this summer.

Neither I nor my wife has met her before, and we introduce ourselves. Her demeanor is calm and pleasant, and she shakes our hands graciously. Nothing has come from the ugly flyer, and she tells us that she now has all the children she has room for. I decide that were my son younger, I would not hesitate to include him among her charges.

To the other side of us sits the owner of the neighborhood pig. This animal—a Vietnamese potbelly—was given to the woman's husband, a doctor, by a dying AIDS patient. The pig itself was losing weight when she was given to the doctor, but she has now regained her health and can be seen walking through the neighborhood every afternoon with her owner and her owner's dog—the dog leashed and the pig free.

After dinner I join a nascent group of volleyball players. As the ball begins arcing back and forth, our numbers increase and soon we have a game. We try to adhere to the rules: no more than three hits per side and the ball must stay inbounds. But our multigenerational composition, our willingness to let servers repeat themselves until they manage to land one in, and the occasional interruption from meandering toddlers all mean that our play is less than pristine. But we do have fun, and we play until dark, when we disassemble the net, help put away the tables and chairs, retrieve our dishes and trash cans, and trickle home, reminded once again of what it is we cherish in those among whom we live.

## SEPTEMBER 13

We have friends, the same who rave about the superiority of Jersey or Michigan tomatoes, who claim that San Diego has no seasons. "In the Midwest," they say, "there are seasons." But while the yearly cycle of hot and cold is elsewhere more dramatic, this is not to say we lack our own seasonal rhythms—they simply require a keener look. Autumn comes subtly to San Diego.

The daily high temperatures are not much different from a month ago, but it is dark now when we wake in the mornings. There is dew on my car when I leave for work, and in the evenings the shadows of the palms lengthen their stretch across streets, houses, and lawns. Some nights we find we need an extra blanket. In the stores the cantaloupes are smaller than at season's peak—soon they will disappear altogether—and the apples are crisp, shiny, and abundant. But the biggest change is in the breezes. Blowing lightly off the ocean, they are somehow fresher than the winds of summer, and the clouds they carry bring with them the fleeting thought, frivolous a month ago, that one day it might yet rain again.

Tomatoes, mine and my neighbors', are a part of this great changing, both signaling its occurrence and subject to its effects. John's tomatoes are gone, the earth where they grew now bare, cleaned not only of tomatoes but also of peppers, borage, and, just a few days ago, eggplants. All that remain are a few sprigs of basil, and he is contemplating what to put in next. "Maybe," he says, "fava beans."

The foliage on my main plants is now mostly brown and withered, with isolated clumps of greenery at the tops. Curious to see what is still alive, and because I still cannot resist the impulse to tidy, and curious to see what is still alive, I pull today handfuls of weightless and shriveled leaves from stems and cages. The stems are brittle, and many break as I work. Several fruit have marble-sized craters gnawed in their flesh, and on finding these, my thoughts run to this summer's many Internet dialogues about what (other than people) might eat tomatoes. Squirrels, dogs, birds, turtles, hedgehogs, cats, rats, slugs, and hornworms were all identified as sometime connoisseurs, but as I clear the plants' dead growth, I encounter yet another suspect: a three-inch grasshopper with bulging eyes and twitching legs. I smash him before he can flee, but I notice he has smaller kin as well. This late in the year, though, I think I will forgo the insecticide.

As always, my labors attract attention. Vito saunters over, and I ask if he would like some fruit. Naturally he says yes, but I soon realize that I have made the offer before apprising myself of what's left to give. The fruit are small, hard, and orangish rather than red; many are cracked and disfigured. They have none of the deep-colored, plump grandeur of their forerunners, and as I comb through the denuded plants to find some respectable specimens, I am struck with a twinge of embarrassment—counterpoint, I suppose, to the satisfied magnanimity with which I dispensed my largesse but a month ago.

After Vito departs, Albert appears with a plate of figs—as delicious as the first—and after Albert, I am greeted by a pair of older women out for a walk. I do not know them, but they stop nonetheless for a chat. After my experience with Vito, I am chagrined as they compliment me on my plants. But still, they are inclined to talk tomatoes. I have one large Lemon Boy left on the vine, and on spotting this, they ask, "Is that as big as it looks? It's like beefsteaks in Alaska."

I was not aware that tomatoes grew big in Alaska, but my visitors assure me that such is the case. "Oh, yes," they say. "They grow really big there because of the long days in summer. It's the same with pumpkins," and one of them holds her arms wide to show me how big the pumpkins grow in Alaska. I refrain from offering them tomatoes, but they are equally interested in my wife's herb garden, and I send them on their way with basil and tarragon.

In the wake of my pruning and cleaning, I pick the few fruit that are ripe. I also spray and fertilize. The latter consumes the last of my second box of Miracle-Gro—I have used three pounds this season—and it occurs to me that I may soon have to think about whether to buy more. This, though, is only one aspect of a larger dilemma. Despite their motley appearance, the plants can limp along like this nearly forever; the indeterminates in particular, notes Ortho, "can grow indefinitely if not killed by frost." This, of course, is not going to happen in San Diego, and so the question is "When to pull the plug?"

For now the answer is "Not just yet." There are still a large number of green fruit on the vines, and at least some have the potential to reach salad size and turn red. It takes, so I have read, thirteen leaves to provide enough nutrients to grow and ripen a one-pound tomato. None of the fruit now left are destined to reach even half that size, but neither are any of the leaves that remain, the big, productive leaves of midseason. And so, as the last step in my tending, I thin the fruit, improving the ratio of leaves to fruit by removing the small and misshapen—sacrificing the weak for the strong. Several plants have even burst forth with an unexpected sprinkling of new flowers, and towards the same end I clip these as well. Finally, I remove the PLEASE DO NOT PICK sign, which now seems a little presumptuous.

In the patio I repeat these same tasks with the container plants, which are in much the same condition. One exception is a Basket King from which I harvest a single red tomato. This picked, there are neither fruit nor flowers on the plant. Its promise exhausted, I throw the whole thing in the trash. Little sentiment accompanies this act, for I found both the yield and the taste of the Basket Kings mediocre, but I do return the container to my son's fort, its substance to be reincorporated into that structure's ever-changing architecture.

Finally, I put away my tools and sweep up. As I am doing so I notice a mockingbird perched among the tomato cages. This I now suspect is the true source of the damaged fruit I discovered earlier, and I find the possibility far more palatable than locusts. High season gone, I am cheered to see the bird in my garden: I will gladly feed him fall tomatoes if he will sing to me in the spring.

### SEPTEMBER 14

Tonight I make Rose's sauce from the tomatoes I picked yesterday. I have only enough to make half a recipe, and it is likely this will be the last sauce I make this year. Afterwards, I store the press away in the garage, where soon I will put the fans we have had out all summer. From now on I suspect we will only have single tomatoes for salads and sandwiches—although I have been saving bacon fat in the hopes of a season-ending splurge of fried green tomatoes.

### SEPTEMBER 19

Tonight is the harvest moon, this being the full moon closest to the autumnal equinox, which occurs in three days. It gets its name, so the newspaper tells me, because this is the time of year for harvesting corn, pumpkins, squash, and beans, and in years past the full moon's light provided extra hours for the work. Tomatoes, I note, are conspicuously absent from this list, they being well past their point of peak harvest and little time needed to pick those still lingering.

Today is also my birthday. For several weeks now I have been trying to telephone my mother. I have been frustrated in this attempt—all I've spoken with has been her answering machine, and she has not returned my calls. But tonight, in honor of the occasion, she calls me. Catching me up on events, she tells me that her company's relocation will be completed and she will be out of work by the end of the year. Her spirits, however, are good: the company has been helping her look for a new job, and she may have an interview this week.

She also takes the opportunity to ask how my son's book is coming. For a moment I am at a loss as to what she is talking about—his writing projects, begun so ambitiously in the spring, have all been in stasis for some time now. But it is the book of odes about which she is curious. By way of answer I put my son on the phone—letting the writer take responsibility for his own work—and after a bit he asks if she would like to hear a poem. Naturally the answer is yes, and so he flips through his *oeuvre*, looking for an appropriate selection. He chooses "Ode to Cats" and follows this with "Ode to a Ship in a Bottle" and "Ode to Tomatoes," all of which my wife and I listen to from our vantage in the kitchen. When he is finished, he asks if she would like to hear my contribution to this creative period in my son's development.

Ten minutes ago I was minding my own business, eating my dinner and with no expectation that I was about to be called upon to read my mother poetry. After my son's performance I can hardly say no, however, and so to her and my sister, who has joined her on the line, I read my "Ode to a Son Who Writes Odes."

They are an uncritical audience and enjoy the reading. But hoping to restore the conversation to the secular, I ask my mother about her tomatoes.

They are, she says, "doing pretty good considering they're not getting any water or sun."

Upon hearing this, my sister, with her gift for directness, interjects that "her tomatoes are wilted and dead, that's what they are."

My mother concedes that this is true. But of late, she says, she has had no time to tend them. The reason—and for that of her recent inaccessibility—soon becomes apparent. She has met a new dance partner. They met this summer, and ever since, they have been dancing three, four, or five nights a week. He lives two hours from her, and when they are not dancing near her home, they rendezvous at points midway and drive from there, often to towns that are yet another hour distant. Just hearing about this frenzy of dancing and driving, I am exhausted; they are pursuing it with the energy of teenagers, and their plans are only growing grander: now, says my mother, they are thinking of going to Cancún.

In my opinion, my mother has had some questionable relationships since she and my father divorced. Mostly they have been based on a common aversion to being alone. But as she tells me of her new friend, I allow myself the hope that she may finally have found someone with whom something richer might develop. "It's really neat," she says, "after all these years to find somebody who wanted me to be his partner. I feel very fortunate."

Even without meeting him, I can tell the man has good qualities. He grows his own tomatoes, and when they meet (and perhaps in recognition of the neglect he has caused to her plants) he brings to my mother bags of *pommes d'amour*. Bags of love apples.

## SEPTEMBER 22

Robert Ehigh, having successfully been kept from committing homicide in the defense of his tomato, is on television today. Yesterday he picked the fruit, and today it will be weighed to see if it breaks Gordon Graham's record. To see, that is, if Ehigh wins the hundred thousand dollars. All of this is to be shown live on television, with Ehigh and the tomato having been flown for the occasion from the hills of Ohio to the studios of New York.

Despite the import of a possible new world record, the weighing of the tomato is preceded by a string of unrelated appearances from minor celebrities. Indeed, the whole event has been delayed by three days because the United States saw fit in the interim to invade Haiti. But eventually there is a voice-over tease ("Behind this door may be the world's most valuable vegetable!"), a commercial, and Ehigh is introduced.

Sixty-three years old and lean, a retired coal-miner from the town of St. Clairesville, Ehigh has thinning hair and age lines on his face. He is dressed in khaki work clothes and carries a bowling bag. A recording of Ella Fitzgerald singing the tomato lines from "Let's Call the Whole Thing Off" is played as he enters, and as he walks onstage Ehigh passes a pedestal on which rests The Tomato, shrouded for the moment from the camera. He rests the bowling bag on a table, near which stand the show's two hosts, a man and a woman, both pert, smiling, and perfectly groomed.

They begin with some introductory banter:

> "Robert, are you a farmer?"
> "No, just a little gardener. Retired."
> "And so you raised this vegetable from the beginning, you noticed its growth, and you knew you had something special?"
> "Yeah, we were going to eat it."
> "Until you went down to the store and some gentleman told you about the contest?"

The specter of making BLTs from a hundred-thousand-dollar tomato elicits laughter from the audience, and it is soon apparent the hosts have little compunction against laughs earned at the expense of their guest. They extract from him the admission that he talked to the tomato, gave it a name, and built a house for it. ("A little A-frame, so it wouldn't break off the vine.") When he reveals that Gordon Graham visited with him during the tomato's gestation, they deadpan that there is a "bonding that takes place among these tomato growers." And when the contents of the bowling bag are revealed to be samples from his garden, including a large red, catfaced tomato the size and shape of a turban squash, the woman scans the assemblage, looks to the camera, and notes, tongue literally in cheek, that "conditions were particularly good this year."

But finally a trumpet fanfare is played, the shroud is lifted, and there on the pedestal sits The Tomato. Like its smaller cousin, it is catfaced and misshapen, with deep furrows and great, uneven lobes—the Elephant Man of tomatoes. It is, though, impressively big. With two hands Ehigh hoists it from the pedestal and carries it to the counter, where an electronic scale is waiting. He places it on the scale, and as the readout flickers, consternation grips the hosts.

"It lost weight," says the man.

"It's losing weight right now," says the woman. "You can see all the water coming out."

And so it is. The Great Tomato, which may or may not have once weighed 6¼ pounds, was kept too long on the vine. Lacking Calgene's Flavr Savr gene, it has begun to soften and rot, and even as it is weighed, it oozes fluid. The scale registers 3 pounds, 2.8 ounces.

"I don't like this scale," says the male host, now suddenly concerned. A technician is summoned, and as he examines the instrument, Ehigh pulls a handkerchief from his pocket and mops up after the leaking fruit. Soon the scale is confirmed as correct, but even were it not so, the problem would now be past remedying, for The Tomato is losing substance by the second. Graham's record remains unbroken.

In consolation, Ehigh is given a check for ten thousand dollars. Music plays, balloons drop from the ceiling, and the scene fades to a commercial.

This is tomato as spectacle. But offstage, another, quieter story has also been playing itself out: that of tomato as healer. Eighteen months ago Ehigh's daughter died of cancer. Since then, says his wife, he has been without a smile. But the tomato has changed that. "It's the first thing he's smiled about since our daughter died." And that, I suspect, is worth more to her than all the money and fame he did or did not earn.

Later today I find that I too have been paid a call by Gordon Graham. Weeks ago when I spoke to Robert Ambrose, he told me that back issues of *The Tomato Club* were available. I sent him a check, and today in the mail I receive the complete, fourteen-issue set.

Here the club's history can be clearly traced. The early issues are black and stern of layout; only later does the two-color design make its debut. The declining frequency of its publication is chronicled—from the initial twelve times a year, to nine, to the final six. And Ambrose's pleas for editorial contributions from his membership can be found increasingly often as the issues progress. But in concept *The Tomato Club* remained unchanged from beginning to end.

From the outset there were Super-Growers, amazing people who grow amazing tomatoes. Gordon Graham, appropriately, was the first. I find that Graham (who says his world-record tomato changed his life) has developed a year-round regimen devoted to the production of world-class heavyweights, and that I can avail myself of his secrets by purchasing his booklet *How to Grow Giant Tomatoes*. Later I learn about Minnie Zaccaria, who bred her own hybrid and called it "Big Zac." I learn about the New Jersey Championship Tomato Weigh-In, now in its seventeenth year. About the five hormones that guide the growth of a tomato. And that Campbell's Soup sold its twenty billionth can of tomato soup in 1990.

I learn that the variety bearing my favorite name is more accurately known as Radiator Charlie's Mortgage Lifter. According to the story, M. Charles Byles had a truck repair business located on a steeply sloped road in West Virginia in the 1930s. Byles worked six years selecting and crossing four other kinds of tomatoes until he had stabilized his own new variety, which he then sold as seedlings to motorists who had overheated and pulled into his shop. This sideline business was so successful that he was soon able to pay off his mortgage.

I learn that Robert Ambrose writes his own poetry:

> Gardeners take heed
> of this valuable directive,
> What you must feed your plants
> is not always subjective. . . .

And I learn that the world of tomatoes has more breadth and diversity, is more all encompassing, than ever I had imagined.

This discovery gives me pleasure enough. But along with the back issues, Ambrose has included a gift. When we spoke, he mentioned that he had found a book of poems devoted exclusively to tomatoes. "I don't like any of them," he had said. And having no further use for it, he sent it along.

Tonight for dinner we eat our first of the frozen sauce made from our tomatoes with Rose's recipe. As we eat, I look through the book—*Some Say Tomato*. Inside are fifty-one poems. There are no rhymed couplets, and some of the poems, as Ambrose complained, have only the most tenuous of connections to tomatoes (one having been included because of its one-time use of the word *ketchup*). But overall the collection gives ample evidence that tomatoes and the muse have long kept rich and fruitful congress.

In these poems, tomatoes are intertwined with celebrations of love and of ripenings, of friendship, and of the unfolding seasons. Included are the ode by Neruda and a pair of poems by Rita Dove, poet laureate of the United States. There is an entry by Maxine Kumin, winner of a Pulitzer Prize. There are poems by the editor's daughters, aged seven and ten. And there is a wonderfully clever word play by Stephen Margulies, curator of the Bayly Art Museum in Charlottesville, Virginia.

## CAUTION: POMMES D'AMOUR

Though in the midst
Of our own garden
And glowed upon
By what we ourselves have grown
And fruitily glowing back,
We let doubt sprout with the love-apples:
To mate? O! O!

—Stephen Margulies

I disagree with Ambrose's assessment—I like *Some Say Tomato*. But I thank him for sending it my way.

## SEPTEMBER 26

Despite the onset of fall and the lateness of the season, I still see tomatoes on my walks through the neighborhood and its surrounding areas. Mostly they look like mine, more dead than alive, their owners waiting out the last few late-ripening fruit. But occasionally I see plants that were set out in July or August and that are now at the peak of their vigor. Today I even discover a newly transplanted seedling, six inches tall and topped by a wire cage, set amidst a patch of roses. By its solitariness, I would guess that its owners' hopes are modest, these being not for a massive summer-style crop but rather for a steady-enough supply of salad tomatoes to get through the winter without having to resort to the grocery store. But truer to the season are the multiple sightings I make of fruit that have fallen to the ground and lie rotting, their disappearing presence the only trace of the plants that bore them and have now been removed.

## SEPTEMBER 29

The tomatoes of my neighbor, owner of Dan the Dog and Stinky the bobcat, are finally gone. Today or yesterday he pulled the bare vines—it could only have taken minutes—leaving in their place a bare patch of earth that now waits for next year's crop and the slow encroachment of the surrounding lawn. These plants never did do well. Although their first fruit ripened before mine, they lived the bulk of their lives shaded by my melaleucas, and I would guess that none of the plants yielded more than a dozen fruit at best. Moreover, Dan's owners have been growing tomatoes in this same spot for four or five years in a row, and I would not be surprised to discover that the soil has become infected with nematodes. These, though, are but the season-ending critiques of a dispassionate observer; I am sure the growing has been deemed a net gain by Dan's owners, and that early next spring the towers will reappear, with new seedlings underneath.

John, too, has been thinking of next year's tomatoes. His strength is returning, and over the last few days he has prepared his soil for a winter garden. He has set out new basil seedlings, planted onions, and sprinkled endive seed over the small patch from whence his winter salads come. He has also worked steer manure—six bags, he proudly tells me—into a dozen holes now filled in and marked by stakes. The nutrients in the manure will percolate into the soil, and in mid-November he will plant fava beans. They will be ripe and harvested, says John, "in time for tomatoes."

# O C T O B E R

### OCTOBER 2

**M**Y WIFE AND SON leave today for a week in Arizona. My son's new year-round school schedule decrees—for him—a multitude of short vacations throughout the year. No doubt this is educationally desirable, but it is hell on parents. Last week we paid an exorbitant sum for his baby-sitter to do double duty, and this week my wife is covering with her own vacation time. Since I can't get away, I will be staying home.

They are bound for the town of Sedona, one hundred miles south of the Grand Canyon. The drive will take them through the low Sonoran desert of Southern California (in El Centro they will pass a water tower with a painted line marked *Sea Level* forty feet above ground) and then into the mountains and desert of the Colorado Plateau, more than a mile high. My wife will have relief on the drive from her sister, who is accompanying them for the week.

When they leave, a deep stillness falls over the house. It is different from the quiet that accompanies their temporary and routine absences throughout the day, when I know they will soon return and with them their chatterings and bustle. Rather, this quiet is unbroken even by the radio, for despite its music and news, I know that for the next week I will not be interrupted or startled by any sound I do not make.

As the day wanes I find also that I am stricken with a strange lassitude and disorientation. I think for a while of pulling up the tomatoes. Except for the California Suns, they have essentially stopped producing. But the effort is more than I can muster, and the act seems far too decisive. Eventually I decide to go to the grocery store, for I do know that I must eat in the coming week. Here it becomes clear that it has been a long time since I have shopped for one person. Every choice poses a host of questions ("Do I really need that much?" "Isn't that more trouble than I want to go to?"), and my progress through the aisles is interminable. Moreover, the evidence at the cash register is that all these questions were for naught. My bill—for one person for one week—is ninety dollars, a total I check and recheck three times in the parking lot.

## OCTOBER 4

I return from work this evening to find Albert standing at the curb by the tomatoes. He hails me desperately, and I hurry over to see what is the matter.

Joined by his wife, he leads me through his patio and into his laundry room, where the air is filled with mist and a thick spray of water is spewing from the handle of a faucet. I have had similar experiences in my house, having once awakened to my wife's complaints that there was no hot water pressure and finding on investigation that my garage was filled with steam and the floor covered with two inches of hot water.

Albert's problem is less acute only because it involves cold water rather than hot. Clearly the first thing to do is turn off the main supply from the street. At the sidewalk, though, I find that his water valve is rusted open. Even using both hands and all my strength, I cannot turn it. Watching me struggle, Albert disappears and returns with a steel crowbar, which he wedges against the valve's leverlike handle and begins to push. Still it does not budge, and he then begins to bang on the handle and to try different angles for more leverage. Quickly I discourage him from further attempts at this sort of do-it-yourself plumbing. If he breaks the valve, he'll increase his mess exponentially.

Using pidgin-English and pantomime, I tell Albert I will call the water department. This is a little forward—normally you don't call to have your neighbor's water turned off. But I can see no other alternative, and so I go home, rummage through a pile of old bills to find the number, and make the call. Naturally they are closed.

A recording does refer me to an emergency number, but just as I finish dialing, Albert knocks on my door. He has begun to feel that this is a great imposition, and so as not to further inconvenience me or the water department, he is willing to let his laundry room flood all night. Right at this moment, however, the phone is answered, and I am assured that help will be sent immediately.

While we wait, I tell Albert that he and his wife will be without water for the night and need to fill some jugs. I do this by pouring an imaginary glass of water from an imaginary vessel and then tilting my head back and drinking the imaginary liquid with loud gurgling sounds. Though crude, the information is conveyed, and they manage to fill several buckets in the short interval before the arrival of the service man—who easily closes the valve using a specially made tool. After an amiable chat—the man tells me he once took Italian in high school but has since forgotten it all—the worker departs, and Albert and his wife retire for the evening.

But first they thank me profusely for the help. I assure them it was no trouble, and indeed it was not. It took no more than a few minutes and a phone call. But what was easy for me was impossible for them. Moreover, Albert was a plate or two of figs ahead of me in the neighborhood reciprocity equation, and this has given me a chance to catch up. It may even have put me ahead.

## OCTOBER 5

I am kept informed of my wife and son's vacation activities via daily phone calls. Today they took a day trip to the Grand Canyon, at which they arrived by turn-of-the-century steam train. My son, Southern Californian that he is, was wearing shorts on this trip, and the adventure seems to have been most memorable to him for the cold. The south rim of the Grand Canyon is seven thousand feet high, and so it was not entirely unusual that when they got off the train, they walked into a hailstorm. Nor, says my wife, could they see across the canyon, because it was filled with rain, sleet, and fog (a scene I can easily envision given the recent conditions in Albert's laundry room).

Besides telling me about the cold, my son tells me also about the town in which they are staying. Although significant portions of the populace are engaged in such fruitful activities as the growing and tending of apple orchards, my sister-in-law, an inveterate shopper, has led my wife and son to enough art and curio shops that my son has concluded Sedona is "one of those towns where the main thing they have for visitors to do is buy little sculptures." Nor have they shopped in vain, for he hints that they have purchased for me an *objet d'art*. Details, though, will have to wait.

## OCTOBER 8

A Santa Ana is upon us, the first since spring. At two in the afternoon, it is ninety degrees in the shade; this on a day when the newspaper weather map shows little circles sketched over northern Michigan to indicate a forecast of snow. Bad as the heat is the dryness: my lips are chapped and my nose is bleeding. Outside, the streets are empty, and dry leaves tumble and blow with a desolate, shuffling sound.

My family is returning home today. Their route will take them through Phoenix and then back through the desert of Southern California, an area the same map tells me will today be the hottest in the nation. At three-thirty my wife calls to apprise me of their progress. She sounds strangely distant, and when I ask her about it, she tells me, "It's one hundred and fifty degrees in the phone booth, and the phone is so hot I can't hold it."

It is little cooler when they arrive home in the evening, but the oppression of heat yields to the joy of reunion. My son has grown, and my wife become more beautiful. Both are bubbling with stories. We unload the car, and inside they tell me about the rope swing they found in an oak tree, the water moccasin they saw in the creek, and the fly fisherman who bewitched my son with the art of casting.

While they talk they unpack, and as they do, gifts and souvenirs emerge: a jar of red chile jam, a *ristra* of tiny red peppers, a paper-cast model of a bicyclist bought by my son for his best friend, and finally, the *objet*: a terra-cotta tomato topped with a cinnamon red glaze. It is good-sized and deep oblate of shape, and were it a fruit I would call it a beefsteak. The purpose of such things I am never sure, but now is not the time for an inquiry, and the object is accorded a place on our living-room bookshelf not far from the hummingbird nest I once found in the desert. And then we turn our attentions again to each other. There are more stories and more catching up, and soon we find it is late. We trundle our son to bed. And then my wife and I look at each other, and a twinkling smile passes between us.

To mate. Oh!

### OCTOBER 9

Today it is hotter than it has been at any time for five years in San Diego. The winds have spawned fires, and all through the day we hear sirens. At noon a fire truck races past our house, but it is well out of the neighborhood by the time it finds its destination.

My energies and resolve have returned along with the return of my wife and son, and briefly I consider pulling the tomatoes. The heat, though, precludes the enjoyment of any outdoor activity, and the thought is short-lived. Instead—great fun—my wife and I draw up a shopping list and plan a trip to the grocery store, my ninety-dollar supply of food now exhausted and the stocks in the refrigerator down to the mayonnaise, batteries, and pickle relish. Feeling guilty about this state of affairs, I offer to make the trip by myself, but my wife says she would like to spend the time together, and I am happy to have her. My son has gone to his best friend's for the afternoon, and so it will be just the two of us.

Our first stop is a local health-food store. We do little of our shopping here, having once too often found bugs in the beans. But today we are in search of a soup mix we know they carry; my wife goes to locate it, and while she does, I survey the fruits and vegetables.

The produce here is all organic—no sprays or chemicals. This is a nicety I have little patience for. The produce's organicity doubles or triples its price, and I can't for the life of me see how it makes a difference whether a plant gets its nitrogen from cow manure or manufactured granules. But I must admit the variety is sensational. They have nine kinds of pear (including French butter pears and Shinseiki). There are red, white, purple, and gold potatoes; passion fruit and Fuyu persimmons; orange honeydew and yellow-fleshed watermelons; white eggplant; a dozen kinds of squash; and tomatoes.

This time of year the selection is less expansive than that of the other offerings and consists principally of red cherries and a nondescript fresh market variety. But they do have a tomato I've not seen before: globe-shaped and golden orange in color, I believe they are Golden Jubilees. Out of curiosity I buy one, and later, when I try it, I find that it's as orange on the inside as it is on the outside. But despite the fruit's handsome appearance, it lacks the juiciness and tang of a homegrown, and the words of Guy Clark's song still hold true:

> *Only two things that money can't buy*
> *That's true love & homegrown tomatoes.*

Money can, though, be put to a great many other uses. For instance, the maintenance of community. The main business street nearest our neighborhood has been in decline for some years now. This year its condition worsened considerably when a national sporting goods company with a local outlet chose to relocate. They chose to be closer to the majority of their affluent customers, which meant nearer to suburban San Diego and farther from the central city. No doubt this was a sound business decision, but in its wake, the company left a ninety-nine-cent store, of which there now seem a dozen within a few-block stretch. The company's departure seemed also the coup de grâce for several nearby small restaurants and businesses, and they in their wake left nothing but boarded windows and paper-strewn sidewalks. Walks down this street now fill me with a mixture of anxiety and despair, and it occurs to me that perhaps it is time to move— thoughts that are hard to reconcile with the affection I have for our immediate neighborhood.

One business on this street is the grocery store at which we have shopped every week for as long as we have lived here. We spend, perhaps, five thousand dollars a year in this store. Recently, however, the store has installed electronic theft detectors and hired a twenty-four-hour armed guard; there is trash in the parking lot constantly, and two weeks ago my son inadvertently stepped in a human fece in one of the aisles. The most optimistic explanation, says my wife, is that it fell from a diaper.

From habit, this is the store to which I now drive. My wife, however, proposes that we shop instead at a more upscale store several miles distant. Although both are owned by the same company, the latter is in a higher income neighborhood, has more selection, and recently received a major face-lift; it obviously is the store in which the parent invests the more money. This store is patently the more appealing, and though farther away, I now head in its direction.

I do so, however, with reservation. If this becomes a permanent decision, we will be shifting a substantial sum of money out of our community; the company that owns our local store will be even less inclined to invest here, and the store will become an even less desirable place to shop. Eventually, our failure to spend locally can only undermine the community in which we live. More than a sporting-goods store, it could cost us a grocery—and even, possibly, a health-food store that sells yellow potatoes and golden tomatoes, and at which we perhaps should shop more often.

## OCTOBER 15

My wife's friends are coming to dinner this evening. In preparation, I harvest all my available ripe tomatoes. This amounts to five modest-sized California Suns and nineteen cherries of assorted types. A small bowl easily holds them all.

The menu my wife has planned will make use of these tomatoes in a salad and *bruschetta*, which has become a new favorite of ours. In addition, she will serve Rose's frozen tomato sauce over fettuccine, fried eggplant, and, for dessert, a baked apple crisp. We will also have pesto. My wife had planned to make her own, thereby making use of the large amount of basil still in our yard, but one of her friends—she of the upside-down tomato cages—said she already had pesto made from basil in *her* yard and couldn't she bring it?

At dinner there is the customary telling of stories and recent life events. My wife and son tell of their stay in Arizona. The game-show winner tells of her recent trip to New Orleans, where she and nineteen friends rendezvoused for a long weekend. All twenty had at one time lived in San Diego. Here they had woven for themselves a network of warmth, ties, and confidences; and though they have since dispersed across the country, they had managed through an amazing feat of coordination to assemble themselves once again in adjacent hotel rooms in New Orleans. There they ate Cajun, had slumber parties, traded radio messages from taxi to taxi, and went dancing. Of the dancing, she says they had a great time, because they all went wild and the other patrons ignored them—"Because who cares what a bunch of middle-aged women are doing?" This is the first time I have heard someone my age refer to him or herself as middle-aged, and her comment gives me long pause.

The pesto-maker's story is of her garden. She and her husband had ample tomatoes from their four plants, their harvest well exceeding the single forty-dollar tomato they had grown years before on their condominium patio. They even collected a troupe of hornworms, which her husband kept alive in a jar and sustained on a diet of bell-pepper leaves, several times bringing them to work for display. The revulsion I feel for these creatures is apparently not universal, for the captives were treated as pets and the captor's co-workers given the chance to stroke their heads and necks. Not only were there takers, but it seems the worms enjoyed the treatment, for when so touched they raised their front ends in worm-ecstasy, which the pesto-maker demonstrates by arching her shoulders, neck, and head backwards, withdrawing her lower jaw, and blankly rolling her eyes skyward.

But their big crop was basil. They had planted lots of it, with the intention of making pesto. But, she says, "We planted so much of it that I became a slave to my basil. Every weekend I had more basil leaves, and every weekend I had to go buy more pine nuts and more mozzarella so I could make more pesto. I kept making more because I had more basil, but I just put it in the freezer, and I had more than I wanted.

"Next year I'm not going to grow so much basil."

The frenzy of her entrapment is evident, but she then digs deep and offers a confession: "You know, to tell the truth, I was relieved when the garden started to die, and I didn't have to take care of it anymore."

Wearied at season's end by their charges' munificence, this is, perhaps, a sentiment shared by more gardeners than care to admit it. And so it is that a garden's expiration can be a synergistic event, with the plants' habits encouraging the gardener's proclivities, which then hasten the plants' decline and the gardener's more studied neglect. I know this, for it has been a month since last I fertilized and sprayed my tomatoes.

After dinner the apple crisp and coffee are brought out, as is a game. This evening we play Matchability. The game's basic play consists of the selection of a word, name, or phrase on the basis of which players write down lists of associated words they hope will be matched by others. "Wars," "bodies of water," and "cartoons" all elicit diverse veins of experiences. But we find that everyone shares virtually the same information about *The Wizard of Oz*. Young and "middle-aged" alike produce lists that include Dorothy, Kansas, Tinman, Lion, Scarecrow, Toto, Emerald City, movie, poppies, Judy Garland, yellow brick road, and ruby slippers. But even here there are some nonmatches. Frank Baum is unknown to those who never read the novel. And my list includes brown sugar. I am astonished to find this item otherwise universally omitted, but the others are equally surprised at my having written it down. What, they ask, does brown sugar have to do with *The Wizard of Oz*? This seems to me a completely unnecessary question, but I proceed to point out that the Wicked Witch of the West was made of brown sugar, which is why she melted when Dorothy threw water on her.

This is a fundamental fact of witch physiology—of which I have known since childhood. It is, however, vociferously disputed by everyone else in the room, my son included. The witch, they say, melted because witches and water are inimical opposites, not because she was made of brown sugar—of which a personage so reprehensible could not possibly be made. How, they ask, could I have harbored such a gross misconception?

Although I am loath to abandon such a central tenet of my worldview, it is, I suppose, possible that this fact was slipped to me extemporaneously by my father during some moment of childhood innocence. Fathers, I have learned, have a deep reservoir of such facts and dispense them freely to their offspring. Indeed, my son has found this well documented in his favorite cartoon, *Calvin and Hobbes*.

CALVIN: Dad, how come old photographs are always in black and white? Didn't they have color film back then?

DAD: Sure they did. In fact, those old photographs *are* in color. It's just the *world* was black and white then.

CALVIN: Really?

DAD: Yep. The world didn't turn color until sometime in the 1930s, and it was pretty grainy color for a while, too.

CALVIN: That's really weird.

DAD: Well, the truth is stranger than fiction.

CALVIN: But then why are old *paintings* in color?! If the world was black and white, wouldn't artists have painted it that way?

DAD: Not necessarily. A lot of great artists were insane.

Only now—now that I am a father—am I discovering that much of this information is actually retained.

## OCTOBER 16

A fine fall day, a Sunday. The skies are blue. Midafternoon temperatures are in the low seventies, though a breeze hints of a chill this evening. On the radio, Garrison Keillor is rhapsodizing about the unfolding of fall in Lake Wobegone. My son's soccer team is holding its picture day. The Chargers are playing football. The Moscow circus is in town. And I pull the tomatoes.

Like patients on life support, I now suspect they could continue in their enfeebled condition almost indefinitely. But our friend's confession of last night has prompted me to realize that the plants have become more chore than pleasure, more bother than sustenance, and that it is time to dispose of them.

I begin with the Celebrity closest the sidewalk. With a pair of pruning shears, I reach through its cage and sever its stems, threading the tired and ossified sections out through the surrounding mesh. When all that remains is a six-inch section of stalk, I grab it and yank out the roots. These I inspect for evidence of nematodes. Largely the roots are as they should be—smooth and slender, like strands of pasta. But in a few spots there are small and distorted swellings, arthritic in appearance; and while they are few in number and less obvious than the glaring and misshapen bulges shown in my stashed-away *Sunset,* still they cause me worry.

This concern is brought more sharply in focus when one of the gay men who lives next door to John stops by on his way home from a walk and asks what I am doing—why I am standing on the sidewalk peering intently at a tangled mass of tomato roots. I tell him I am looking for nematodes, and when he asks what that means, I tell him about the swellings on the roots, last year's Vapam treatment, and the perils of growing tomatoes in the same spot year after year. Mostly this is strange stuff to him, but he does understand what I am saying, for he tells me that he and his partner used to grow tomatoes in their yard. For lack of space, they too grew them in the same place repeatedly. "But after a while ours just quit producing. So we stopped planting them. That must have been why." This is confirmatory but less than consoling.

After he leaves I remove the remaining Celebrity. The roots of this plant show no sign of nematodes, but on several stems I encounter interlopers of another sort. Lines of ants are making their way up and down the plant to sections of stem that are covered with dense colonies of tiny reddish brown insects. They look like miniature galactic battlecruisers, bristling with spikes, spines, and odd protrusions, but their true identity is *Antianthe expansae:* nymphs of the solanaceous treehopper. They have been brought in by the ants, who harvest from them droplets of honeydew, which the nymphs produce from the plant's juices. Had I noticed the menagerie earlier, I could have controlled it with a shot of malathion or a blast of water; but its presence speaks, I suppose, to my declining vigilance of the last few weeks.

In like fashion I make my way down the row of tomatoes. I find no more nymphs, but I do find ants, aphids, and a lone green worm. I check also for evidence of the self-diagnosed virus that did in the beefsteak; one of the Champions and the Lemon Boy show signs that they too may have been infected. Both have some stunted leaves and stems, and at their tips both have tinges of the interior discoloration I noted on the Beefsteak. Whether its roguing prevented more extensive damage I cannot know.

As I work I toss the cuttings in a pile. Those few green fruit worth salvaging—those larger than a golf ball—I pick and place in a bowl. Faced with my plants' heaped and withered remains, the full extent of their afflictions now revealed, I am tempted momentarily to think of my season as a failure and of my efforts as but slovenly bumbling. Forgotten for the moment are the glorious and perfect first Lemon Boy—the fruit that caused John to gasp with wonder—the potfuls of tomatoes cooked into sauce, and the bagfuls given away.

But I also pull up the plants' roots as I work, and on none do I find further evidence of nematodes. All are clean, smooth, and slender. I am increasingly perplexed by the meaning of the little nodules on the first Celebrity—do I, or do I not have nematodes?—when I make an unexpected discovery. A short distance from where the Lemon Boy had stood, and beyond the boundaries of last fall's Vapam-ing, is a small volunteer I first noticed a month ago. The plant is slight, less than two feet tall, and never produced more than a handful of tiny fruit. I believe it to be a Sweet 100 sprouted from last year's crop. Sweet 100s are not resistant to nematodes, and so I am startled when I find that for all its waifish appearance, the plant's roots are as thick as my fingers and marked by a riot of gnomelike twistings and swellings.

This is the work of nematodes unfettered, and it tells me many things. It tells me the nodules I found on the first Celebrity were trivial—the plant was infected but the damage insignificant. It tells me, as I need constantly to be reminded, that it is impossible to make sound judgments in the absence of references for comparison: I needed the unaffected plants to see that the Celebrity's roots were diseased, and I needed the volunteer to see that the Celebrity had nonetheless fared well under the circumstances. It tells me I haven't done such a bad job as a gardener after all—even the master gardener's plants die in the end, and in the interim I'd done what could be done with the soil I'd been given and picked varieties that had withstood well the assaults they had faced. It tells me, too, that things won't be perfect in the future—without more Vapam I'll be disarmed— but that I'll manage.

All these musings are interrupted when the mother across the street brings her new baby boy out to her car. As she fits him to his seat, she sees me working and calls out a greeting. Must tomatoes be replanted every year? she asks. Yes, I reply, they must. Well, she says, you certainly had a nice crop—"real prizewinners." Clearly she is not a gardener, and clearly I grew no prize-winning tomatoes—not in height, weight, or fecundity; not nationally or locally. I posed no threat to Gordon Graham and raised no candidates for the New Jersey Champion Tomato Weigh-In. But I did have fun, and my neighbor's compliment helps lift me from my despondency and is appreciated.

With the plants removed, I use wire cutters to detach the bailing wire that has bound the cages together since spring. I work each of the cages out of the ground and carry them to storage behind the house, where they will spend the winter as guard towers in my son's fort. I gather up the mound of refuse on my driveway and wad the stems, roots, and unripe fruit into plastic trash bags, which I then lug to the street to await removal.

And finally, I rake the soil of the patch smooth and sweep the driveway and sidewalk clean.

In the patio I repeat these steps, following the same sequence and rhythm. Having grown in sterilized soil, the potted plants are free of nematodes. With the exception of a few aphids, they are also free of bugs and blight. Rather, the primary problem faced by these plants was insufficient sunlight. The California Suns had the sunniest corner of the patio, and they produced the best. The other plants mostly grew tall—searching for light—but bore few fruit.

Absent passersby to stop and chat, my work is now silent. One plant startles me when its stem cracks loudly as I loosen its supports, but gradually all the plants make their way into trash bags. All, that is, but one Floragold. Unlike its miniature companions, who are outright dead, this plant has sent from its base a new green stem from which are growing new green leaves. I trim off all the old and dead stems, give it water, and leave it— now three inches high—otherwise undisturbed in its pot. Whether anything will come of this rejuvenation—whether we'll get a new plant with new fruit—I do not know. It will be an experiment.

Eventually, the pots and poles are put away, the patio is swept, and all is as it was a year ago. The only botanic residents that remain are the once-scorched lime tree and the potted palms. My work is done. Inside, the house is dark; my wife, my son, and my son's best friend have gone to the circus. Later this evening they will return with tales of dancing bears and juggling acrobats. In the meantime, I will shower, make dinner, and wait contentedly.

## OCTOBER 17

When I return home from work today and my yard comes into view, my eye is drawn first and unavoidably to where the tomatoes had stood. Not yet accustomed to the spot's vacancy, I am momentarily taken aback. Something is missing. But though I have no plants, I do have fruit.

From the green tomatoes I salvaged yesterday, six are big enough to fry. To accompany them I have purchased some yellowtail, and my first step in starting dinner is to heat the grill for the tuna. Then I prepare the tomatoes. In anticipation of this event, I have collected a pound of bacon fat—lagniappe from the summer's bacon, sprout, and tomato sandwiches and the remains of which will be tossed after tonight's dinner. I scoop the bacon fat—layered in its jar like sedimentary rock, white on brown on white on brown—into a cast-iron skillet, and as the fat melts, I slice the tomatoes. I roll the slices in flour sprinkled with salt and pepper, and when the fat is hot, I drop in the whitened disks, causing the fat to bubble and hiss.

When they have browned, I turn them over; and when they are cooked on both sides, I remove them from the heat, replacing them with newly floured raw slices. Frying is a skill, and no skill can be maintained through disuse. And so it is that as the cooking progresses, the grease begins to blacken and a dark sludge of fried flour accumulates on the bottom of the pan, for I am clumsy at modulating the fat's temperature in concert with the addition and removal of tomatoes. Unavoidably, I also fill the air with the smell of bacon fat and generate a layer of aerosolized grease on my skin. But when I am done, I have produced a satisfying heap of fried tomatoes.

Simultaneously, I have been grilling the fish, and my wife has been making a salad and microwaving a squash. My son sets the table, and when we are all done, we eat. Although a single and infrequent dish does not a diet make, my wife is nonetheless squeamish about the fried nature of the tomatoes, and she takes but a few—mostly, I think, out of deference to me. My son, who wouldn't eat green tomato pie, shuns them entirely. But I load my plate, diverting several slices directly to my mouth. Compared to the dry and tasteless things I cooked this summer, these are an infinite improvement, and I rapidly inhale the equivalent of three or four tomatoes. But somehow they are not like those I remember my mother made. I think perhaps I sliced them too thin and was too restrained in my use of the salt shaker.

Andrew Smith, who wrote *The Tomato in America*, a history seven years in the writing, has also written of the recent popular quest—inspired by Fannie Flagg's book and the resulting movie—for the "authentic" recipe for fried green tomatoes. In southern Europe, he says, green tomatoes have long been fried like eggplants—in olive oil with a little salt and pepper. The first American recipe for "Fried Green Tomatoes," says Smith (who has compiled a personal database of more than fifty thousand tomato references), was published in 1870 in a book with the no-nonsense title *What to Eat and How to Cook It*. The recipe, he says, was "relatively simple."

## THE FIRST PUBLISHED RECIPE FOR FRIED GREEN TOMATOES

*Green or half ripe tomatoes fried, or rather browned, make a nice relish for breakfast, but they require care and patience. Wipe the fruit clean, cut in slices one-fourth of an inch thick, dip in corn meal, and brown on a griddle till tender, say ten or fifteen minutes.*

From *What to Eat and How to Cook It*, by John Cowan, New York, 1870. Reprinted in "Authentic Fried Green Tomatoes?" Andrew Smith. *Food History News*, Summer 1992.

Over the next several decades many recipes followed, with dozens of variations. Some called for dipping the slices in beaten egg before rolling them in the breading material, which in turn ranged from cornmeal to cracker crumbs to flour. Some called for slicing the tomatoes thin, some thick; some for green tomatoes, some for red; some called for frying in butter, some for bacon fat, and some a mixture of both. Some called for ladling the finished product with gravy.

In the twentieth century, spices such as oregano and curry started to find their way into the recipes, and liquid oil was recog-

nized as an acceptable medium for frying. One concoction speci-
fied the placing of fried green tomatoes on toast, "sprinkling with
grated cheese, and topping off with whipped cream."

In the face of this variability, Smith's conclusion is that there is
no one "authentic" recipe for fried green tomatoes. To those who
seek this holy grail, he suggests abandoning the search and beginning instead to experiment "with the procedures . . . spices and
condiments that *you* like."

No doubt this is wise advice. But it is hard to accept when the
authenticity you seek is a lost and elusive bit of your childhood.

### OCTOBER 24

On the subject of brown sugar and witches, my father is exoner-
ated. Haunted by the possibility that the explanation I had
believed in for the witch's solubility was not fabrication, I stop by
the library today and check out a copy of Frank Baum's *The
Wizard of Oz*. In it I find that when Dorothy doused the witch,
she melted away "like" brown sugar. Clearly I had missed this sub-
tlety as a child, and took instead the simile for fact.

I feel it a minor triumph to have cleared up both the misconception and the misattribution of its source. But still it is certain I
harbor within me many more such erroneous beliefs, some indeed
traceable to my father and some of my own creation, and not all
of which will resolve so neatly.

On the subject of tomatoes, the Internet has been quiet of late. Last
weekend there were 414 postings to *rec. gardens*. These included
comments and queries about the planting of bulbs, the feeding of
citrus, techniques for composting, and how to kill bamboo. There
are questions about entomology ("What are these crawlies?"), squirrels, and sources for heirloom corn. But nothing about tomatoes.

A few days ago, however, a discourse arose concerning how to
make use of the last of the season's green tomatoes. Rob F., location unknown, wrote that he had "a ton of green tomatoes that I
had to pick when closing my garden. I know I can make fried
green tomatoes or pickle them, but I wondered if anybody would
have other suggestions."

I like Rob's businesslike "closing" of his garden—it eliminates neatly the opportunity for angst I felt at the uprooting and decimating of my plants. But most of his respondents are more attuned to the immediate substance of his query. He is told he can wrap his tomatoes in newspaper, store them in a dark, cool place, and have them ripen "through Thanksgiving." There's a recipe for a Savory Green Tomato Pie, made with Swiss and Muenster cheeses, and another for marinated, grilled green tomatoes.

But the recipe that attracts my attention is for Cream of Green Tomato Soup. Loath to throw them away, I have kept for the past week a pound of tiny green tomatoes in a bowl on my kitchen countertop, their continued presence demanding that I do

## CREAM OF GREEN TOMATO SOUP

1½ cups sliced onions
3 garlic cloves, minced
2 tablespoons olive oil
2 pounds green tomatoes, cored and chopped
1½ pounds potatoes, peeled and chopped
2 cups chicken stock
1½ cups water
2 teaspoons sugar
½ teaspoon thyme
1 cup heavy cream
½ teaspoon cayenne

*Sauté onions and garlic in oil until soft and golden. Add tomatoes, potatoes, stock, water, sugar, and thyme. Cover and simmer about 45 minutes or until soft. Purée and stir in cream and cayenne. May be served hot or cold.*

From the Internet

something with them. This recipe seems the perfect solution, and so I acquire the necessary ingredients and make it for dinner. Having deviated from our low-fat diet with last week's tomato fry, tonight I substitute nonfat yogurt for the heavy cream. The result is a fine dispersion throughout the soup of tiny bits of curdled yogurt. Strictly speaking, I have blown it—presumably the recipe's creator had a *creamier* texture in mind. But even so the soup has a wonderful lemonlike tang, and with a loaf of fresh bread, it makes a fine meal. And when we have finished, so have we finished the last of this year's tomatoes.

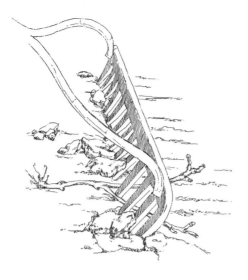

# NOVEMBER

## NOVEMBER 6

TODAY I BEGIN AN experiment, the last of this season, first of next. This summer I read in a magazine of a new method for growing tomatoes. The tomato-vetch connection, the magazine called it.

The article reported on the work of researchers seeking a replacement for black plastic mulch. By slowing moisture loss and blocking weeds, black plastic improves yields, but it's expensive and difficult to dispose of—not to mention ugly. As an alternative, the researchers had experimented with a variety of winter cover crops, known also as green manure.

The crop they settled on is called hairy vetch *(Vicia villosa)*. When planted in the fall, it grows to three or four feet over the winter. In spring the vetch is cut close to the ground and left lying where it falls; tomato transplants are then planted directly through the fallen vetch, which acts as a water-retaining, weed-controlling mulch. In addition, the vetch conditions the soil and acts as a natural fertilizer. The resulting yields are said to exceed "plastic-and-fertilizer plots by about twenty-five percent and fertilized bare soil by one hundred percent."

Intrigued, I purchased a pound of vetch seed. This will be enough to last me to the next millennium, but it was the least I could buy and it was cheap, costing all of a dollar and a half. More costly (but still cheap) was a pouch of legume inoculant. Legumes, which include not only vetch but peas, beans, and clover, have evolved a symbiotic relationship with bacteria called *rhizobia,* which live in nodules on the host's roots and convert atmospheric nitrogen into organic forms usable by the plant; when the legumes die and decompose, this organic nitrogen is then available for use by other plants. The inoculant itself is a fine black powder—zillions of rhizobia, I suppose—into which the vetch seeds are rolled prior to planting, thereby seeding the seeds with their vital symbionts.

This latter is a task I delegate to my son. But first I take the opportunity—never to be missed by a parent—to give him an applied math problem: The article says to plant the vetch at the rate of one ounce per ten square feet. Our tomato plot is three feet by thirteen feet. Rounding the square footage to the nearest ten, how much vetch seed will we need? This of course brings both puzzlement and protest ("Aww, Dad, do we have to do that?"), but before getting out shovels and rakes, we spend a few minutes drawing three rows of thirteen squares to determine that we have nearly forty square feet of tomato patch, meaning we will need four ounces of seed.

While my son weighs the seed and dusts it with inoculant, I begin turning the soil, much as I did last spring. He soon joins me, and together we work, the sun on our backs and the sky blue overhead. There isn't much work really, and it takes us but a short time—we level the soil, I rake back a thin layer, he spreads the seed, and I cover it. But there is pleasure in the teamwork and the working of father and son, side by side. My son, too, enjoys our shared task. And though his thoughts are mostly of anticipation—his best friend will be coming soon to play—I would like to think that years from now he will remember this, or some similar afternoon of planting or harvesting or tending the yard, as a part of his growing up that brings him a smile.

What grown vetch looks like I have no idea. I may have just sown a weed patch in my front yard. In sum I am more ignorant than informed about what I have just done (although I did call my father beforehand, concerned the vetch would encourage the nematodes—an occurrence he thought unlikely). And so it is that I am a little fearful lest Albert come out and I have to explain what I am planting and why. But instead it is his wife who appears, stowing items in their car for an outing. She is resplendent in a black dress with a pattern of gold sequins across her chest, and I tell her she looks pretty.

"Church?" I ask.

The compliment transcends our language difficulties, and she smiles self-consciously while offering a one-word reply: "Party."

Later, John comes by, and he does ask what we are doing. I tell him about the vetch, that it is supposed to be good for the soil and good for the tomatoes I will plant next year. Mostly, I tell him, it's an experiment.

He nods as I tell him this, and he agrees the experiment is a good idea. "It's good to learn. I like to learn." It is clear, too, that he is familiar with the concept I am describing. Fava beans, he says, also make the soil better for other plants—and it is tomatoes that will follow his fava beans in the spring.

As he tells me this, I recall the catalog from which I ordered my vetch. Listed among the winter-growing nitrogen-fixing cover crops was fava. I could, in short, have performed this same experiment—and likely achieved the same results—by growing fava beans. Not only would I have improved my soil, but I would also have produced an edible crop of beans. No doubt I would have tickled my Italian neighbors as well.

Momentarily I am stricken with regret at the lost opportunity. I could have done it differently, could have done it better. But it is, after all, only gardening and next year I'll have another chance. For now, my season is over.

# ENDINGS

AND SO, WHAT HAVE I REAPED?
I have this year harvested 547 tomatoes; 388 were full-sized and 159 were cherries. To grow them, I spent $120.

### EXPENSES: YEAR END

| | |
|---|---:|
| seeds and potted plants: | $17.32 |
| equipment and miscellaneous supplies: | 35.60 |
| potting soil and soil amendments: | 20.31 |
| sprays and fertilizers: | 26.92 |
| water (estimated): | 12.00 |
| taxes and shipping: | 8.32 |
| TOTAL: | $120.47 |

All together, my large tomatoes probably weighed about 175 pounds; my cherries probably equaled about six baskets. At mid-season retail (say, 39 cents a pound for large tomatoes, and 99 cents a basket for cherries), my crop was worth about $75. Figured this way, I lost money. At early-winter prices (99 cents a pound and $1.99 a basket, respectively), I can claim a small profit. Alterna-